Pg. 41
Pg. 62 war & peace

D1259377

THE BIRTH
OF A VISION

THE BIRTH OF A VISION

Edited by
David F. Hartzfeld and Charles Nienkirchen

Essays by members of the faculty of
Canadian Bible College
and the faculty of
Canadian Theological Seminary
Regina, Saskatchewan
the official College and Seminary of
The Christian & Missionary Alliance in Canada
on the occasion of
the Centennial of the
Christian & Missionary Alliance
1887-1987

HIS DOMINION Supplement No. 1

THE BIRTH OF A VISION

Library of Congress Cataloging in Publication

Main entry under title:
    The birth of a vision: essays on the ministry and thought of
    Albert B. Simpson, founder of the Christian & Missionary
    Alliance.

    (His Dominion Supplement; no. 1)

    Includes bibliographical references.

    1. Christian and Missionary Alliance — History. 2. Simpson,
Albert Benjamin, 1843-1919. I. Hartzfeld, David F. II. Nienkirchen,
Charles. III. Series.

BX6700. A4B4   1986   286.4

ISBN NO: 0-88965-074-8

Produced by
BUENA BOOK SERVICES
A Division of Horizon House Publishers
Box 600, Beaverlodge, Alberta, Canada

Printed in Canada.

CONTENTS

ABBREVIATIONS

CA   The Christian Alliance

CAFMW   The Christian Alliance and Foreign Missionary
            Weekly

CAMW   The Christian Alliance and Missionary Weekly

CMAW   The Christian and Missionary Alliance Weekly

CPI   Christian Publications, Inc.

HCL   Hymns of the Christian Life

LT   Living Truths

WWW   The Word, The Work and The World

FOREWORD

The future of the church of Jesus Christ is in heaven. For the present, though, God is building it in human history. That building is a process that spans the centuries and has a cumulative character to it.

Because of this, the battle line in one generation is not always the scene of greatest conflict in another. There is ebb and flow. That does not change the fact, however, that what is at the forefront of discovery in one generation may be assumed in another. The process is dynamic. Thus, what is creatively revolutionary in one age may seem almost trite, if not sterile, in another.

Consequently, the church is in continual need of those souls who can discern where the crucial issues are in their day and can devote their energies to providing leadership in these areas. There will always be those intent upon reinventing the wheel, i.e., rewinning battles already won. These individuals are of minimal significance to the movement of God's Spirit in history. Some hardy souls occasionally get beyond the front line. Their isolation, however, reduces their effectiveness. The sensitive soul who perceives the moment's crucial issues and gives guidance in dealing with them is the prophetic figure that every generation needs. Albert Benjamin Simpson was such a person.

From Canadian stock that had its roots and associations in Presbyterianism, Simpson was an heir to the best of the Reformation. In his teens he came to see and know for himself that a person is justified by faith in Christ alone. This experience brought with it a quickening that enabled him to hear the call of God into the Christian ministry. With that quickening came a hunger that was to propel Simpson beyond traditional lines and structures into new frontiers of truth and grace. This was to give him singular influence in his day and make him a means of special blessing to the many who have followed him.

Simpson was the product of his century, though he transcended it. In the 19th century, revival stirred much of the heart of the American church. Forensic categories that showed the way to right standing before God, though not to be depreciated, did not satisfy fully those hearts which had sought and found justification for themselves, but still cried out for more. There was a widespread hunger among believers to know God more perfectly and to give themselves more totally to Him and to His world. A concern for evangelism was broadened so that it now began to be inclusive of the needs of the whole world. The cry of the believing heart to the holy, and the passionate sense of responsibility for the world, made an emphasis upon the work of the Holy Spirit inevitable. To all of this was added the conviction that Christ was not remote from human history. He Himself would conclude the historic process with His own appearing, an event that might be far more imminent than the world imagined. This gave the concern for holiness and world evangelism an immediacy that proved remarkably creative. Simpson was a willing participant in this ferment.

He found himself the pastor of a prominent and respected congregation in a major American city. A holy discontent grew within his spirit as he assessed his congregation in the light of the city and its need. As he prayed and sought divine help, the conviction deepened within him that before something would happen in his church and in his city, something must first happen to him.

We know the story from his own hand as to how he sought God, the surrender to which he came, and the fullness in which the Spirit met him. The result was a deeper knowledge of God and His grace and an anointing of the Spirit that transformed him and his ministry.

Now began the crystallization of those emphases that led to what we know as Simpson's Fourfold Gospel. The result was that traditional patterns, structures, and associations could no longer circumscribe him. Old wine skins needed to break and break they did. He belonged to the Christ of the Church, not just to the church of Christ.

New things had to be tried. New methods had to be developed. Laymen had to be drafted and trained. All parts of the world must know; here lay the inspiration for the Bible school movement. Literature had to be produced, at a popular level and on an extensive scale. Resources had to be found to send the missionaries and to maintain them. This necessitated structure and organization. Other efforts with which he had only a tangential relationship but which were committed to common goals, must be encouraged and supported. Christ and His cause had totally captured him.

The results that have come from Simpson's expenditure of himself are very substantial. It is the hope of some of us that the Centennial of the Christian & Missionary Alliance in 1987, will be the occasion to collect that story and to publish it far and wide for the glory of Christ. His children owe that to themselves and to the larger church. The reality is that Simpson's wingspread extends far beyond the Christian & Missionary Alliance and the institutions and organizations it has spawned.

On one occasion, when Simpson was speaking for Mr. Moody in Chicago, a young Methodist couple who had recently been converted, slipped in to hear him. They were profoundly impressed. That couple ended up overseas. Today, there are eleven Bible schools and graduate schools of theology scattered across the world that are the result of the life work of that young couple. The wife was to have her own ministry as well. It was she who authored *Streams in the Desert* and other devotional works that have been the source of much blessing in the church.

Sometime ago, the story of a prominent thoracic surgeon in one of the significant third world countries was brought to my attention. The surgeon, a woman, had been financed in her training by the widow of a Presbyterian elder in the United States. The major inspiration in that widow's life was the weekly contribution of A.B. Simpson to *The Alliance Weekly.*

Simpson belongs obviously to the Alliance. The reality is, though, that his influence extends far beyond his direct lineal descendants. But then, that is always true of pioneers. The centennial will never be able to tell the full extent of his influence. Only eternity can reveal that.

Dr. Dennis Kinlaw
President, Francis Asbury Society
Wilmore, Kentucky
October, 1986

ACKNOWLEDGMENTS

This project was made possible by the assistance of many persons. We would like to express our special appreciation to President Rexford Boda and the Board of Directors who both encouraged us and made available the necessary finances for this venture.

During the past four years, the archives at Canadian Bible College/Canadian Theological Seminary were enlarged and catalogued through the efforts of John Sawin, former archivist at the Albert B. Simpson Historical Library in Nyack, NY, and Adjunct Professor of Alliance History and Thought at Canadian Bible College/Canadian Theological Seminary. His gathering of sources, numerous discussions with faculty, and personal oversight of archival development have made possible the research of Alliance origins at the College and Seminary campus. His colorful presentations of numerous incidents in Alliance history and the life of its founder, have inspired the writers of this book.

A general survey of sources was provided by Ron Baker whose spirited interest in archival materials assisted each writer in becoming familiar with the sources.

Our proofreaders, Sandy Ayer, Librarian, Ted Goshulak, Assistant Librarian, and Milson DeGaris (Associate Pastor at 10th Avenue Alliance Church in Vancouver) spent many hours beyond the call of duty to purge the final text of lingering errors. Their offers of numerous stylistic suggestions made each writer indebted to them. However, the editors assume full responsibility for any errors that eluded their watchful eyes. We owe a large measure of thanks to Cheryl Bird, secretary to the Seminary Dean, for her long hours of entering the text and its revisions into the word processor.

The Editors

INTRODUCTION

The year 1987 represents the centennial anniversary of the Christian and Missionary Alliance. The approach of this celebration has stirred a number of activities. First, and most fitting, has been an emphasis on evangelism in which, during the last decade of its first century, great effort has been expended to double the membership of the Alliance churches, not only in North America, but in other continents and regions as well. Measurable goals were set, and to date, these goals overall are being met. Without question, such an effort would be pleasing to the founder of the C&MA, Albert Benjamin Simpson, and fits the spirit and practice of his own purpose and strategy.

The approach of the centennial has also prompted a number of studies in the history and writings of the Alliance and its founder. It is imperative for any movement, as it reaches a level of maturity, to review and analyze its beginnings and the principles and practices which produced it. This is particularly important if its earlier years have been crowned with significant success. What were the specific principles which brought about its success? How can these principles be applied in relevant ways in a new age? What needs to be done to retain the dynamic of the earlier years?

It is further imperative, with the rise of a new generation which includes both the children of an Alliance heritage and those who have joined the movement from other traditions, to share with them the things God has accomplished at the beginning and in the ensuing decades. The instruction of the Lord to the parents of Israel in Deuteronomy 6 underlines this obligation and its importance.

In recent years, a number of people on the administration and faculties of Canadian Bible College and Canadian Theological Seminary have suggested the value of a comprehensive listing of historical Alliance literature and a collection of articles which would examine the views and practices of A.B. Simpson. In 1983, specific impetus was given to such an endeavor through the formation of a committee composed of John Dahms, David Hartzfeld, Charles Nienkirchen and Samuel Stoesz. A proposal was formulated for a Simpson *Festschrift*, a technical term which literally translates as a "festival of writings" and which is published as a tribute to a person who has made a significant contribution in a particular field. The Christian and Missionary Alliance, as the lengthening shadow of its founder, gives witness to this *Festschrift* being an appropriate project. This proposal was submitted to the College and Seminary Board of Directors who generously approved the project and the needed financing.

The men and women who have contributed to this collection are members of the faculties of Canadian Bible College and Canadian Theological Seminary. They have contributed according to their particular interest and expertise. The volume has been prepared under the diligent supervision of its two editors, David Hartzfeld and Charles Nienkirchen. A word of appreciation must also be expressed to three other colleagues for their painstaking assistance in preparing the manuscript — Milson DeGaris, former CBC faculty member and the librarians of the Archibald Library, Sandy Ayer and Ted Goshulak.

In publishing this *Festschrift*, no claims are made to this effort being exhaustive or fully comprehensive. It has been our intention that this volume, along with others currently coming into print, will be a solid beginning which will spur others on, both at the scholarly and popular level, to examine in increasing detail the heritage of the Christian and Missionary Alliance in all its breadth and depth. It is our concern to share these things with our students on campus and our many friends off campus. It is our hope and prayer that we all, both the older and the newer generation, will focus on these principles which have made a significant and lasting impact for Christ and His Kingdom.

I commend this volume to its readers, not to bring glory to a man, A.B. Simpson, but to the glory of his Lord with whom he walked in obedience. Praise God that he was faithful as he led a group of men and women whose goal was to bring back the King through the preaching of the gospel to all nations and whose joy was walking in the power of the Spirit of the Lord with the awareness that it was Christ in them who was their hope of glory.

Rexford A. Boda
President, Canadian Bible College/
  Canadian Theological Seminary
Regina, Saskatchewan
October, 1986

THE FOURFOLD GOSPEL

by

John Sawin

INTRODUCTION

The Fourfold Gospel is an integral ingredient of the life-blood and ministry of the Christian and Missionary Alliance.[1] When Simpson apprehended and realized the totality of its truth, his ministry altered course dramatically. The same was true for others who came into contact with Simpson.

The importance of the Fourfold Gospel to Simpson is quickly seen as one reads through his periodicals (1882-1919), peruses his books, or looks at the several constitutions of the Alliance. His sermons, articles, book reviews and editorials, as well as the writings of other authors that he published, all bear witness to the prominence of the Fourfold Gospel in his thought and ministry. His experience and observation taught him that the personal apprehension of the Fourfold Gospel was the key that would unlock people's hearts so that the burden of evangelism for neglected people around the world could gain an entrance. Worldwide evangelism was the ultimate objective of the Alliance and a deeper, richer Christian experience was the starting point toward that objective. The Christian Alliance (North American support groups) would promote the starting point and the Missionary Alliance (training and sending agency) would pursue the ultimate objective.

In 1889, the incorporation papers of the Missionary Alliance

1

read: "...its particular business [is] the promotion of evangelical, domestic and foreign missions and also the training of missionaries for such work."[2] For the Christian Alliance, its particular business was:

A. To bear united testimony to:

  1. Salvation through Christ

  2. Sanctification through Christ for all who fully yield themselves to Him

  3. Healing through the name of Jesus for those who believe and obey Him

  4. Christ's personal and pre-millennial coming

B. To promote the wide diffusion of these great truths and to lead all the children of God into the practical experience of all the fullness of Jesus.[3]

The 1911 *Manual* described the setting out of which the Fourfold Gospel emerged and delineated it more precisely: "...during the past quarter of a century and more, large numbers of God's people have been united in a deeper spiritual life in Christ as a complete Saviour and indwelling presence by the Holy Spirit as Sanctifier, Healer and Keeper"; and stated further that the Alliance had been organized "to give a more emphatic testimony to these great truths." Accordingly, "the Alliance stands for the full Gospel, Christ our Saviour, Christ our Sanctifier, Christ our Healer and Christ our Coming Lord."[4]

Membership in the Alliance was granted to all who could state, "I believe in the Lord Jesus Christ as my Saviour, Sanctifier, Healer and Coming Lord."[5] In the words of the 1912 Alliance Constitution, Alliance members were those persons who recognized "the truths of the Lord Jesus Christ as Saviour, Sanctifier, Healer and Coming King as taught by the C&MA."[6]

Similar wording can be found in Alliance Manuals until the Constitution was revised in 1975. At that time, the requirement remained the same: "Acceptance of the doctrines of the Lord, Jesus Christ as Saviour, Sanctifier, Healer and Coming King."[7]

So today, the Alliance is committed to the truth and experience of the Fourfold Gospel and dedicated "to [discipling] people of all nations, particularly where Christ has not been named, emphasizing the Lordship of Jesus Christ and the person and work of the Holy Spirit, and looking for the coming of the Lord."[8]

ORIGIN AND MEANING OF THE TERM

One may well ask who originated the term "Fourfold Gospel" and what each of the "folds" stand for. At the opening of the March, 1890 Convention at the Gospel Tabernacle,[9] Mr. Simpson stated that the expression "Fourfold Gospel" came to him by inspiration. He reminded the eager audience:

We have met here to make emphatic our testimony to the blessed fulness of the Gospel of our Lord Jesus Christ. I know not why the term, Fourfold Gospel, should have been suggested by the Holy Spirit, but it seems to have been taken up all over the land by those who have known something of the blessing which it represents. This Gospel seems to grow more sweet each year, and I have not yet begun to fathom its incorruptible richness and infinite fulness.[10]

Two of Mr. Simpson's close friends also attributed the source of the phrase to him. One was the saintly and erudite Episcopalian clergyman, Dr. Kenneth MacKenzie.[11] In May 1922, at the Missionary Training Institute in Nyack, N.Y., MacKenzie referred to the Fourfold Gospel "having been given to Dr. Simpson," and stated that "after it had stood the test of a generation, there was no occasion to add anything to it or to take anything from it." And that, furthermore, "today it is just as clear, full, fresh and powerful as in the beginning."[12]

William T. MacArthur was also a close personal friend of A.B. Simpson,[13] and said of him: "The facts of the Fourfold Gospel became like a fire in his bones. He coined the expression, The Fourfold Gospel, or Jesus our Saviour, Sanctifier, Healer and Coming King."[14]

Simpson viewed the Fourfold Gospel as an entity in itself as well as the sum of its constituent parts. For example, when in 1887, on the eve of the formation of the Christian Alliance and the Evangelical Missionary Alliance, he wrote an article for his "paper parish" friends to remind them of the distinctive teachings upon which these two organizations would rest, he declared that:

> First, we believe and teach all the evangelical doctrines of the Christian Church in the strictest sense; and secondly, even in what might be called distinctive teachings, we hold nothing that is not directly founded upon the Word of God. And even these are in accord with the spirit and sense of all the great standards of the Protestant churches.

Regarding the aforementioned distinctive teachings, he wrote:

> ...these are precious truths, like hidden mines, and are being brought into light and life from age to age in the development of Christian experience and in the progress of the Church. Each age has its emphatic message, its 'present truth,' its contemporary testimony.[15]

He enumerated the content of these teachings as follows:

1. Christ is our complete Saviour from guilt...from inbred sin, from sickness...for time and for eternity.

2. Christian holiness is...Christ life, perfection in Christ, abiding in a perfect Christ.

3. Christian holiness is a free gift of God through Jesus Christ...received by faith and retained by abiding in Him....We do not grow into it, but we go into it and grow out from it into all the fulness of the stature of Christ.

4. Healing is the purchase of Christ's atonement and the gift of Christ's indwelling and resurrection life. Through the indwelling Christ, we are supernaturally quickened, sustained and enabled to rise above the power of disease, to overcome infirmity and to fulfill all of the work to which He calls us until our life work is completed and we rise to the higher life of immortal resurrection.

5. The age we live in points to a speedy consummation. The

4

Holy Scriptures meet this expectation with the personal and pre-millennial coming of the Lord Jesus Christ to set up His kingdom on earth.[16]

Speaking of the goal of these distinctive teachings, he declared:

God is calling us as never before to look on the fields, they are white unto harvest, and to go into all the world and preach the Gospel to every creature. Are not these distinctive truths in which we can all unite and go forth to save a dying generation and prepare for the close of the world's most marvelous century and the coming of the Lord Himself in His Kingdom of glory?[17]

It should be noted that Simpson's first sermon at the 1887 Old Orchard Convention was entitled "The Fourfold Gospel."[18] When he returned to New York City, he preached four sermons on each of the "folds" which were published as Vol. 5 of *Tabernacle Sermons*, and entitled *The Fourfold Gospel*. (The latter book is still in print; the 1925 edition added two more chapters: "The Walk With God," and "Kept," also sermons of Mr. Simpson.) A few years later, in 1891, in an article entitled, "Fourfold Unity," Simpson elaborated further on the subject:

A single note in music is melody, but not harmony. A repetition of that note by a thousand voices is not harmony. You may have a chorus of soprano singers that would rend the sky, but you can never reach the highest effects of music until you add a second part. It is the blending of the notes that are not the same, but yet are in accord, that constitute the power of harmony.

And when, instead of two parts you have three, the deep bass, the chorus swells with a grandeur that no simple melody could ever give. And then when the lofty tenor completes the whole effect and swells the chorus to the very heights of triumph, there is no one who understands the merest rudiments of music but knows that there is breadth and length and depth and height in the harmony which all the voices and instruments in the universe could never produce with a single melody.

...this imperfect figure enables us to understand how, in the Fourfold Gospel, we have the elements of a Christian unity which no other fellowship could give.[19]

At about the same time, a convention speaker remarked that the Fourfold Gospel required all the "folds" to give any one of them its true emphasis and proportion. Simpson commented:

> Christ our Saviour is not enough. The new convert must be led forward into the baptism of the Holy Spirit. Every Christian needs the inspiration and support of a deeper life and an abiding union with the Lord Jesus Christ.... Divine healing alone will surely lead you into fanaticism and distortion. It must spring in its truest meaning from a deep spiritual intimacy with the Lord Jesus.[20]

And the fourth "fold," Christ's return,

> is dependent upon all the other constituent truths of the Fourfold Gospel. It is the climax of all other teaching and experience and it needs a deep hold of God to steady us as we rise to its heights of vision.[21]

Simpson considered "...the theology and theory of the Fourfold Gospel [to be] sublimely high in its ideal of Christian living [because it] presents the highest life possible for redeemed men...a Christ life, a reproduction of Christ Himself, a miniature and living epistle of the Son of Man. Surely it ought to develop practical results as high and as glorious."[22]

SIMPSON RESPONDS TO HIS CRITICS

Simpson's theology of the Fourfold Gospel had its critics even among conservative Christians, as Simpson acknowledged in 1892 in declaring that "we have risked the good opinion of thousands [of Christians] by fearless testimony to the advanced truths of the Fourfold Gospel."[23] In 1919, the editor of the Alliance Witness responded to an oft-asked question, why these phrases?

6

The Fourfold Gospel
The Full Gospel
The Whole Gospel
The Whole Bible to the Whole World

These phrases were applied to several organizations including the Alliance. The answer, then and now, was that too many Christians, churches, and Christian denominations had narrowed God's salvation to only an escape from hell. But Fourfold Gospel people and their kind perceived that the Scriptures also required God's people to be holy, to stop sinning, to obey God and walk in His ways. They also saw that God met His own requirement with promises to His people, whereby they might perform His expectations. These requirements and promises they viewed as neglected truths and intended to restore them to the life of the Church. Simpson was persuaded that his exegesis of Scripture was accurate, and that it had been verified in his personal experience. He knew he had been blind, but from the time of his pastorate in Louisville, he enjoyed new sight and a Christian life that he had not previously known.[24] Innumerable Christians, both inside and outside the Alliance, bore similar testimony to the reality of Fourfold Gospel truth.

One may wonder if the Fourfold Gospel is unique to the Alliance. Certainly the phrase itself and the particular theological expression given to it by Alliance writers originate within the denomination. However, today other so-called "full gospel" denominations adhere to the concepts of the Fourfold Gospel, but express their views somewhat differently. Among these are the International Church of the Foursquare Gospel, the Assemblies of God, some of the many denominations known as the Church of God, the Missionary Church, et al.[25] The theological differences among these groups usually concern their respective definitions and experiences of sanctification and/or the baptism of the Spirit.[26] But together they hold in common the view that the Gospel includes another critical decision in addition to the conversion experience of repentance, justification and regeneration. They maintain that Christians should be taught higher and deeper Gospel truths and be persuaded to appropriate them personally and live according to them.

JESUS OUR SAVIOUR

The first "fold," salvation, probably requires little explanation, but its position among the "folds" is primary. It signifies the beginning of all Christian life and identifies the chief business of the Church. Christian people are commissioned to bring lost to a saving faith in Jesus Christ. The Gospel of redeeming grace is the first "fold," salvation, the first formal step into the family of God. Simpson's all-consuming burden was to preach such a gospel and evangelism has always been the ultimate object of the C&MA. Simpson expressed his concern for evangelism in the following hymn:

Saving and serving our watch-word shall be;
Living for others and living for Thee;
Help us, dear Lord, to be true to our trust,
Serving the Master and saving the lost.

Saving the lost ones wherever they roam,
Seeking the wanderers and bringing them home;
Going where sorrow and darkness are found;
Seeking the lost to earth's uttermost bounds.[27]

JESUS OUR SANCTIFIER

The second "fold," sanctification, is not as easily explained because of the problems of semantics and biblical exegesis, but Simpson's point of view can easily be ascertained from his books on the subject, and particularly from *Wholly Sanctified*.[28]

Simpson used the term "sanctification" as it pertains to the Fourfold Gospel in its subjective sense of "holiness,"[29] not in its more frequent objective sense of "setting apart." The two meanings are interrelated, but as far as the second "fold," sanctification refers to holiness of heart and life that results from the abiding presence of Christ or from the indwelling of the Holy Spirit. When Simpson was sanctified, or filled with the Spirit, he testified that "across the threshold of his spirit there passed a being as real as the Christ who came to John on Patmos."[30] The indwelling Spirit and the Christ who abides within are simply different expressions of the same truth. It is the truth that prompted Simpson to preach the sermon "Himself" and to write the poem/hymn of the same title.[31] To Simpson, this was the essence of the second "fold," sanctification. He believed that to enter this experience necessitated a critical decision, but he also knew that growth and deeper fillings of the Spirit ought to characterize the sanctified life. Subjective sanctification, then, to Mr. Simpson, was a distinct experience.[32]

Simpson, in his printed sermons (books), articles and editorials, sought to define precisely his view of sanctification and he sought to lead people into the experience of it. A few examples of his writing on sanctification follow:

What is Sanctification?

First, it means to be separated from sin. This carries with it the idea of cleansing, of crucifying, of putting off. It is the renunciation of all evil.

Second, it means to be dedicated to God. This is the offering of ourselves to God after we have turned away from all evil. It is the dedication of our whole being to God to belong to Him.

Third, it means to be filled with or baptized with the Spirit and carries along with it the idea of the indwelling of Christ in the heart. Jesus dwells within us and becomes the power and substance of our new life. The indwelling of Christ and the indwelling of the Spirit represent different sides of the same experience. The Spirit-filled life therefore is a Christ-filled life. When Christ fills our life with Himself, it is then meet for the Master's use and prepared unto every good work.[33]

When does this decision and experience take place?

[Sanctification] is a crisis just as distinct as the experience of conversion, but it is fraught with issues unspeakably important. Even after we receive the Holy Spirit to dwell within us, there are measures and degrees of His fullness into which the soul does not immediately pass. As He shows us clearer light upon ourselves and our deeper

9

needs, we are led to take Him in larger measure and for still deeper cleansing and filling. Therefore, the fullness of the Spirit is a matter of growth and maturity. It is like the great waves that sweep in from the sea and fill the little pool to its utmost capacity. But while it fills, it also enlarges and the next wave leaves a deeper fullness than the last.[34]

Simpson related his view of sanctification to the Wesleyan and Keswickian view in the following article:

We believe that the Alliance teaching on this subject is neither Wesleyan nor an echo of the excellent teaching given at Keswick. While speaking in greatest appreciation of all who endeavor to hold up the true Scriptural standard of Christian life, yet we believe that the view of the teachers and workers in the Christian Alliance regarding personal holiness is what we might term the "Christ life." There is always a little danger of seeing our experience more than seeing the source of that experience, the Lord Jesus. We have been led to rise above all our experiences and recognize our new and resurrection life as wholly in Him. [We need to maintain] an attitude of constant dependence and abiding so that our holiness is dependent every moment on our union and communion with Him.[35]

A few years later, Simpson's teaching of sanctification came into conflict with the Pentecostal tongues movement and their view that speaking in tongues is the definitive evidence of the baptism of the Spirit. Simpson taught that the gift of tongues remained a present manifestation of the Spirit, but he objected to the Pentecostal teaching that speaking in tongues was the unique initial evidence of the Spirit-filled experience.

The Alliance doctrine of sanctification continues unchanged to this day, as evident from the current Statement of Faith:

It is the will of God that each believer should be filled with the Holy Spirit and be sanctified wholly, being separated from sin and the world and fully dedicated to the will of God, thereby receiving power for holy living and effective service. This is both a crisis and a progressive experience wrought in the life of the believer subsequent to conversion.[36]

With Simpson, Alliance people sing today:

I long, oh, I long to be holy,
Conformed to His will and His Word;
I want to be gentle and Christ-like,
I want to be just like my Lord.[37]

JESUS OUR HEALER

As far as the third "fold" is concerned, we have already noted that Simpson was cautious regarding the place he accorded divine healing. He refused to allow it to predominate the first two "folds." He knew that it could easily become a sensational attraction and the press would delight in making it so. As he himself put it:

Divine healing is not the most important truth of the Gospel, but it is a truth that God has shown to us. Holding it in its subordinate place, let us hold it fearlessly and confess it manfully....[38]

Though cautious, Simpson wanted divine healing to receive proper emphasis, as the following excerpt from the preface to *The Gospel of Healing* shows:

The importance of this subject and the emphatic way in which the Holy Spirit is pressing it upon the attention of His people demand for it the most careful and thorough Scriptural study. This doctrine is becoming one of the touchstones of character and spiritual life in all the churches of America, and revolutionizing the whole Christian life of thousands. It has a profound bearing upon the spiritual life. No one can truly receive it without being a holier and more useful Christian.

It is most important that it should be ever held in its true place in relation to the other parts of the gospel. It is not the whole gospel, nor perhaps the chief part of it, but it is

11

a part, and in its due relationship to the whole, it will prove to be, like the gospel itself, "the power of God to everyone that believeth." [39]

Simpson taught that the basis of faith in divine healing was the atonement of Jesus Christ. He did not conceive its availability as equal to the offer of salvation, "whosoever will may come," but as a provision by the Lord for His children:

> ...if disease came through the fall of man, it must be undone by the Saviour. [40]

Drawing his conclusions from Scripture verses such as Isaiah 53:4,5; Matthew 8:17; Psalm 103:2,3; Exodus 15:25,26, he maintained that:

> the atonement of Christ takes away sin and the consequence of sin for every believer who accepts Him;

and added that Jesus

> healed all who came to Him for healing...and He is still the same today.

Hence, for Simpson,

> the personal ministry of Jesus when on earth is our ground for claiming healing. [41]

Simpson also perceived a parallel source of divine healing, Christ's resurrection. Early in his independent ministry, he wrote:

> His death took away your liability to disease, but His resurrected body is a positive fountain of real vital energy....His bodily energy vitalizes your body....I think whole people need it as much as sick people....I take it every morning and it has given me many times more the strength of my natural energy....He, the living One, comes into you and henceforth, lives in you Himself so that your bodies are members of Christ and you are members of His body, of His flesh and of His bones. [Divine healing] is Jesus Himself, His life manifested in your mortal flesh....We must live in Him; we must take

12

our healing as we do our life, breath by breath, from Jesus.
We must live in His bosom under the shadow of His
wings.[42]

Later on in his ministry, he elaborated on this point as
follows:

Divine healing is not giving up medicines or fighting with
physicians or against remedies. It is not even believing in
prayer or the prayer of faith or in the men and women
who teach Divine healing; nor is it believing the doctrine
to be true. But it is really receiving the personal life of
Christ to be in us as the supernatural strength of our body
and the supply of our physical life. It is a living fact and not
a mere theory or doctrine.[43]

Such an elevated concept of divine healing places Simpson in
a category somewhat different from other exponents of the
doctrine of healing.[44] Yet their objectives are the same, to
appropriate by faith a provision of the full Gospel.
How does a person receive Divine healing? Certainly, it is by
faith and not by works, for

if it is part of the Gospel, it comes by faith and not by
sight. Faith takes God at His Word.[45]

The seeker must come to

a definite point and cross it, put down a stake and take it
forever.

He will say,

this is God's truth and I stand upon it.[46]

But there is a preliminary condition prior to definite faith. The
seeker

must be right with God. The holy Gospel only remains in
a holy life and heart.[47]

He must ask himself,

Am I myself right with God? Am I in a position where I
have a right to claim this? Any doubt...would hinder the

13

rest of faith. If there is any sin...anything the Lord would frown upon, then lay it at His feet, choose His will in the matter. Take His faith and depend upon it. He does not promise that you will never die, but He does promise that until His purpose is fulfilled concerning you, He will be the strength of your life. Go forth in His strength moment by moment with sweet and thankful rest, like one who is healed, like one who has Christ walking by His side giving you all of His physical strength to lean upon."[48]

How effective was this subordinate third "fold" during Simpson's lifetime? His periodicals published testimonies week after week throughout his life of remarkable healings. Almost every known human malady was cured by the divine touch.[49] Though Simpson was cautious as to the time and place of healing meetings, miraculous cures that electrified the audience also occurred in large public gatherings.

Many of the leaders in the Alliance during the formative years were men and women who had been delivered from life-threatening and incapacitating sicknesses.[50] Though Simpson was cautious and though he kept the doctrine of healing subordinate to evangelism for lost souls and the Spirit-filled life, nevertheless God's healing grace and power exercised towards hundreds of people during early Alliance history accounts in some measure for the remarkable ministry and influence of Simpson and the Alliance. Many healed persons gave themselves unstintingly to the ministry of the Gospel. They served in churches, in Alliance branches, in rescue missions, and in overseas missionary work. Simpson's belief in divine healing as a continuing reality is summed up in one of his better-known hymns entitled "The Branch of Healing":

There is a healing branch that grows
Where every bitter Marah flows;
This is our health renewing tree,
'I am the Lord that healeth thee.'

There is an old appointed way
For those that harken and obey;
Above the gate these words we see,
'I am the Lord that healeth thee.'

14

There is a great Physician still
Whose hand has all its ancient skill;
At His command our pains will flee,
'I am the Lord that healeth thee.'[51]

JESUS OUR COMING KING

The fourth "fold" of the Fourfold Gospel proclaims Christ's personal and premillennial return to earth. Simpson's reading of the Scriptures, however, convinced him that the Lord would not return until his followers had fulfilled certain requirements. They must "disciple all the nations," and "preach the Gospel to all creation from Jerusalem unto the extremities of the earth."[52] Alongside these great commission verses, Simpson also placed another verse which, to him, linked the return of the Lord to earth with missionary responsibility.

This gospel of a kingdom shall be preached in the whole world for a witness to all the nations, and then the end shall come.[53]

Students at his Missionary College and those who attended the conventions felt the urgency of this verse. Failure to take the Gospel where Christ was not known simply delayed His return. Therefore, to the work!

The Alliance historically is a pioneer missionary society and part of that pioneer motivation came from Matthew 24:14. Simpson could become quite excited when he contemplated the Church playing a significant role in "bringing back the King."[54] Walter Turnbull asserted that Simpson was the only missionary leader that associated the coming of the Lord with the completion of the missionary task.[55]

Simpson viewed the Lord's return to earth "as an ever impending event."[56] In his view, the millennium was not an intervening period, although apostasy and terrible iniquity would precede Christ's return. He also believed that the

...Gospel of the kingdom will be preached among the nations first, but this does not imply that it will be

15

universally accepted. Its design is to be a witness, to utter the warning cry, to leave the nations without excuse, and 'to gather out of them a people to His name,' and complete 'the fullness of the Gentiles.' Then shall the end come and the fulfillment cannot now be very far in the future.[57]

He also taught that the truth of the Lord's return tends to sanctify Christian character and to stimulate true Christian effort....It must lead every honest Christian to a life of holy vigilance and purity....It is one of the strongest influences to separate us from an evil world."[58]

Moreover, in his opinion, people with this hope

are not likely to bury their souls in a defiling or doomed world, that the Lord's return is the most powerful of all incentives to missionary effort. If we are really looking for the end, and if the preaching of the Gospel to all nations is to be the last condition before His coming, then all who 'love His appearing' will seek to hasten it by fulfilling this condition. Surely there can be no more all-constraining impulse than the hope that we may be permitted to complete the great commission and then turn our face to the heavens and welcome Him back to earth again.[59]

CONCLUSION

Holiness, hope and heralding the Gospel to all nations! This trilogy of biblical concepts expresses the essential impact of the fourth "fold" upon those who embrace the Fourfold Gospel. It also shows how all the "folds" mesh together into a beautiful unity of Christian life and ministry. Like the Trinity, it would seem most unfortunate if any one of the "folds" were lessened in emphasis or subtracted from the total number. God stands unique in His tri-unity and all three equal Persons must remain ever the same to maintain the wonderful Godhead. The four "folds" of the Gospel are not equal, but each "fold" contributes to the worth of the whole. Thus, Simpson and Alliance people conceived the concept of a Fourfold Gospel, and thus we continue that emphasis today. To do otherwise would lessen

16

the spiritual impact of the Alliance upon each subsequent generation.

ENDNOTES

1. In 1892, letters of inquiry were addressed to the Board of Managers regarding the doctrines of the Christian Alliance. The following is part of their response:

   "We, the Board of Managers of the Christian Alliance, desire publicly to state that while the Christian Alliance is not in any wise an ecclesiastical body, its bond of cohesion being simply a belief in the doctrines of the Fourfold Gospel, viz. Jesus as Saviour, Sanctifier, Healer and Coming Lord; yet its principles are thoroughly evangelical and such as constitute the basis of the Evangelical Alliance (the London based organization).

   "Inasmuch as the specific object of the Christian Alliance is to bear testimony to the truth of the Fourfold Gospel, it does not feel called upon to institute special inquiry into the private views of its members on other points. Yet as an avowed evangelical body *it does not* feel at liberty to publicly recognize or allow any to speak upon its platforms who are known to hold views contrary to evangelical truth."

   Christian Alliance [Hereafter C.A.] (April, 1892), p. 274.

2. *Manual of the Christian & Missionary Alliance* (New York: Christian Alliance Pub. Co., 1911), p. 8.

3. *The Word, the Work & the World* (Sept. 1887), p. 110. [Hereafter, W.W.W.] See also the *Manual of the Christian & Missionary Alliance* (New York: Christian Alliance Pub. Co., 1900), p. 6 & 9; the *Manual of the Christian & Missionary Alliance* (New York: Christian Alliance Pub. Co., 1917), p. 15, 19, 26. [Hereafter, *Manual*]; *The Annual Report of the Christian & Missionary Alliance, 1911/12*, p. 39-40. [Hereafter, *Annual Report*). The incorporation charter of the Christian Alliance 1890 read, "its particular business is the wide diffusion of the Gospel *in its fullness*, the promotion of a *deeper, higher Christian life.*" One of the objectives of the amalgamated C&MA (1897) was "to bear witness to Christian truths, especially those relating to the *deeper Christian life.*" In 1912, the Alliance constitution was updated, but the objectives remained the same: "to *promote* ... the deepening of the spiritual life of Christians everywhere; *to afford* fellowship for "Christians of different church affiliations and in sympathy with the truths for which the Alliance stands," and *to stimulate* them "as loyal witnesses to Jesus Christ in His fullness."

17

4. *Manual, 1911*, p. 5.

5. Ibid., p. 11.

6. *Annual Report, 1911/12*, p. 41; *Manual, 1917*, p. 29.

7. *Manual, 1975*, p. 38, and *Manual, 1983*, p. 48.

8. *Manual, 1983*, p. 5.

9. The Convention was the delayed October convention of 1889. The new Gospel Tabernacle complex on 44th St. and 8th Ave. was being constructed and not ready for occupancy in October of 1889.

10. *Christian & Missionary Alliance Weekly* (March 1890), p. 157. [Hereafter, C.M.A.W.]

   Simpson's first use of the phrase has not yet been discovered.

   In 1882, when writing about Luther and the Reformation, he made this comparison: "It was reserved for others to unfold in succession the deeper mysteries of *full salvation*, the doctrine of the Holy Spirit in Christian Experience, the doctrine of the Lord's personal coming, the doctrine of Christian sanctification, the doctrine of physical healing." W.W.W. (May 1882), p. 148.

   Later he published an article entitled *The Twofold Gospel*. It was his response to a missionary's plea for medical missionaries to fulfill "the Divine command, heal the sick, preach the Gospel." W.W.W. (April 1883), p. 61. In 1885, he advocated a Christian Alliance of all those who hold the *Gospel of Full Salvation*, W.W.W. (Oct. 1885), p. 280. He had recently returned from the Bethshan Conference in London, England.

   The phrase was probably used at the 1886 Old Orchard Convention. He followed through on a suggestion made there "to unite the host for prayer, fellowship, cooperation and testimony" by encouraging his readers to send him "names and addresses of all God's children who believe in the Fourfold Gospel." W.W.W. (March 1887), p. 192. The request made at Old Orchard is not surprising. Simpson's sermons and testimonies alone would have prompted the request. In his public addresses in 1886,

   1. He related his testimony of healing at Old Orchard, p. 130.

   2. He preached five sermons, the topics of which were:

       a. The Holy Spirit, p. 138
       b. The Perfect Christ, p. 148
       c. Divine Healing, p. 154
       d. The Lord's Coming, p. 167
       e. Consecrated Service, p. 172
          This sermon records his own experience and testing about giving.

11. Dr. MacKenzie first met Simpson in 1883 at a dinner engagement. Two sisters, members of MacKenzie's parish, frequented Simpson's meetings and desired their pastor to meet Mr. Simpson. MacKenzie immediately participated in some private Bible studies with Simpson and others. Simpson, in turn, invited MacKenzie to minister in the meetings of the Tabernacle and teach at the Training College. He taught at the College as late as 1935.

12. *Alliance Weekly* (Oct. 1922), p. 477. See also article in W.W.W. (March 1890), p. 157.

13. In 1898, when Mr. Simpson first encountered Wm. MacArthur, he told his wife that he had "caught a rare bird." A.E. Thompson, *The Life of A.B. Simpson* (Harrisburg, PA: Christian Publications, 1920), p. 206. MacArthur was unique in his presentation of truth and ministered widely in the Alliance as local branch superintendent, assistant pastor of the New York Gospel Tabernacle, et al. His writings are witty, pungent and succinct. Two of his sons rose to considerable fame, Charles, the playright and husband of Helen Hayes, and John, the billionaire insurance and real estate broker.

14. W.T. MacArthur, *Twenty Sermonettes* (n.p.: published privately. n.d.), p. 48.

15. *W.W.W.* (July 1887), p. 2.

16. Ibid., p. 2.

17. Ibid., p. 3.

18. *W.W.W.* (1887) supplement, p. 18f.

19. *Christian Alliance & Missionary Weekly* (Nov. 1891), p. 274. [Hereafter, C.A.M.W.]

20. *Christian Alliance & Foreign Missionary Weekly* (Nov. 1896), p. 420 [Hereafter, C.A.F.M.W.].

21. Ibid.

22. *C.A.F.M.W.* (Mar. 1896), p. 300.

23. *C.A.M.W.* (Feb. 1892).

24. One may conclude from the prominence of Mr. Simpson in this history that he was an authoritarian figure; and there is probable reason for that conclusion. But, on the other hand, the historical account of the first 35 years of the Alliance is found primarily in Simpson's periodicals, and he was the editor most of the time. So, of necessity, he is our primary source. Generally speaking, Alliance people supported his views; indeed, that is one reason they became members of the Alliance. Simpson personally recoiled from any

authoritarian concept of himself; indeed, he rejected a proffered honorary Doctorate of Divinity lest he be above his brethren. However, others treated the proffered degree as conferred and addressed him as Dr. Simpson.

25. The original *Missionary Church Association* were German speaking people who formed local assemblies that were associated with the C & MA. Rev. A.E. Funk, Simpson's close associate, was their earliest leader.

26. In October 1899, Simpson penned an article entitled *Phases and Phrases of Higher Christian Life.* He wrote:

> There is often much needless controversy about phases of truth and phrases in which it is expressed. We hear the "Second Blessing," "Entire Sanctification," "a clean heart," "eradication," "separation," "a deeper life," "the rest of faith," "the consecrated life," "the baptism of the Holy Spirit," "the fullness of Jesus," "Christian perfection," "perfect love." Simple hearts become perplexed while dogmatic people become warlike over these various lines of battle. Perhaps, after all, we shall find when we reach the land of perfect light that these various parties were nearer together than they dreamed, and that amid an infinite diversity of expression there was a substantial oneness of spirit. Let us learn to recognize the Christ life behind every variety of temperament and theological expression....Let us seek for Scriptural holiness and the Holy Spirit will meet us in the promises of His own inspired Word; and where our brethren differ from us in matters of expression, let us see if we cannot find a deeper unity in the image of Jesus reflected from their hearts and lives.

27. *Hymns of the Christian Life,* 1978, edition (Harrisburg, PA: Christian Publications, 1978), p. 468. [Hereafter, *H.C.L.*]. The first printing was in the third edition of *H.C.L.* in 1904, p. 157.

28. *Wholly Sanctified* is a series of sermons preached early in 1890. They were followed by another series preached from July through October, 1890, and published in the book, *A Larger Christian Life,* see especially ch. 10. An earlier series, May - Sept. 1886, will also prove helpful. They can be found in *The Fullness of Jesus* or *Christ Life in the New Testament.* The earlier sermons have a number of interesting personal illustrations.

29. "Pursue holiness with all men..." Heb. 12:14, "perfecting holiness in the fear of the Lord." 2 Cor. 7:1 et al.

30. *Alliance Weekly,* (Oct. 1915), p. 11.

31. The impromptu sermon, *Himself,* can be purchased as a tract. The

hymn is in every edition of *H.C.L.* from 1891 to the present (except the 1897 edition).

Over one-half century ago, Mr. Booth-Clibborn wrote in *The Christian Herald* (January 13, 1927) that above a million copies of A.B. Simpson's sermon *Himself* had been published in many languages. The following is the story of that sermon:

In 1885, the subject of *True Holiness and Divine Healing* was becoming more prominent on both sides of the Atlantic. Simpson was led into holiness in 1874 through W.E. Boardman's book, *The Higher Christian Life*. This same man was now the spokesman for a group in London that issued a call for an International Convention on Holiness and Divine Healing to be held at Bethshan, London, the first part of June, 1885. Delegates came from Australia, America and Europe, some 120 of them. Up to 3000 people attended the public sessions. Space at Bethshan was inadequate and the Conference was moved to Agricultural Hall.

Mr. Simpson published in his magazine immediately after the Conference many of the addresses given at the Conference, including three of his own, but not *Himself*. He also described his impressions and evaluation of the Conference. Mrs. Elizabeth Baxter, a co-hostess of the Conference, first published *Himself* in her journal, *Thy Healer*. Later, Mr. Simpson published it in *The Word, Work and World* "by request," *W.W.W.* (Oct. 1885), p. 258.

At the Conference, there were those who held the Keswick view of holiness, others who sided with the Wesleyan view (sometimes classified as "suppressionists" and "eradicationists"). Regardless of the different approach, the conferees were in dead earnest about a life of "true holiness." Mr. Simpson had listened to these two emphases and in his experience he knew that the truth of holiness, indeed all Christian experience, could be understood and realized in a much more beautiful way. To him, the truth was the ever-present Jesus abiding in the believer's life, Jesus Himself, a daily companion in the Christian's life. Or in a word, it was "habitation."

Mr. Boardman moderated the meetings and he chose not to have a formal program. At the proper moment during the addresses and discussion on 'holiness,' Mr. Simpson requested time to speak. The result was the impromptu address, *Himself*.

What was the immediate impression upon the hearers? Mr. Booth-Clibborn wrote: "The present writer still remembers (in 1927) the glow coming with the message as he sat near him on the platform." The message eventually gave birth to Simpson's matchless poem, *Himself*, and then the hymn.

32. *C.M.A.W.* (Dec. 1905), p. 769f. Also, in March 1906, an announcement was sent to Alliance workers. The heading read: *Conference for Prayer and Counsel* respecting uniformity in the Testimony and Teaching of the Alliance, May 25-28, 1906.

It continued:

The Committee appointed by the Board to prepare a plan for a conference on the matters above stated, recommend that such a conference be held immediately before the annual Council at Nyack in the beginning of June and that as many as possible of our Alliance workers throughout the country be invited and urged to attend.

The importance of Unity upon a common basis of testimony and teaching is becoming more and more urgent and the need of prayer for the great objects which we hold in common is emphasized at this time as never before. In connection with this conference, the following plan is suggested:

1. That it shall be held for at least three days and that at least one hour of each session shall be given to prayer and the rest of the time to conference respecting our Alliance testimony and teaching.

2. That the various subjects covered by this report be introduced by a short paper not exceeding fifteen minutes and followed by five or ten minute addresses by the members of the conference.

3. That a Committee be appointed by the conference for the purpose of carefully following the various discussions and drawing up a brief paper to be submitted to a subsequent meeting and adopted as the sense of the conference upon the matter in question.

4. That specific subjects be taken up at the various meetings of the Council for prayer and made the subject of earnest, united, believing intercession.

5. The following outline of subjects to be discussed is respectfully submitted as a basis for the deliberations of the proposed conference:

I. OPEN QUESTIONS

That the conference recognize certain matters of teaching and testimony as not within the direct province of the Alliance, but open questions about which our brethren agree to differ and hold in mutual charity their individual convictions according to their various denominational connections and previous teachings.

These open questions include:

1. Church government

2. The subjects and mode of baptism

3. The doctrines known as Calvinism and Arminianism

4. Various ceremonies and practices such as feet washing, etc.

II. OUR DISTINCTIVE TESTIMONY

1. Christ, our Saviour, always assuming that we stand unequivocally upon the Diety of Christ, His vicarious sacrifice and the necessity of regeneration through the power of the Holy Spirit.

2. Christ, our Sanctifier, assuming the following essential points:

a. A definite second blessing, *distinct in nature*, though not necessarily far removed in time, from the experience of conversion;

b. The baptism of the Holy Ghost *as a distinct experience*, not merely for power for service, but for personal holiness and victory over the world and sin;

c. The indwelling of Christ in the heart of the consecrated believer *as a distinct experience;*

d. Sanctification by faith *as a distinct gift* of God's grace to every open and surrendered soul;

e. Growth in grace and the deeper filling of the Holy Spirit as distinct from and the result of the definite experience of sanctification.

It is understood that all our Alliance officers and teachers are at liberty to present the truth of sanctification in such phases and phrases as his own convictions warrant, in general accordance with the above specifications, but with the understanding that such extreme views as are sometimes taught under the name of "eradication" or "suppression" shall not be presented in an aggressive or controversial spirit toward those who differ.

III. DIVINE HEALING

It is understood that the Alliance holds and teaches:

1. The will of God to heal the bodies of those who trust and obey Him by His own direct power without means.

2. The atonement of Christ for the body.

3. The life of the risen Christ for our mortal frame received by faith.

4. The ordinance of anointing and laying on of hands with proper recognition of the necessity of faith on the part of the individual anointed.

5. Power over evil spirits through the name of Jesus.

6. The disclaiming of all merit or individual power on the part of the worker and the constant recognition of the name of Jesus as the source of all supernatural power.

IV. THE LORD'S COMING

1. The Alliance holds and teaches the personal and pre-millennial coming of the Lord Jesus.

2. (blotted out—unreadable)

3. Liberty is accorded to our teachers in connection with the various opinions about Anti-Christ, the Tribulation, the Last Week of Daniel, Rapture, etc., but with the understanding that any spirit of antago-

nism and strife toward those who may hold different opinions is
discountenanced.

Signed: Henry Wilson
         J.D. Williams
         A.E. Funk
         F.H. Senft
         A.B. Simpson
           Committee

NOTE: This Conference was called for and planned prior to the out-
break of "tongues" at Azusa St., Los Angeles, California. See *C.A.*,
(Dec. 1905), p. 817; *C.A. (Mar. 1906), p. 185*; *C.A.* (May 1906), p. 297;
C.A. (June 1906), p. 329; and *C.A.* (July 1906), p. 33.

Unfortunately, whatever minutes were made of the Conference, were
not published in anything discovered to date. Mr. Simpson highly
commended a paper read by Dr. G.P. Pardington entitled *Sanctification*.
He published it both in *Living Truths* (July 1906), p. 397, and the
C.M.A.W., June 9, 1906, p. 348. Dr. Pardington, at the time, was also
writing *The Crisis of the Deeper Life*. It was published in July, 1906.

33. *C.M.A.W.* (Nov. 1899), p. 380. This editorial is a succinct summary of
Simpson's book, *Wholly Sanctified*.

34. *C.M.A.W.* (July 1899), p. 238.

35. *C.M.A.W.* (June 1899), p. 8.

36. An analysis of the declaration may be helpful.

NOTE:
1. the substance of the experience
2. the result of the experience
3. the kind of experience
4. the time of the experience

The substance is:
1. each believer should be filled with the Holy Spirit
2. each believer should be sanctified wholly
3. each believer should be separated from sin and the world
4. each believer should be fully dedicated to the will of God

The result is:
1. thereby receiving power for holy living
2. and receiving power for effective service

The kind:
1. this is both a crisis
2. and a progressive experience wrought in the life of the believer.

The time:
1. subsequent to conversion

37. *H.C.L.*, 1978 edition, p. 236; see also Simpson's hymn, *Christ in Me,* p. 166, and the hymn, *Not I, But Christ,* Ibid., p. 264, for which Simpson wrote the music.

38. *C.A.F.M.W.* (1896), p. 300.

39. A.B. Simpson, *The Gospel of Healing*, 4th edition (New York: Christian Alliance Pub. Co., 1890), p. 7, 8.

40. *W.W.W.* (July/Aug. 1887), p. 75. See also, "Divine Healing in the Atonement," *C.M.A.W.* (Aug. 1890), p. 122.

41. *W.W.W.* (July/Aug. 1885), p. 204.

42. *C.M.A.W.* (Aug. 1890), p. 124.

43. *W.W.W.* (July/Aug. 1887), p. 75.

44. *C.A.F.M.W.* (1896), p. 300.

What is written here is a very limited synopsis. To understand properly the full orb of Simpson's view of Divine healing, consult *The Gospel of Healing*. This book is a written treatise, not a collection of sermons as are so many of his books. The first chapters were published in his periodical in 1883, and then published as tracts. He took with him to Bethshan, London, in 1885, either the tracts or the first edition of the book. The book, as we know it, has been continuously in print since 1887.

Simpson published three other books on Divine healing, but they are sermons entitled *Friday Meeting Talks*. (See "The Writings of A.B. Simpson" at the end of this volume.) Articles and editorials on the subject abound in his magazine and usually can only be read therein. Following is a list of some of the early articles and editorials in the *W.W.W.* (1882-1887).

Articles

1882   The Credentials of the Gospel, May, p. 148
       For Us or For the Apostles, July, p. 245
       The Scriptural Ground of Physical Redemption, ibid.

1883   The First Promise of Physical Healing, Feb., p. 23
       The Gospel of Healing, April, p. 57
       The Gospel of Healing, No. 2, June, p. 77
       The Gospel of Healing, No. 3, Oct., p. 150, and Dec., p. 172

1885   The Principles of Faith Healing, May, p. 154
       The Past Year at the Berachah Home, ibid., p. 158
       Testimonies of Healing in the Bible, June, p. 175
       Testimonies of Healing, concluded, Aug., p. 189
       How to Receive Healing, Aug., p. 203
       Homes of Divine Healing, Oct., p. 253

1886   Divine Healing and Demonism (or Spiritualism) not Identical,
       a reply to Dr. Buckley's criticism of Healing, July, p. 52, and
       Aug., p. 114
       A testimony at Old Orchard of his own healing, Sept., p. 130
       Divine Healing, Sept., p. 154
       Testimonies of Healing at Old Orchard, Sept., p. 160-167
       The Scriptural Basis of Divine Healing, Oct., p. 208
       Inquiries and Answers (re: Divine healing), Nov., p. 290, and
       Dec., p. 338 (can be read in Simpson's book, *The Lord for
       the Body*)

1887   The Gospel of Healing in the Old Testament:
       1. In the writings of Moses, Jan., p. 26
       2. Joshua and Judges, Feb., p. 71
       3. In the book of Job, April, p. 205
       4. In the Psalms, May, p. 262
       5. Under the Kings of Judah and Israel, June, p. 326
       6. The Prophets, July, p. 13

       Divine Healing in the New Testament:
       1. The Gospels, but not printed in 1887
       2. The Acts and Paul's Epistles, Dec., p. 187

Editorials

1882   The Ministry of Healing and the Lord's Coming, May, p. 146
       Response to Dr. Hepworth's criticism of healing by faith,
       Nov., p. 261
       Faith and physicians, a response to adverse criticism in *The
       Independent*, Dec., p. 327

1883   Healing by Faith in God receiving much attention, Feb., p. 17
       Healing the handmaid of foreign missions, March, p. 47

1885   N.Y. Presbyterian ministers discussed faith healing with alarm,
       Jan., p. 31
       Simpson responds to a S.S. Times article against Divine
       Healing, Dec., p. 347

45. *W.W.W.* (July/Aug. 1885), p. 204.

46. Ibid.

47. *W.W.W.* (July/Aug. 1887), p. 75.

48. *W.W.W.* (July/Aug. 1885), p. 205.

49. Iona Moses at Old Orchard. See *W.W.W.* (1887) supplement, p. 77
    and *C.A.M.W.* (Jan. 1888), p. 6.

50. See A.B. Simpson, *A Cloud of Witnesses* (New York: W.W.W., Pub. Co.,
    1887); Sarah Lindenberger, *Streams From the Valley of Berachah* (New York:
    Christian Alliance Pub. Co., 1893; and *A Cloud of Witnesses* (New York:

Christian Pub. Co., 1900).

Names of some of the more prominent early leaders are:

Rev. John Cookman	Mr. and Mrs. E.G. Selchow
Rev. John Salmon	Ellen A. Griffin
Dr. Kenneth MacKenzie	Harriett Waterbury
Dr. Henry Wilson	Mrs. Henry Naylor
Rev. E.D. Whiteside	Mrs. Emma Mott Whittemore
Dr. Geo. P. Pardington	Sarah Lindenberger
Rev. E.J. Richard	Mrs. M.J. Clark

51. *H.C.L.*, 1978 edition, p. 275.

52. *Matt. 28:19; Mark 16:15; Acts 1:8.* The Biblical verses here and else-where are not always an exact quotation from a particular version of the Bible, but are free translations from the Greek text for purposes of emphasis.

53. *Matt. 24:14.* Many interpreters do not understand this verse as Simpson did. Then and now, Bible interpreters' understanding of scripture conform to certain prophetic frameworks and consequently, they interpret various verses of scripture within those parameters. Simpson honored differences of opinion and set forth his views for all to read. (See note 32, this chapter, no. IV.)

Regarding *Matt. 24:14*, Simpson argues that there is only one Gospel and that the requirement to witness to it here in Matthew and Acts 1:8 are similar stipulations. The scope of the witness in both verses is the same—all the nations and the earth's extremities. He did not believe that Matt. 24:14 represents a post-second advent enterprise as did the dispensationalists. (*C.M.A.W.* Jan. 1897), p. 60.

Earlier in a sermon, Simpson said regarding this verse:

"This is the consummation. We are preaching the Gospel...for a witness unto all nations, and when we have accomplished this, He will come. He has given to us the key to the future. God's great chronometer...measures...by preparations and conditions, and the hour of the Marriage of the Lamb may be fixed by the bride." *C.A.M.W.* (Dec. 1892), p. 387. See also, *W.W.W.* (July 1883), p. 98; A.B. Simpson, *Missionary Messages* (New York: Christian Alliance Pub. Co., 1925), p. 37; and *Alliance Weekly* (Dec. 1914), p. 157f.

54. During the birth of the Bold Missionary Movement and at the Old Orchard Convention in July 1891, Simpson preached a sermon en-titled *Missionary Wings*, Rev. 14:6. *C.A.M.W.* (Aug. 1891), p. 118.

He concluded his fourth point, "Wings of Faith," with this challenge:

"Our faith will give us wings that will lift us above the difficulties, above the possibilities and above the impossibilities, until we stand in Him around a world, ransomed, evangelized, girdled with the gospel of His glorious grace, and lifting up our faces to the heavens, cry

"Lord, it is done as Thou has commanded. Now, Master, come!"

See also *W.W.W.* (May 1882), p. 166
See also *Chapter 10 Leap Forward*, p. 230

55. *Alliance Weekly* (Nov. 1919), p. 98.

"But he was not only a herald of the dawn, but he had a message from God, as to the meaning of the injunction, 'occupy till I come.' He was the only great teacher we know who linked the evangelization of the world as a necessary preparation for Christ's return with the study of prophecy. It was this pouring out of life and love in missionary channels which was the supreme meaning of his life."

See also Thompson, op. cit., p. 111, 123; *H.C.L.*, 1978 edition, p. 462, stanza 3. The hymn, *A Missionary Cry* was first published in 1891.

56. *W.W.W.* (May 1882), p. 166.

57. Ibid.

58. Ibid.

59. Ibid.

JOHN SAWIN

John Sawin has served as missionary in Viet Nam and as a pastor with the Christian and Missionary Alliance. He has been archivist and librarian at the C&MA Headquarters in Nyack, New York and has compiled considerable historical data relative to the history of the C&MA. He is a graduate of Nyack College and Gordon-Conwell Seminary. He presently serves as Adjunct Professor of Alliance History and Thought at the Seminary.

THE MISSIONARY ESCHATOLOGY OF A.B. SIMPSON

by

Franklin Arthur Pyles

One never attends the annual American Council or the Canadian Biennial Assembly of the Christian and Missionary Alliance without singing stirring hymns about the second coming of Christ. Any visitor would assume that such a display of strong feeling reflects a deeply held doctrinal position which is crucial to the life of the church. But is this so?

More and more people think that the Alliance emphasis on the soon return of Jesus to reign personally on this earth is not really part of the gospel, but simply one of several possible interpretations of obscure biblical texts. However, this was not the case for A.B. Simpson. For him, eschatology was the fountain from which was to issue the work of the church in his day. But, as we shall see, the Alliance has not only moved on to an eschatological emphasis quite different from that personally held by her founder, she has also lost the connection between this doctrine and the missionary mandate.

OVERVIEW

Let us first take an overview of Simpson's basic position. The inner spiritual struggle that he experienced in Louisville,

29

climaxed with his being filled with the Holy Spirit. He tells us that at approximately the same time he became convinced that the pre-millennial teaching concerning the Lord's return was correct.[1] Pre-millennialism says that Jesus Christ will visibly return to earth and establish a kingdom over which he will personally rule for a thousand years. In the closing decades of the nineteenth century, this teaching rapidly grew in popularity as it was proclaimed in Bible conferences across England and the United States.

A particular stream of pre-millennialism is an interpretive system called dispensationalism. Dividing the Bible into seven epochs, it is claimed that God's saving activity is organized differently in each. Thus, the word dispensation is akin to the word management. One of the teachings of dispensationalism is that the present age will end with a terrible seven-year manifestation of the wrath of God upon the whole earth. However, the true church will not partake of this tribulation, for immediately prior to it, Christ will have secretly come and taken the saints away to heaven..This coming, it is taught, may occur at any moment.

Certainly, this school of thought influenced Simpson. He was in close contact with its leadership as can be seen by his speaking in 1892 at a convention at the Congregational Church pastored by C.I. Scofield of Scofield Bible fame.[2] Nevertheless, as shall be demonstrated, he never fully accepted dispensationalism. Although he believed that the church would escape the tribulation, he did not think it possible to say how long this period would be. As well, he did not believe that the coming of the Lord could occur at any moment.

One Bible teacher with whom he had almost perfect agreement on the doctrine of last things was the Baptist theologian and holiness preacher, A.J. Gordon. Gordon interpreted the Book of Revelation using a method called historicism. According to historicism, the visions given to John prophesied the future of the church. However, most of those prophesied events have already occurred. Simpson and Gordon were of one mind in their firm adherence to historicism.

On one issue, Simpson disagreed with Gordon and agreed with the dispensationalists, that is, on the relation of the second coming to the tribulation. Gordon thought that the tribulation would happen and the church would live through it.[3]

Simpson, however, was certain that the saints would be raptured into heaven by Christ before the Great Tribulation began on earth. He based his belief in a pre-tribulational rapture on Luke 21:28, "Lift up your heads, for your redemption draweth nigh," and Luke 21:36, "Watch that you may escape."

Before we look more closely at the implications of these verses for the time of the Lord's coming, it is necessary to address Simpson's apparently temporary adherence to a view known as "partial rapture." This view links the attitude of "watching" (Luke 21:36) to sanctification and eschatology by claiming that only those believers who have been baptized by the Holy Spirit will be caught up in the rapture.

In his sermon on the wise and foolish virgins, reprinted in the two-volume set titled *The Holy Spirit*, Simpson says that those Christians who have not been filled with the Holy Spirit will be left behind by the returning Bridegroom, presumably to undergo the tribulation. It is easy to understand why he might get caught up in such a theory. It strongly links the second coming to personal holiness, by stressing that the hope of seeing Jesus is a motivation to purity (1 John 3:2,3) as well as to seeking the fullness of the Spirit. However, it is certain that "partial rapture" was a fleeting fancy in Simpson's thinking, for after this one reference to it, he never mentions it again.[4] But, he always stressed that the second coming is a motivation to holiness. He loved to tell A.J. Gordon's story of how his daughters knew he would return on the train sometime during a given week, but they did not know on which particular day. So every day that week, they dressed in their finest and waited at the station, hoping each time that this train would bring their father.

This story aptly drives home the implications for both holiness and imminency of the word "watch" in Luke 21:36. The church is to wait eagerly in her best garments, garments of holiness. She is to watch, for while the exact time of his coming is unknown, there are signs that tell us it will be very soon. For Simpson, it was almost as if the church was standing on the station platform on the last day of the week. The very fact that trains have arrived and departed on previous days only serves to strengthen hope, for they are, as it were, the signs that have already occurred. Thus, for Simpson, imminency means

31

precisely this: Christ will appear when the last sign has been fulfilled, and there is only one last sign to wait for.

Here we turn the key that unlocks both his doctrine of last things and his view of the mission of the church. We are not to watch passively for the last sign, as the daughters at the station. We are to bring it about, for the awaited last sign is the preaching of the gospel to every tribe and nation. Thus, all of the Bible's diverse prophetic teachings were held together in Simpson's mind by their relation to the missionary task. Every single point of his end-time thinking had a definite impact on his plan to preach the gospel across the world. And, at the same time, his missionary theology guided his eschatology, for if a point of prophecy had no impact on missionary strategy, he had little concern for it.

An examination of Simpson's eschatology in more detail will reveal how each point served and was served by his missionary theology.

HISTORICISM

Simpson's conversion to pre-millennialism did not result in a complete acceptance of the dispensational format because he viewed its futurist method of prophetic interpretation as a mistake. Instead, he vigorously advanced historicism, which, as we have noted above, believes that the visions of the Book of Revelation denote events that have already occurred and which can be identified in church history. Thus, historicism radically differs from the futurist school which, in its interpretation of the Book of Revelation, considers the seven churches of chapters two and three to be a portrayal of seven periods of church history, while the remainder of the book, after chapter 4:1, is thought to deal with the future Great Tribulation and subsequent events.

Simpson's historicism would most likely have been learned as an intimate part of his Presbyterian upbringing. An example is his commitment to viewing the Pope as the Antichrist, a view that is incorporated into the Westminster Confession. Referring to a prophecy conference address by A.J. Gordon[5] in which Gordon forcefully denied that the Antichrist is an individual, arguing instead that the Antichrist is none other than the papacy as it has existed throughout church history, Simpson says,

> ...in Dr. Gordon's address especially, the full and able presentation of the historical rather than the futurist view of the Antichrist, the only view we are persuaded consistent with Scripture, the face of ecclesiastical history, and the true testimony of the church of Christ respecting the vital issues and real perils of today.[6]

As we have already seen, the soon return of Christ dominated Simpson's view of the Bible. For him, the historicist interpretive method strengthened this conclusion, for the more Scriptural prophesies that have been fulfilled, the fewer remain to be fulfilled before the Lord returns. Thus, the view that the papacy at all its stages in history is the Antichrist, relieved him of any necessity to anticipate Antichrist in the future. This sign then, is past.

Hand in hand with his literalist-historicist model is Simpson's penchant for date-setting. For him, the papacy, as the Antichrist, corresponds to the little horn (Daniel 7) and the beast of Revelation 13. To the decrees of Emperor Phocas in A.D. 607-610 establishing the supremacy of the Bishop of Rome, he adds 1260 years, the days of the beast.[7] This brings us to 1867-70, when, as a result of the Franco-Prussian war, the Pope was virtually put under house arrest by Italian patriots. Of that event, Simpson says, "the Pope fell forever from his throne, and the little horn, as a political system, ceased to exist."[8] Thus, he believed he had already witnessed the end of the Antichrist.

The destruction of the little horn was not the only prophetic countdown Simpson was listening to. There is also the little horn of Dan. 8:9-12, which "was to rise in the East, out of the subdivisions of the Greek Empire, and become the most prominent figure in the subsequent history of the Jewish people."[9] This, Simpson says, is Islam, and the Bible predicts not only the rise, but also the time of the fall of this world religion.[10] The significant date is A.D. 637, when "Omar captured Jerusalem and set up the Mosque of Omar on the site of Solomon's Temple. The place of the sanctuary was indeed cast down and the old Bishop went out of the city crying, 'The Abomination of desolation is set up.'"[11] Although his calculations on the dates are again confusing, this much is certain—

he expected the Ottoman empire to collapse and for that event to signify the end of the little horn of the East, the False Prophet. When World War I did indeed bring its end, Simpson wrote, "We are in the time of the end, we are in the border zone. We are on the edge of everlasting things."[12]

However, while believing that the chronology, as he projected it, was both correct and significant, he realized that God might be operating in a different fashion. In 1910, he wrote, "God does not count time by chronology, but by spiritual conditions, and a single year may count as much for the Lord's appearing as a century."[13] In 1914, he cautioned that, although it was a special year in the prophetic calendar, there might still be years left. And, in 1917, he says,[14]

> Behold, I come quickly [or swiftly is perhaps better], at the same time there is evident provision for a long procession of fulfillments of providential developments and political and spiritual preparations.[15]

Such a view is compatible with his date-setting because he did not hold to an absolute distinction between dispensations, but rather, an overlapping of ages. Drawing from Romans 8:23, he points out that the leaf is contained in the bud which the tree has had all winter.[16] Every age contains the bud of certain evil characteristics that will become a full leaf in the end. As well, certain blessings that properly belong to the millennium can, to an extent, be appropriated by the believer now, especially healing and holiness.

Because of these hedges, Simpson was saved from plunging into the abyss of predictions concerning the exact year of the Lord's return. In fact, Simpson criticized the Millerites (forerunners of the Seventh-Day Adventists) for this very thing.[17]

But why did he involve himself in date-setting at all? Because these studies convinced him that the return of the Lord was very soon. Again and again he recites current events and comments on them in relation to prophecy. He was, as it were, a man who read holding the morning newspaper in one hand and the Bible in the other. But, his historicist perspective protected him from foolish attempts at forecasting the next event in international relations, economic cycles and what-not, on the basis of a supposed correlation with prophetic Scriptures. For example, only after an event such as the British capture of Jerusalem had occurred, was he willing to comment on what he considered to be its significance, not before.[18]

This brings us to the place where we can understand that, in Simpson's thinking, historicism and imminency went hand in hand. Futurism, in his opinion, effectively denied imminency by reason of the sheer number of things yet to happen. If we are yet to see a ten-nation confederation that corresponds to the ten toes of the image in Daniel, the rise of the little horns of the East and West, and the introduction of an individual who is the Antichrist to the world, then there are yet these many things that must occur before Christ can come, in which case the second advent is not imminent by any stretch of the imagination. Thus, it is not only in Simpson's writings, but in those of the writers he published that one sees a consistent promoting of the historicist's view that the ten-nation league has come and gone; the papacy as an institution is the Antichrist, the little horn of the West, the great apostasy, but it is now fading away; Islam is the false prophet, the little horn of the East, and it is being destroyed before their very eyes in the destruction of the Ottoman empire; and the Jews are even now returning to the land.

IMMINENCY

However, while Simpson used the word imminent, he did not think the Lord could come at any moment. He was quite clear on this, writing in 1894:

> We cannot truthfully say that we are expecting the instant return of the Lord Jesus, but rather, that we are looking for it as an imminent event, that is, as one that is impending and rapidly approaching.[19]

The key here is his correlation of the terms "imminent," "impending," and "rapidly approaching." Because of his historicist view, he could say that most of the signs of the Lord's return were already past. Only two remained to be fulfilled: the restoration of the Jews, and the mandate of Matthew 24:14 — "For this Gospel of the Kingdom shall be preached to the whole world as a witness and then shall the end come." He was certain that the Jews were being restored to Palestine and would soon re-emerge as a national state. Subsequent events have shown him to be correct in this, even though the State of Israel was established at a later date than his calculations led him to believe. That left the missionary task as the one sign yet to be accomplished. Once a testimony had been established in every tribe and nation, this last sign would be complete, and the church would then expect the Lord's return at any moment. To this end, he and the people who, with him, founded the missionary society, committed themselves to "bring back the King" by fulfilling the missionary mandate.

MILLENNIAL REIGN

Implicit in this program is the conviction that the second coming of Jesus Christ will occur prior to the inauguration of this kingdom; in other words, pre-millennialism. Simpson understood the Bible to teach three truths about this kingdom which form three pillars that uphold pre-millennial teachings. These are: the personal reign of Christ, the establishment of justice, and the total evangelization of the world. Let us examine each of these along with their implications.

Of great importance in Simpson's interpretation is the implicit relationship between a kingdom and the King.[20] To him it is a truism that a kingdom can only be established by, and ruled over by, an actual King. Thus, *the personal rule of Jesus Christ* on this earth forms the first and central pillar of this millennial theology.

Implicit in this affirmation of the necessity of a personal rule is his polemic against post-millennialism. Simpson asks, what kind of kingdom does post-millennialism offer, with no King? He seems to imply that post-millennialism strips the word kingdom of its majesty, offering instead a vague vision of a worldwide church.

Furthermore, he contends that a coming of Christ that is anterior to the victory removes the anticipation of a personal encounter with the returning Lord as an effective motivating force in the life of the individual and the church. In post-millennialism, only those who live at the close of the golden age can hope to see Christ return and all know that we are not now living in the last days of a peaceful millennium.

> Instead of looking for Christ, multitudes are looking for
> the millennium, the conversion of the world, the regen-
> eration of the nations....His charge was, "Watch not for
> the millennium, but for the Lord."[21]

Simpson's point is that if the millennium must come and go
before the second advent, then we would know for a certainty
that the Lord is not coming in our lifetime, nor in the lifetime
of our children. Why then should we be commanded to
"Watch!"?

> If it were true that 1000 years of spiritual blessings and
> universal righteousness must certainly precede His per-
> sonal coming, then, how irrelevant, how absurd, the
> command to watch for His coming as an ever impending
> event?[22]

Thus, for Simpson, while post-millennialism speaks of a
personal return of Christ, it destroys whatever impact that
return might have on the daily Christian walk. In practical
effect, the personal return is nullified.

Post-millennialism was also rejected because Simpson felt
that the vision of the church converting the whole world was
impossible and impractical. The spread of the truth of
Christianity to the whole world is obviously something that
requires time, more than a lifetime, and thus no one living
could reasonably expect to see even the inauguration of such a
kingdom.

> So long as our theology puts it far distant as a condition of
> the world at large which is to come about through the
> gradual spread of truth and righteousness, we can scarcely
> expect to live to see that consummation.[23]

Simpson's argument is very unconvincing here since post-
millennialism says that this is precisely where we are called to
have faith in the sovereign ability of God to send great revival
to the church and for her to be so Spirit-empowered that she
will rise up and sweep across the world bringing in a great
missionary harvest and inaugurating the golden age with the
conversion of the nations.

In the "Queries" column of the *Weekly*, a response to this very issue was once requested. The answer given was that pre-millennialism does not deny the power of the Spirit to convert the world, it is simply that such a thing is not part of God's program as revealed in the New Testament.[24] But, one is left to wonder, why, if Simpson really believed this, he continued to assert that it was unrealistic to say that the church could see the conversion of the world in this dispensation.

Simpson rejected not only any post-millennialism, but any understanding of prophecy that denied Christ's personal reign. He relates that the Scottish school of theology in which he was raised, considered that Christ's coming meant:

> His manifestation to the Soul of the believer by the Spirit, his coming at death to the saint, and his coming spiritually by the spread of the gospel.[25]

This interpretation may be a variant of either post-millennialism or a-millennialism. The spiritualization of the personal appearing eliminates the basic difference between those two views, leaving only the post-millennial claim that the church will evangelize the world, and the a-millennial denial of such a total victory as a point of divergence. While Simpson's deep reaction to post-millennialism might lead us to believe that he somehow identified it with the teachings of his youth, we must not think that he was unaware of the a-millennial alternative. Although he never mentions it by name, he was as firm in his rejection of it as he was in his rejection of post-millennialism.

His focus was on a-millennialism as it appears in Roman Catholic doctrine. In this strand, the Kingdom of God began with the ascension and is now active in the Church. Simpson rejected this for three reasons.

First, a-millennialism made the kingdom "of this world" in contradiction to the words of Jesus that "my kingdom is not of this world."[26] The fact that the same verse could be used as an objection to pre-millennialism did not seem to deter him.

Secondly, he saw the church as called to engage in warfare to prepare for the King's coming. The kingdom parables of Matthew 13 were, for him, a positive proof that the church is not the kingdom, but labors for the kingdom. In an analysis that cuts against both traditional post-millennialism and a-millennialism, he says that these parables teach that "much of the

38

work of the church would apparently be a failure," but that after the angels have separated the wheat from the tares, "then shall the righteous shine."[27]

His final objection to this brand of millennial interpretation is that it confines the reign of Christ to the spiritual, whereas he saw it as being historical, and therefore having social implications. He affirms that wherever you find "goodness, and love, and peace, and purity, there you have the Kingdom." Yes, "the holy heart and the unselfish life are the sign manuals that you belong to the Kingdom." But, after each admission, Simpson emphatically asks the rhetorical question, "But, is that all?"

> Is right forever to be on the scaffold and wrong forever on the throne, and goodness and patience only manifested through the tears and sorrows of the oppressed?[28]

And Simpson was indeed very sensitive to the issue of economic oppression. He speaks out directly against the injustices visited on the working man[29] and attacks "modern business methods...hoarding, having and holding, immense wealth, luxury, and the oppression of working people."[30]

> Go to the sweat shops of our manufacturing cities, see the poor, attenuated women and children that are toiling for a pittance in suffocating workrooms with long hours of half-remunerated toil, and read the sickening story that has sometime come to us of struggling girls that have been told to their face that they cannot expect to earn a living merely by honest toil, but must also expect to sell themselves as well as the labor of their hands to eke out a sufficient livelihood or help those who are so often dependent on them.[31]

At times, Simpson switches to the second person, showing that he knew of working people sitting before him as he preached, and he speaks to them of going home and seeing their little family hungry and ill-clothed and of shedding tears.[32]

What is the answer? The only satisfying answer, says Simpson, is the advent of a King who will restore to the poor all that was lost.[33]

> That day will bring the righting of our wrongs. That day will pay us the long-deferred hire. That day will put us in

our right place and displace the sons of pride.[34]

Thus, in contrast to a-millennialism, we see that the second pillar of Simpson's pre-millennial view is *justice*. We must be patient for the return of the King.

Perhaps his thinking on the relation of the future kingdom and justice could be summarized in this way. A-millennialism with its spiritualization of all things contains no cry for justice. Post-millennialism, with its unrealistic expectations, proposes an impractical program for justice (in places, Simpson speaks directly against the socialist programs of his contemporary post-millennialists). Only pre-millennialism has a final answer to injustice: the coming of the King who will, in this world, set all things to right. Without the pre-millennial hope we are, in Simpson's opinion, left only with the words of Solomon:

> So I returned and considered all the oppressions that are done under the sun, and beheld the tears of such that were oppressed, and they have no comforter.[35]

Regrettably, Simpson, who began his New York ministry with a strong practical ministry to the poor, gradually turned his back on philanthropy. In so doing, he was following the lead of some pre-millennialists as well as reacting to the rising social-gospel.

This abandonment of any attempt to have an impact on society, including even the early promotion of the temperance movement, left Simpson with evangelism as the sole kingdom activity, but not evangelism in the sense that as one by one people are converted, their lives will change, and thus gradually the world will change. He would identify that with the rejected post-millennarian view. For him, the relation between evangelism and the kingdom is this: God has decreed that a witness be established throughout the whole world and then the end will come.

Evangelism is the third pillar of Simpson's millennial view. Through the witness of the church in this age, a people of God will be gathered out of the Gentiles, some from every tribe and nation. The task of evangelism is to give to everyone at least one chance to hear the gospel and to see some from every group converted. Rightly understood, Simpson tells us, this commission saves us from discouragement with the actual results of missions and gives a simple and practical aim within reach of the church.[36]

However, the story does not end with the second coming of Christ. The world is to be converted, but not by the church in this dispensation. This great missionary harvest will be brought in by the converted Jews during the time of the millennium.[37] In this way, the nations will be converted and a rule of peace will cover the earth.

This conviction, that the church was to establish a testimony, but the millennial Jews would carry forward the work of converting the world, guided the early missionary strategy of the Alliance. Men and women were hastily sent overseas with a minimum of training, sometimes as little as six months, because of the felt urgency of the hour. It was not expected that a national church would rise up, but only that a few would be converted as a testimony. Hence, indigenous principles were not used. Yet despite many mistakes, national churches did begin to emerge, and Alliance missionary methodology began to run on tracks other than those laid by Simpson's eschatology.

Simpson was convinced that the completion of this missionary mandate was the key to the return of the Lord. The clues given by dates were important, but that timetable would be hurried or delayed in accordance with the obedience of the church.

> The Lord has left to us in some degree the determination of the time of His coming. There is a sense in which our chronology may be condensed into briefer limits by intense activity.... There is such a thing as accelerated as well as retarded time and we may accelerate the time of the Lord's return by meeting the spiritual conditions and preparing the way.[38]

Thus, eschatology was the life blood of Simpson's missionary theology. That the imminent return, not in the sense of "any moment," but in the sense of an event that could be soon, could be within this generation, if the church obeys, was the well-spring of his missionary motivation. His fascination with the "signs of the times," his playing with date-setting and his support of Zionism, all are colors on the spectrum of the truth of the soon return of Christ, shining through the prism of the missionary task.

CONCLUSION

The Christian and Missionary Alliance has stood in a certain tension with the eschatology of its founder since his death. Perhaps nothing better illustrates this tension than the refusal of the society's book publishing house to reprint any of Simpson's four books on that doctrine. Yet, the society claims to stand now, as it did then, on the assertion that part of the gospel is that Jesus is the coming King. What are the causes of this ambivalent attitude and how might a solution be formulated?

The central tension is between imminency and practical theology. For Simpson, these two concerns interlocked. However, they so interlock for very few today. The reason for this is that Simpson's rather elastic definition of imminency has been rejected by many in favor of the "any moment" version. But, any moment imminency cuts the nerve of missionary motivation as it should arise out of Matthew 24:14, for it leaves no relation between the church's obedience and Christ's appearing.

As well as this tension caused·by redefinition, there is the problem of the overall shift in missionary strategy caused by the church-growth movement and the recent hidden-peoples movement. Simpson and his contemporaries thought that the number of language groups to be reached was relatively small. Missions researchers now know that there are a vast number of languages, and some estimate there are 17,000 distinct people groups without a Christian church.

Neither the Alliance nor any other missionary agency could be satisfied with merely winning a few converts from each of these groups as "a testimony." We now realize that people are not truly having the gospel communicated to them until it is being communicated by a church indigenous to their culture. To this end, the contemporary goal of missions is to establish churches and for these churches to grow until every idol is cast down and the cross is lifted over the people.

But is this pre-millennialism? Perhaps, but at first it sounds suspiciously like the old post-millennial goal of converting the world. Hence, there lies before the Christian and Missionary Alliance a theological task: once again to develop a missionary-eschatology. In the next few paragraphs, I will endeavour to propose a profile for such an eschatology.

The statement of Jesus in Matthew 24:14 is quite clear and should continue as the foundation for our missionary work. We must once again realize that imminency is compatible with the fact that there is yet something to do. Even as the apostle John prayed, "even so come, Lord Jesus," we must be active in prayer and obedience in order to hasten the day of His appearing. To that end, we, along with evangelical churches around the world, must double and redouble our efforts at sending missionaries, especially targeting the yet-unreached people groups. In this way, imminency will cease to be a slogan and will again be a pulse beat for our churches.

Simpson's view that the conversion of the world is too great a task for the church and must await the millennial work of the Jews is self-contradictory. If it is too great a task now, why will it be any less difficult then? The presence of Jesus on this earth would not, in and of itself, reduce the stubborn pride of men's hearts. Without at all denying that there is a future work for converted Israel (Romans 11:12), it must be said that the church has been commanded and empowered by the risen Lord and the descended Spirit to preach the gospel to all the world, to disciple and to baptize the nations.

Here, Simpson's concept of "the overlapping of the ages" comes to our aid. We tend to think of the beginning of the millennium as a clear-cut moment, the moment of Christ's return. This is certainly true. But, there is a sense in which the reign of Christ is manifested in the church now. Wherever the church pushes forward its boundaries, the darkness and terror of Satan's kingdom is pushed backward. Simpson is right— this will not be done completely by the church, but awaits its consummation when Christ returns. But this inability to complete the task before He appears is not because of an inherent weakness of the Holy Spirit and the church, it is simply a decree of God. This is seen in Psalm 2:8, "I will give you the nations as your inheritance," and Philippians 2:10,11, "Every knee shall bow...and every tongue confess that Jesus Christ is Lord." These verses indicate that the worldwide recognition of Jesus as the Messiah will be a result of the Parousia. That the church is now doing kingdom work provides us with an eschatological foundation for building churches, for we are indeed building for the future, even the future millennium. At the same time, it provides us with a standpoint

43

from which we can act as citizens in the world, even though our true citizenship is in heaven. It must be said with sorrow that many evangelicals in the generations that followed Simpson not only rejected any action to alleviate the oppression of the poor, they took the side of the rich and denied the existence of oppression.

A truly missionary church must be ready to proclaim clearly that it is the Bible, not Marxism, that not only condemns the exploitation of the poor, but provides whole societies a way of escape from the grinding wheel of economic privation. The Bible teaches that the individual has worth because he or she is made in God's image; work is a God-honoring activity; all buying and selling is to be done in fairness, including the buying and selling of labor; and it also gives many other teachings on the family and society. Whenever a people have accepted these teachings as a whole, they have risen above the poverty that binds them. This is not simply because they, as individuals, one at a time, change their ways. The church itself, as a viable community, becomes an agent to change the structures of society that promote oppression.

This total message must be seen as part of the gospel of the kingdom, for it is an extension of the call to practical holiness in light of the second coming. Again, Simpson was right. Justice is an integral part of the millennial kingdom, and it is the failure of either post-millennialism or a-millennialism to provide for justice that causes us to insist that there must be a personal rule of our king. But, we must understand that we are no more allowed to await passively His appearing to establish justice than we are to wait for the trumpet to sound before we seriously begin the task of converting the world.

The current divorce between our missionary practice and our eschatology can be overcome by again asserting the strengths of pre-millennialism: a real kingdom will soon be inaugurated on this earth by the personal presence of Jesus Christ. But, even now, the church prepares for and, to an extent, can share the victory and blessings of that kingdom. To that end, she purifies herself and presses ahead with the task of evangelizing, discipling and modeling the life of a spiritual community that functions on the basis of love. The church can know that every day that she lives in such obedience, she hastens the return of the king.

ENDNOTES

1. A.B. Simpson, "How I Was Led to Believe in Pre-Millennarianism," *Christian Alliance and Missionary Weekly* 7, no. 19 (November 13, 1891): 298-299.

2. Simpson, *Christian Alliance Weekly*, 8, no. 24 (June 10, 1892): 370.

3. However, he did not believe that the tribulation is the 70th week of Daniel, and therefore, he denied that we could know its length. His exegesis of Daniel's weeks from Daniel 9 is as follows: "The decrees" is that issued by Artaxerxes in 457 B.C. In 7 weeks (49 years), the walls were rebuilt in troublous times. In 62 more weeks (434 years), we are brought to the Messiah, in A.D. 26. Because of an error in dating Christ's birth, Simpson says that makes Christ 30 years old. "He shall confirm the covenant." Simpson says the "pronoun refers to Christ who is the subject of the whole prophecy." Christ confirms the covenant by calling Israel to himself and the apostles continue to preach to Israel for about three and a half years after the crucifixion. "In the midst of the week shall cause sacrifices and oblation to cease." "After three and one-half years of public ministry, in the midst of the final week, our Lord and Savior, Jesus Christ, was offered on the cross ...and that caused other sacrifices to cease." The other half of the week was spent by the apostles offering the covenant to Israel until the martyrdom of Stephen.

   Simpson, "The Seventy Weeks of Daniel," *The Christian and Missionary Alliance*, 27, no. 22 (June 1, 1907): 254,255. This view is virtually identical with that set forth by A.J. Gordon in his book, *Ecce Venit*. See also the works of H. Grattan Guiness.

4. Simpson, "Just one thing they lacked, but it was enough to prevent their entering in," *The Holy Spirit*, or *Power From on High Part II* (New York: Christian Alliance Publishing Co., 1924), p. 31. Again, "but it will be too late to enter into the joys of the marriage and escape the sorrows of the great tribulation," p. 33.

5. This address by A.J. Gordon was subsequently printed in *The Word, Work and World* (November 1886): 296-309.

6. Simpson, *The Word, Work and World*, 7 (October 1886): 251.

7. Simpson, *The Coming One* (New York: Christian Alliance Publishing Company, 1912), p. 83. Simpson here specifically says he is using solar years (365 days) for the calculations.

8. Ibid.

9. Ibid., p. 102.

10. Simpson, *The Coming One*, p. 102-109; *Gospel of the Kingdom*, p. 153-164.

11. Simpson, *The Coming One* (New York: Christian Alliance Publishing Company, 1912), p. 108.

12. Simpson, "The Fall of Jerusalem in the Light of Prophecy," *The Alliance Weekly*, 49, no. 20 (February 16, 1918): 307.

13. Simpson, *The Christian and Missionary Alliance*, 35, no. 5 (October 29, 1910): 72.

14. Simpson, *The Alliance Weekly*, 42, no. 13 (December 26, 1914): 193.

15. Simpson, "Were the Apostles and Early Christians Disappointed and Mistaken in Their Expectation of the Lord's Immediate Return?," *The Alliance Weekly*, 47, no. 25 (November 24, 1917): 386.

16. Simpson, "Overlapping of the Coming Age," *The Alliance Weekly*, 49, no. 16, p. 242.

17. Simpson, *The Word, Work and World*, 1, no. 1, p. 3.

18. Simpson, *The Alliance Weekly*, 49, no. 12, p. 177.

19. Simpson, "Editorials," *The Christian Alliance and Foreign Missionary Weekly*, 12, no. 20 (May 18, 1894): 527.

20. Ibid., "How I Was Led to Believe in Pre-Millennarianism."

21. Simpson, "That Blessed Hope," *The Word, Work and World*, 1, no. 4 (May 1882): 166.

22. Ibid., Also, see "Looking For and Hastening Forward," *The Christian and Missionary Alliance*, 20, no. 23 (June 8, 1898): 533.

23. Simpson, "Looking For and Hastening Forward," *The Christian and Missionary Alliance*, no. 23 (June 8, 1898): 533.

24. Simpson, "Queries," *The Christian Alliance and Foreign Missionary Weekly*, 12, no. 21, p. 577. It is possible that this column was not written by A.B. Simpson himself.

25. Ibid., "How I Was Led to Believe in Pre-Millennarianism."

26. Simpson, "Thy Kingdom Come," *The Alliance Weekly*, 43, no. 4 (October 24, 1914): 51.

27. Ibid.

28. Ibid.

29. Simpson, "Our Attitude Towards the Lord's Coming," *Christian Alliance and Missionary Weekly*, 40, no. 16 (October 20, 1893): 244.

30. Simpson, "The Practical Hope of the Lord's Coming," *The Christian and Missionary Alliance*, 34, no. 19 (August 6, 1910): 305.

31. Ibid., p. 306.

32. Simpson, "The Practical Value and Influence of the Doctrine of the Lord's Coming," *Christian Alliance and Missionary Weekly*, 9, no. 15, 16 (October 7, 14, 1910): 305.

33. Simpson, "Times of Salvation; Times of Refreshing; Times of Restitution," *The Christian and Missionary Alliance*, 34, no. 22 (August 27, 1910).

34. Ibid., "The Practical Hope of the Lord's Coming," p. 306.

35. Ibid.

36. Simpson, "Christ our Coming Lord," *Christian Alliance and Missionary Weekly* (July 15, 1892): 42.

37. Simpson, "Editorials," *The Christian and Missionary Alliance*, 28, no. 3 (January 15, 1897): 60. See also *The Coming One*, p. 64.

38. Simpson, "The Scriptural Principles of Missions," *The Christian and Missionary Alliance*, 24, no. 24 (June 24, 1905): 398.

FRANKLIN ARTHUR PYLES

Franklin Arthur Pyles received a B.A. from Fort Wayne Bible College, an M. Div. from Wheaton College Graduate School and a Ph.D. from Garrett Seminary and Northwestern University. His doctoral studies centered on Philosophy and Systematic Theology; his dissertation deals with the Philosophical Foundation of C.S. Lewis' Apologetics. Dr. Pyles served with Youth For Christ in Fort Wayne, and pastored Alliance Churches in Chicago and Detroit before joining the faculty of Canadian Theological Seminary in 1982 as Assistant Professor of Theology.

THE SOCIAL INTEREST AND CONCERN
OF A.B. SIMPSON

by

John V. Dahms

Albert Benjamin Simpson's foremost concern was to bring man to Christ. Evangelism was his primary interest. Closely bound up with this was his emphasis on the deeper life. He realized that the effectiveness of evangelistic effort was largely proportional to the quality of the spiritual life and experience of those who preached, laboured and prayed for the salvation of those men and women who needed to become members of God's kingdom.

Because he was so concerned with the calling of the lost to repentance and the redeemed to the deeper life, he could so express himself as to leave the impression that Christians should not be involved in social welfare activities. In 1897, he urged,

> Philanthropic schemes and social reforms are absorbing the interest and enthusiasm of thousands of redeemed men and women who ought to be giving their strength and wealth to do the best things and not the second best. We admit there is something good in these enterprises. They have a place and a value, but let the world take care of them.... There are...plenty of people to run social reform and temperance societies; plenty of people to fight the political battle. God wants you to give the gospel to the world, to rise to the highest calling, to do the best things.[1]

49

There is considerable evidence, however, that this was an overstatement. Though they are not numerous, there are occasions when Simpson expressed himself somewhat differently and implied that it was right and proper that Christians devote time, energy and financial support to philanthropic and welfare activities.

In 1882, he lauded the missionary efforts overseas of various churches, which had resulted not only in souls being saved, but also in "hundreds of Christian colleges and schools, hundreds of benevolent and charitable societies, disbursing millions to the suffering and the poor," and added that "the heart would be false to every Christian instinct if it did not bless and thank the Lord of Harvest."[2]

In 1886, he wrote,

We should give for the relief of God's poor and suffering children...allowing no true child of God to be in want or suffering....Nor should the unworthy poor be altogether neglected, but so aided as to prevent the abuse of our gifts for sinful indulgence, and so as to promote industry, independence and trust in God.[3]

It was probably in the same year that he also stated,

He (Christ) wants His church to be complete in every department of work; He wants us to have not only the mere preaching of the Gospel, but work for the poor and lowly; work for the destitute and the sick; work for the rich and worldly. He wants us to be a people who will combine every department of Christian beneficence which it is right for the church of God to sustain.[4]

In 1889, he affirmed that the Parable of the Good Samaritan "in its first application...is...designed to exemplify the duties of humanity and kindness to our neighbour,"[5] a statement he repeated in a sermon preached on December 10, 1905.[6] Also in 1889, he wrote that the Parable of the Great Supper in Luke 14 urges us to do "all that sympathy and consideration can do" for those suffering physical ills and material want, and, in this connection, promoted "the Christian philanthropies and blessed agencies of consecrated evangelism."[7] It is reported further that in 1895, he interpreted that same parable to imply that

Christians should be involved in meeting "the physical needs and material miseries" of mankind by providing "real help for human suffering as well as human sin."[8]

In 1896, Simpson stated, "The law of Christ is the bearing of others' burdens, the sharing of others' griefs, sacrificing yourself for another."[9] Also in 1901, he interpreted the exhortation in James 2:15-16 as follows:

> It is doing things to relieve and help the temporal needs of our suffering men....Our acts of love and help may be His links in bringing them to see the attraction of His love and listen to the Gospel of His Grace.[10]

In 1905, he encouraged "charitable relief for the orphans and the helpless."[11]

Perhaps Simpson's most significant statement relative to Christian social action was published in 1893:

> We should aim to bring all the work of God within the sphere of the church of Christ....There is room not only for the worship of God, the teaching of sacred truth and the evangelization of the lost, but also for every phase of practical philanthropy and usefulness. There may be, in perfect keeping with the simple order and dignity of the church of God, the most aggressive work for the masses and the widest welcome for every class of sinful men; the ministry of healing for the sick and suffering administered in the name of Jesus; the most complete provision for charitable relief; industrial training and social elevation for the degraded classes, workshops for the unemployed, homes for the orphaned, shelter for the homeless, refuges for the inebriates, the fallen and the helpless; missions for the heathen; Christian literature for the instruction of the people, and every agency needed to make the church of God the light of the world and the mothering of the suffering and the lost. And there is no work that will be more glorifying to God than a church that will embrace just such features and completeness.[12]

Even more eloquent than such statements is the testimony of Simpson's activities. Three months after resigning as pastor of Thirteenth St. Presbyterian Church in New York City, he and thirty-five others met in February, 1882, and founded the Gospel Tabernacle Church "for the especial purpose of Gospel work, particularly among the neglected classes, both at home and abroad."[13] That "the neglected classes" were especially in view is evidence of great social concern. Even if it was only the evangelization of such classes that was envisaged at that time — and we are not sure that it was — Simpson was well aware that there is nothing so powerful to effect social uplift, at least in the long term, as the experience of Christ's regenerating grace followed by walking in the Spirit. Indeed, he himself said, in elaborating on the Parable of the Great Supper recorded in Luke 14,

> The provision of the Gospel for the temporal needs and physical in humanity is surely set forth in this picture.... It (the Gospel) alleviates their physical condition. It is of infinite value even in improving the material condition of the poor, and leading to prosperity and success in temporal things.[14]

Worthy concern for the spiritual welfare of people cannot long be divorced from active concern for their physical, material and social deprivations, however much the spiritual concern may be primary, as it ought to be. Such proved to be the case in the early years of the Christian and Missionary Alliance, years in which A.B. Simpson was its guiding light and its towering inspiration.

Due to the influence of the Alliance and its leadership, the ministry in "hospitals, almshouses and charitable institutions" in New York City was so considerable by 1894, that it was said that even A.B. Simpson would have been at a loss to tell "how much the Alliance was doing for all (such) agencies of Christian work in that city."[15] At the turn of the century, the annual report of the Gospel Tabernacle in New York City, the "mother" congregation of the Christian and Missionary Alliance where Simpson was himself in charge, contained the statement that members of the congregation were involved in "much useful work...in nearly all the missions and charitable institutions of the city."[16] And in 1907, it was reported in *The Christian and Missionary Alliance Weekly* that many of the charitable institutions "within the limits of New York City, and, indeed, for many miles around" had benefited from the influence of the Gospel Tabernacle, and that many of their leaders were adherents of the Christian and Missionary Alliance.[17]

Highly influential in this connection was the annual Rescue Day which grew out of the Gospel Tabernacle's monthly "all-night prayer meeting...for the city mission workers of New York." The Rescue Day program, which included reports and presentations concerning welfare agencies and institutions of various kinds, generated widespread interest and support.[18] It must be added, moreover, that the sample and inspiration of the Gospel Tabernacle and its pastor spread with the Alliance throughout North America and overseas so that, along with a mighty evangelistic enterprise, there developed social enterprises of various kinds in many of the places where the representatives of the Alliance made their influence felt.

From such general statements concerning Simpson's impact on welfare work, we turn now to more specific material.

Rescue Homes for Women

Though the Alliance as such did not establish or maintain homes for fallen women, Alliance people closely connected with the movement did so.[19] Indeed, there is report of such a home as early as 1882, under the direction of a Mrs. Henry Naylor.[20] It is also reported that the following year (1883), the ministry of the Gospel Tabernacle inspired a Miss Margaret Strachan to open a home for women in a section of New York City where there were many houses of ill fame.[21]

In 1889, the Alliance "'solemnly set [Mrs. Emma Whittemore] apart' for a special rescue ministry to girls," and on October 25, 1890, she established in New York City, the Door of Hope, "a refuge and a home for girls of the better class who have been tempted from home and right."[22] Dr. Simpson's support of the venture is evidenced by the fact that he gave the address at its dedication. As a result of her efforts, by 1903, sixty-one Doors of Hope missions were established in various parts of the United States of America.[23] One of these was opened in Fort Worth, Texas in 1891 by a Mrs. Delia Collins, member of a family prominent in Alliance work in that city.[24]

Alliance support for such ventures is further evidenced by the fact that Henry Wilson, who became associate pastor at the

Gospel Tabernacle in 1891, and field superintendent for Alliance work in the United States in 1901, an office he retained until his death in 1908, became chaplain of the Magdalene Home for Women in 1894, and thereafter promoted that home and other institutions of the kind at the annual Rescue Day described above.[25] From 1893 to 1902, the Alliance gave its support to what was known as the Rescue Band, which provided temporary lodging for many girls, and, beginning in 1895, provided training for girls in an industrial department.[26] Indeed, the relationship of Alliance branches and members with homes for "fallen" women in a number of cities is reported.[27]

Orphans and Orphanages

One of the welfare institutions most closely connected with the Alliance was the Berachah Orphanage,[28] opened in 1886 at College Point on Long Island, New York, and later relocated in Nyack, New York. It provided a ministry to needy children beginning in 1888.[29] In an 1897 article, apparently by Simpson, it is stated,

> The work of caring for the little ones, and especially the orphaned ones, is a fully recognized and important department of our Alliance work.[30]

Other orphanages in the continental United States besides Berachah were later to receive "direct and indirect support" from the Christian and Missionary Alliance.[31] In addition, famine in India in the 1890s led Alliance missionaries there to provide care for hundreds of children.

Articles by A.B. Simpson in *The Christian Alliance and Foreign Missionary Weekly* helped secure financial support for the "helpless children" in famine-stricken India.[32] Henry Wilson, Simpson's associate, became especially known for his activities and accomplishments on behalf of needy children. For a number of years, the contributions he secured from U.S. children underwrote the care of one hundred of the orphans who were provided for by Christian and Missionary Alliance missionaries in India.[33]

Rest Homes and Medical Missions

In 1883, "Mr. Simpson...felt impelled to open his own home

for personal ministry to the afflicted," and on May 16, 1883, it was dedicated "as a Home for Faith and Physical Healing." It was said at the time that "any sufferer who is really willing to exercise and act faith for healing will be received for a limited time for instruction and waiting upon God for temporal and spiritual blessing."[34] But the need for separate facilities was evident, and a year later, on May 5, 1884, Berachah Home was dedicated in another part of New York City, an institution to which Simpson devoted a good deal of his time, and which he described as a "delightful" place "of rest or spiritual blessing."[35] Moreover, it was so fruitful a venture that it is reported that in its first fifteen years of ministry, 10,000 had been "transformed" through "rest, quickening, and Divine healing."[36]

With respect to this report, it is to be kept in mind that though Berachah Home was dedicated as a home for rest and healing, the healing in view was divine, not medical. Simpson believed that others should avail themselves of medical means, but he taught that Christians should rely on divine power alone for relief from physical ills.[37] In this connection, it is instructive to note that he says concerning the physical ailments of children in the Berachah Orphanage, an institution separate from Berachah Home:

> In the case of the children of our Orphanage, we would not feel justified in taking this responsibility [i.e., the responsibility of trusting solely in Christ for their healing], in view of the law of the state requiring the care of an attendant physician.
>
> In all cases of sickness in others where there is danger involved and you have the responsibility to meet the obligations of the law, it is a great matter, if possible, to have some regular physician who believes in Divine Healing within call, so as to be responsible if necessary.[38]

Though Berachah Home was the most important of the homes established by or connected with the Alliance, a variety of other homes came into existence[39] and/or were supported in one way or another because of the influence of Simpson's ministry.[40]

Miss Kate White opened her home near the Gospel Tabernacle where she was a member and devoted herself to "caring for, feeding and clothing the poor and needy, worthy and unworthy."[41] In her obituary (1898), it was stated that her home was "a shelter for the homeless and unfortunate.... She often even denied herself a bed and food to be hospitable to others."[42] Carrie Judd Montgomery, "a close friend of Simpson's from the early 1880s," established rest homes in Buffalo, New York, and in San Francisco, California. Though she and her husband joined the Salvation Army in 1892, they and their work continued to enjoy the appreciation and support of Simpson himself and of the Alliance, to which they also belonged.[43]

Typical of various other homes in North America bearing some connection with the Alliance was a home in Philadelphia directed by Mrs. Sarah Beck, which existed for the sake of people "weary or sick in body or mind."[44]

In the area of health ministries, mention must be made of the ministry of Berachah Mission in the section of New York City known as Hell's Kitchen. There "Dr. Dowkonut...held a free dispensary and gave medical attendance without charge to the poor of the neighbourhood."[45] No doubt, Alliance inspiration led to similar ministries elsewhere.[46]

Besides the Alliance-inspired efforts on behalf of physical needs in North America, Alliance missionaries overseas engaged in extensive medical programs in alleviation of physical distresses. As early as 1882, Simpson praised medical missions overseas[47] and in that same year called for prayer and counsel concerning a proposed sanitarium on the Bosporus.[48] In 1892, he not only defended medical missions but also invited volunteers for medical missionary service in Africa.[49] It should be noted, however, that he frequently emphasized that medical missions are justified because they open people's hearts to the reception of the Gospel.[50]

Industrial Missions

The Christian and Missionary Alliance Weekly, July 4, 1890, reported a sewing school at Catherine Mission in New York City. In 1891, a movement to provide work for men in Rescue Missions was sanctioned.[51] As already noted, beginning in 1895, the Rescue Band lodged and trained girls, a ministry which enjoyed Alliance support until 1902. Beginning in the mid-1890s, William Raws of Germantown, PA, operated a plant employing 125 people on a "work-for-what-you-can-get plan."

This provision, whereby the needs of otherwise unemployed people were met without undermining their self-respect, was featured in the annual Rescue Day program of the Alliance.[52] Door of Hope establishments, mentioned above, provided training for their residents. In the New York City Door of Hope "homemaking, dressmaking and fancy serving" were taught. On the Door of Hope property at Tappan, New York, there was "training in gardening and poultry care as well." A Women's Industrial Center was part of the Door of Hope establishment in Fort Work, Texas.[53] In Buffalo, New York, there was an "Alliance-related 'Industrial School' for girls."[54]

In 1893, A.B. Simpson reported on a visit he had made to India. One of the things that excited his interest was an Industrial School and Workshop operated by Alliance people in Akola, India, for the teaching of "useful trades to the native boys." He considered it desirable that the operation be "considerably enlarged" and "two or three manufacturing departments added." Though he held that "the missionary society ought not to put its funds into this work," he encouraged readers to invest their lives and their money in the project.[55]

In the years which followed Simpson's visit to India, famine conditions in that sub-continent led Alliance workers to a greatly expanded program of aid. A major project in this respect was the operation of a 350-acre farm in Sanand, India, where orphans were settled and taught how to earn their own livelihood.[56]

Famine Relief

In 1891, relief was sent through the Alliance to flood victims in China.[57] During a severe famine in South China in 1903, Alliance missionaries provided food for as many as 3,000 per day.[58] With respect to this famine, Simpson wrote, "We cannot too strongly appeal for help in this hour of need and opportunity."[59]

As indicated earlier, famine relief was also provided for thousands in India at the turn of the century. A.B. Simpson wrote at length describing the desperate need and appealed to North American members of the Society to contribute generously. On one occasion he declared, "It would seem to be the duty of God's children...to...plan for systematic gifts...

for the next few months...." He added that "enemies of the truth are not neglected" in Alliance relief efforts, though "special provision (was made) for the native converts and their families."[60] Again in 1912, he appealed for famine relief in India.[61]

Such relief was not only provided overseas in places like China and India. Needy people in the United States were assisted as well. There is on record the appreciation of a Kansas family which had received eight barrels of clothing as well as a gift of money in 1896, meeting not only its desperate need but that of neighbours as well.[62] A similar letter of gratitude for "food and clothing" assisting "the drought stricken in many districts" was received from Springfield, Montana, in 1903.[63] In response to the San Francisco earthquake and fire of 1906, A.B. Simpson immediately sent aid, and appealed in the Christian and Missionary Alliance for general contributions. Within a week the members of his Gospel Tabernacle alone contributed some $700 for the purpose.[64] In 1913, he urged contribution for flood relief in the Central and Western districts of the C&MA.[65]

Immigrants

Alliance people were assisting immigrants from Germany as early as 1887.[66] In 1890, the Alliance began mission work in the section of New York City known as "little Italy." By 1895, this effort included a home for girls. Students and faculty of Nyack College conducted services in Italian in surrounding communities and offered night school classes three times a week.[67] It may be assumed that such efforts had the support of Simpson himself.

M. Nardi, "a lifelong friend of A.B. Simpson," aided Italians in hospitals, prisons and elsewhere. In one of the poorest areas of Chicago, he established a vocational school for children, a kindergarten, a Sunday School and a sewing school. In another part of the city, he instituted evening classes in English. And in other places, he initiated similar programs for needy newcomers from Italy. That Simpson compiled a biographical volume honouring Nardi, indicates at least general appreciation of his work, if not outright support.[68]

Temperance

Miss J.E. Dougall, a friend of Simpson, provided leadership for the Women's Christian Temperance Union in Montreal, and played a considerable part in its development across Canada, becoming the national vice-president in 1903. At her death in 1904, tribute was paid to her in the columns of *The Christian and Missionary Alliance Weekly*.[69] Mrs. Delia Collins of Fort Worth, Texas, and Mrs. John Best of Pittsburgh, PA, were prominent in WCTU work in their respective states as well as being strong supporters of the Alliance.[70] Josephus Pulis, whose life and leadership in Alliance work inspired Simpson to write his biography, was on the staff of the Christian Home for Intemperate Men.[71] In addition, Henry Wilson, Associate Pastor of the Gospel Tabernacle during Simpson's leadership there, was president of a mission which emphasized the pledging of total abstinence.[72]

A.B. Simpson himself delivered daily Bible lectures in the mid-1890s at the World's W.C.T.U. Evangelistic Training School.[73] The weekly magazine he edited included a temperance column for a number of years.[74] In 1907, he praised the temperance movement, and added, "All hail to every social, political and religious influence and effort that can further restrain this sinful curse."[75] In subsequent years, however, he points out that despite social efforts, the consumption of alcoholic beverages had increased.[76] He emphasized that without Christ, social and political effort is of no permanent help.[77]

General Education[78]

In his earlier writings, Simpson strongly favoured educational work on the part of Christian organizations. In 1882, he praised educational missions overseas.[79] In 1885, we have reference to a "Chinese School" in connection with the Twenty-third St. Tabernacle in New York.[80] In 1887, a kindergarten in connection with Simpson's church in New York City is reported.[81]

Beginning in 1891, Simpson repeatedly spoke of the desire to establish a "preparatory school for the education of children connected with the Christian Alliance."[82] The *First Annual Report of the Christian and Missionary Alliance*, 1897-98, pp. 13, 85, contains a recommendation urging the provision of schools for Alliance children in the United States. Such provision was said to be "one of the greatest needs" and of "great importance." In 1894, we read of a day school in Stockton, California, under Alliance auspices, the purpose there being "to bring the children, young and old, to Christ, and to prepare them for missionary work at home and abroad."[83] However, it appears that Alliance-sponsored education of a general nature did not begin in the New York area until 1906. For a number of years thereafter, college courses and an academy initially for higher school grades were provided, but their existence was temporary.[84] According to D.W. Cartmel, "the Academy had been justified on the grounds that it supplied an alternative to the state or local schools controlled by a philosophy not consistent with Alliance views of the Bible."[85]

Provision of a liberal education to white boys and girls of the southern U.S. mountains who could not afford to go to the regular schools was reported in 1908.[86] Moreover, in the 1917-18 Report of the Alliance, schools in India and in South China were reported, including a school for blind girls in the latter area. The need for more schools in India was noted.[87] No doubt many more Christian schools both in North America and overseas were sponsored and/or inspired by Alliance people who had been influenced directly or indirectly by A.B. Simpson.

Simpson's support of educational enterprises seems, however, to have been a response to practical needs as he perceived them, rather than being rooted in his fundamental convictions. In 1893 he declared, "We are not called to build up great educational institutions" overseas, though he conceded that in such areas as South China "a certain amount of educational work seems to be necessary, as the native schools compel their pupils to learn and practice heathenism."[88] Indeed, in that same year he declared, his view is influenced by the conviction that the gospel could be quickly taken to all the world and then Christ would come.[89] Perhaps one can discern how he would have harmonized his support of educational institutions with such a view in a statement he made in 1912:

> Whereas educational work may be justified on the grounds of expediency, direct evangelism and Bible training work rest upon the distinct command of Christ, as well as His personal example and that of the apostles.

The former may be a matter of opinion, the latter never. It is binding. Evangelism is the first and great business of the church, and it must always remain so.[90]

Race Relations

In a day when racial prejudice was widespread, A.B. Simpson referred to the blacks who supported him as his "beloved coloured brethren."[91] In 1896, Simpson's periodical published an article by an Alliance worker in the southern United States in which the living conditions of Negroes, and attitudes toward them, were strongly criticized.[92] The Alliance constituency supported schools for coloured people, the most important, perhaps, being the Lovejoy Missionary Institute in North Carolina, which opened its doors to needy people of all colours in 1906.[93] A variety of homes and institutions ministering chiefly to Negroes were either sponsored or heavily supported by Alliance people. Moreover, the columns of the *Alliance Weekly* publicized and commended such efforts, including Peter Robinson's rescue home for women established in 1904, the social work of Miss Joanne Moore of Nashville, Tennessee (Alliance responsibility for it beginning in 1906), and the Steele Home in Chattanooga, Tennessee.[94]

The attitude and efforts of A.B. Simpson and his co-labourers with respect to the racial situation in the United States is important evidence that they were people of noble Christian stature.

War and Peace

Simpson's views on war and peace seem to have been complex. On the one hand, he made clear that he supported international efforts which made for peace. In 1896, he criticized the policy of Britain and the United States with respect to Venezuela.[95] In April, 1911, he indicated his support for President Taft's proposal of an Arbitration Treaty between Britain and the United States, and called upon the Alliance constituency to give hearty support to "Arbitration Sunday."[96]

It is true that early in 1914, Simpson declared that peace propaganda and effort are of little value. Only Christ brings peace. "The best peace propaganda...is the preaching of the Gospel of Grace to sinners of all nations."[97] It may be that the clouds of war on the horizon were making him pessimistic about human peace efforts. It may be, however, that his earlier support for international peace efforts was always with the conviction that it was only a very little that they could accomplish.

Despite his concern for peace, Simpson voiced opposition to those who held that war is always wrong, declaring,

> While the spirit of Christianity is preeminently for peace, yet God has also a providential purpose of dealing with sinful nations, and sometimes war is one of His scourges.[98]

It seems to be Simpson himself who stated in 1896, "President Kruger showed an excellent spirit in offering troops to assist the English, if necessary, in repelling the Matabele rising."[99] Moreover, he supported the United States in its war with Spain, declaring that it was right for the American government "to interpose for the protection of the outraged Cuban people," and urging his readers to pray that "this war shall utterly and speedily accomplish God's highest purposes for the world and the coming of His Son."[100] He opposed restoration of the Philippines to Spain after that war,[101] and rejoiced when it was announced that this would not take place, because it would now be possible to "share with them (the Philippine peoples) the holy privileges of our Christian heritage as well as our liberty and civilization."[102]

In 1905, Simpson judged that Russia's defeat by Japan was "well deserved," and stated that "God...(was) compelling the proud oppressor (i.e. Russia) to stop a war which has been in defiance of every sentiment of justice and humanity."[103] A few months later, he added that Japan was "manifestly used by Him (God) as the instrument of His providence."[104]

In 1915, the *Alliance Weekly* described the sinking of the steamer Ancona as "another shocking outrage" and "another drop in the full cup of Teuton iniquity," this at a time when the United States was not yet at war with Germany.[105] After it had become involved, Simpson called for unreserved support of the war effort and described the Allied armies as "forces of liberty and righteousness."[106]

The Social Order

A subject which necessarily requires attention is Simpson's attitude to the social order. He drew attention to "the

62

oppression of the poor" and to the

> sweat shops of our manufacturing cities...women and
> children...toiling for a pittance in suffocating workrooms
> with long hours of half-remunerated toil...struggling
> girls that have been told...that they cannot expect to earn
> a living by honest toil, but must also expect to sell them-
> selves as well.[107]

He declared that "the whole system is harsh and selfish to the core."[108] However, there was no suggestion that the government should act to alleviate such circumstances. He only encouraged liberality by the wealthy.[109] In fact, to the oppressed he said, "Do not go and fight your battle; do not get up a strike or a political party; leave your vindication to Him."[110] In 1896, he described Labour Unions as "a step toward the universal democracy and lawlessness which is to be the condition of the last days, as symbolized in Rev. 17 — by the kings without their crowns."[111]

Why was it that Simpson seems to have thought that the restructuring of society was not to be encouraged? Was it because of his expectation of the very imminent return of Christ? Was it because he believed that such effort would encourage people to fix their hopes on this world rather than on the world to come? Was it because of the laissez-faire spirit of the times? Was it because he shared the widespread optimism of the day concerning the American "way of life"? His positive view of "our liberty and civilization" quoted above may so indicate. One could legitimately conclude that all of these considerations, and perhaps others as well, may have had a part to play in shaping his view of the matter.

Simpson was not unaware that there were those who believed that social change was necessary. He was strongly opposed to socialism and repeatedly condemned it. In 1885 he declared, "Socialism has become a hideous war against civilization and humanity."[112] In 1911, he called it "a substitute for the kingdom and coming of the Lord Jesus Christ."[113] Previously he had said, "God does not come...to sweep away all differences and bring a hopeless socialism."[114] Nor did he associate it solely with theological liberals.[115] He criticized Frances Willard, renowned national president of the WCTU, for her socialist views, despite such a regard for her that he could speak of her as "our dear sister."[116] Moreover, he criticized Salvation Army leaders in England for their views in this respect, making mention of William Booth's book, *In Darkest England and the Way Out* (1890), and of the reception given to General Booth's views in Paris, France. He commented, "The grand basis of spiritual regeneration is ignored, but the wedge is in and a failure on any other basis will open the eyes of leaders in the work."[117] Nevertheless, the work of the Salvation Army in the United States could be featured in Simpson's periodical and high praise given to it for its "love for the lost."[118]

Simpson's view of efforts at improving the social order is evident when he urges us to "cease from wasting our lives on good but secondary things." Our purpose, he says, is "to gather out of the world a people for His name and then to prepare the way for His kingdom and His benignant reign."[119]

CONCLUSION

Whatever one may say about Simpson's views on world peace, and his lack of support for change in the structures of society, the social welfare impact of his movement was both enormous and magnificent. Moreover, it has been rightly described as "essentially a by-product of the deeper spiritual life Simpson and his co-workers sought to cultivate."[120] As F.W. Farr wrote in *The Christian and Missionary Alliance Weekly* in 1907, what was done of this nature was done "incidentally and immediately." It was the result of lives transformed by the power of the Gospel.[121] It seems to this writer that it is fair to say that so much was accomplished because what was of foremost importance was kept foremost without forgetting that what is secondary must be accorded its proper significance.

Only one closing comment is necessary. Whatever the reasons, there seems to have been a decline in concern about social needs beginning in the last years of the first decade of the twentieth century. The pages of the official organ of the Alliance contain much less material having to do with the meeting of man's material and social needs. (Almost all of our quotations are from the earlier years.) There are intimations that Simpson was always somewhat ambivalent about the institutional and welfare aspects of Alliance work. In 1893 he wrote, "If we had a hundred million dollars, we would not spend one cent of it in establishing another school at home, or an institute abroad, unless it were simply for the purpose of training persons directly to preach the gospel."[122]

However, the first clear intimation of a tendency to reduce such involvement surfaces in relation to the work of the Alliance in India. There a very large program of educational, industrial and relief activities had developed. The evidence shows that the Rev. M.B. Fuller came home on furlough in 1907-08 to the United States "to consult with the Board of the Christian and Missionary Alliance about 'practical questions of missionary policy.' Some of the items under discussion were orphanages, education and industrial work." As was to be expected, the consultation concluded with a reaffirmation of evangelism as the concern of the Alliance. It appears, however, that orphanage work, which had been very prominent in Alliance work in India, was only "conceded a temporary place" in the program.[123] In accord with this decision, the *Annual Report of the Christian and Missionary Alliance* in 1910, recommended the phasing out of orphanage work in India, a decision that seems to reverse the position commended in the *First Annual Report of the Christian and Missionary Alliance*, 1897-98, which recommended the establishment of schools and orphanages at home, and the recognition of "homes, orphanages and schools under proper limitations...as part of the Alliance on the foreign field."[124] Following the decision reported in 1910, efforts toward the alleviation of physical and welfare needs were still being reported. Industrial work flourished "as late as 1914."[125] Schools in South China, including a school for blind girls at Kwai Ping, were reported in 1917-18.[126] Other welfare efforts continued to have Alliance sponsorship as well, but such concerns had much less prominence and are given much less attention.

Priority must always be accorded to evangelism and any program or activity which threatens that priority must be pruned. On the other hand, evangelism which does not result in the fueling of social concern is a distortion of what Christian evangelism is meant to be. It needs to be asked in all seriousness whether the turn away from social action taken by the Alliance about 1908, a turn which Simpson apparently ac-

cepted, if he did not inspire it, was a needed pruning or a retro-
grade step.

ENDNOTES

1. *The Christian and Missionary Alliance Weekly* (October 27, 1897): 417 (Hereafter, *CMAW*). Cf. *The Christian Alliance & Foreign Missionary Weekly*
(October 2, 1896): 303 (Hereafter, *CAFMW*); *The Heavenly Vision*
(1896): 88.

2. *The Word, The Work & The World* (January 1882): 23 (hereafter, *WWW*).
For reports of social welfare activities in the New York area published
by A.B. Simpson during this period see, e.g. *WWW* (1882): 122;
(October 1886): 241.

3. A.B. Simpson, *The King's Business* (New York: The Christian Alliance
Pub. Co., 1886), p. 134. In an article published in *WWW* (1885), W.S.
Rainsford declared, "You cannot present the Gospel to a hungry man
with any hope of success until you have ministered to his physical
wants...Jesus Christ means His church...to feed the hungry, shelter
the homeless, clothe the naked, visit the sick, bury the dead, and,
above all, preach the Gospel...." (p. 313). A.B. Simpson was the
editor of *WWW*.

4. A.B. Simpson, *The Fullness of Jesus* (New York: The Christian Alliance
Pub. Co., 1886), p. 25.

5. A.B. Simpson, *Christ in the Bible*, Vol. IX (New York: The Christian
Alliance Pub. Co., 1889), p. 227.

6. *CMAW* (December 23, 1905): 805.

7. Simpson, *Christ in the Bible*, Vol. IX, p. 237.

8. Norris Magnuson, *Salvation in the Slums* (Metuchen, NJ: Scarecrow
Press, 1977), p. 44, apparently quoting *CAFMW* (November 27, 1895):
345, which has not been available to me.

9. *CAFMW* (September 25, 1896): 227. In 1899, P.W. Philpott, in an
address to Alliance people, declared, "A good way to test your love
to God is by the way you treat your brother...God is more concerned
about my conduct toward my brother than by my prayers to Him."
This address was reported in *CMAW* (August 19, 1899): 188.

10. A.B. Simpson, *Practical Christianity* (New York: Christian Alliance Pub.
Co., 1901), p. 80. It is noteworthy that Simpson seems to have con-

sidered that the value of charitable and philanthropic activities lay in their power to make people more receptive to the Gospel of spiritual salvation.

11. *CMAW* (December 23, 1905): 806.

12. *The Christian Alliance & Missionary Weekly* (March 13, 1893): 165 (Hereafter, *CAMW*), cf. *CMAW* (October 31, 1908): 78. It should be noted, however, that in *CMAW* (July 14, 1897): 54, he objects to "humanitarian schemes and social reform movements to better the human and social condition of men without regard to their supreme spiritual and immortal needs." And his social interest seems to decline not long after the turn of the century.

13. G.P. Pardington, *Twenty-five Wonderful Years, 1889-1914: A Popular Sketch of the Christian and Missionary Alliance* (New York: Christian Alliance Pub. Co., 1914), p. 26.

14. *CMAW* (December 23, 1905): 806. See *CMAW* (August 3, 1907): 51, for similar statement.

15. Report by Dr. S.E. Furry in *CAFMW* (August 17, 1894): 160.

16. *CAMW* (January 20, 1900): 41.

17. *CMAW* (March 9, 1907): 111-112.

18. Magnuson, *Salvation in the Slums*, p. 17. See also *CMAW* (October 20, 1897): 404-406. *CMAW* (October 20, 1900): 225, reports on Rescue Day presentations with respect to Florence Crittenden Homes, Bowery Mission, Salvation Army, Dr. S.E. Furry's Midnight Mission on Doyer Street, New York, and Mr. Raws' Industrial Home in Germantown, PA.

19. Magnuson, *Salvation in the Slums*, p. 83.

20. Pardington, *Twenty-five Wonderful Years*, p. 29.

21. A.E. Thompson, *The Life of A.B. Simpson* (Harrisburg, PA: Christian Publications, Inc., 1920), p. 100. *WWW* (1885): 307, contains a report of the Florence Mission which included, among its ministries, a temporary refuge for fallen women. The relationship of this mission to the Alliance is unclear to the present writer.

22. Magnuson, *Salvation in the Slums*, p. 82, and E. Whittemore, *Records of Modern Miracles*, pp. 18-31.

23. See *Year Book of the Christian Alliance and the International Missionary Alliance*, 1893, p. 51; Magnuson, *Salvation in the Slums*, p. 82, in dependence on the *Christian Herald* (September 9, 1903): 750.

24. See *CMAW* (June 10, 1892): 370; *CAFMW* (March 30, 1894): 351; *CMAW* (January 22, 1897): 89; *CMAW* (October 20, 1897): 405; *CMAW* (September 2, 1899): 220.

25. M. Wilson and A.B. Simpson, *Henry Wilson, One of God's Best* (New York: The Alliance Press Co., 1908), p. 78, 112-113, 147; *CAFMW* (October 16 & 23, 1896): 346; *CMAW* (October 20, 1897): 405.

26. For a description of the work of the New York Rescue Band, see *CAFMW* (May 8, 1896): 446-447.

27. Such a home in Denver, CO, *CMAW* (June 8, 1898): 544; and in Pittsburgh, PA, *CMAW* (July 2, 1904): 76-77. The Denver home was but one of the complex of social services making up the "Haymarket." Simpson encouraged financial support thereof.

28. There was also a Berachah Mission and Berachah Rest Home.

29. See Pardington, *Twenty-five Wonderful Years*, p. 96; *CMAW* (December 9, 1899): 445; *CMAW* (December 30, 1899): 492; *CMAW* (June 6, 1908): 157.

30. *CMAW* (October 6, 1897): 356. *The First Annual Report of the Christian and Missionary Alliance*, 1897-8, p. 84, contains the statement, "The Committee would recommend that the advisability of establishing orphanages in connection with our work to be taken up by the Board and commended to the liberality of our people... That the matter of homes, orphanages and schools under proper limitations be recognized as part of the Alliance on the foreign field."

31. For orphan work in Fort Worth, TX, see *CMAW* (January 22, 1897): 89; *CMAW* (October 20, 1897): 405; in Chattanooga, TN, *CMAW* (June 24, 1899): 61; in Richmond, VA, *CMAW* (August 12, 1899): 173; in Newbern, VA, *CMAW* (October 12, 1907): 185.

32. See *CAFMW* (December 4, 1896): 517, ibid. (December 11, 1896): 529-532; ibid. (December 1900): 300.

33. A.B. Simpson in M. Wilson and A.B. Simpson, *Henry Wilson: One of God's Best*, p. 104-105.

34. See Thompson, *Life of A.B. Simpson*, p. 140-141. Was this the real beginning of Berachah Home?

35. Ibid., p. 142-143; *CMAW* (May 4, 1898): 420. For the "objects" of Berachah Home as officially set forth in 1893, see *Year Book of the Christian Alliance and the International Missionary Alliance*, 1893, p. 48-49. In this connection, see also *CMAW* (June 6, 1908): 157. In 1897, Berachah Home was relocated in Nyack, NY, where it carried on its

ministry for twenty years. See Thompson, *Life of A.B. Simpson*, p. 142-143.

36. *CMAW* (April 23, 1897): 387; cf. *WWW* (May 1885): 158-159.

37. See A.B. Simpson, *The Lord for the Body* (New York: Christian Alliance Pub. Co., 1925), p. 129.

38. Ibid. (original text 1900?), p. 131-132.

39. A Berachah home in Bombay, India is mentioned in *CMAW* (November 25, 1899): 406.

40. In *CAMW* (January 23, 1891): 50, Simpson speaks of a home for invalids not yet ready to trust the Lord completely for healing.

41. Magnuson, *Salvation in the Slums*, p. 200, n. 15; *CMAW* (March 1899).

42. *CMAW* (July 6, 1898): 17.

43. See Magnuson, *Salvation in the Slums*, p. 70; *CMAW* (April 22, 1892): 257.

44. See *CMAW* (1905): 700. For other Alliance homes, see *CAMW* (November 24, 1893): 334; *CMAW* (April 23, 1897): 393; *CMAW* (May 14, 1904): 362; *Alliance Weekly* (November 18, 1911): 110, (hereafter, *AW*).

45. Pardington, *Twenty-five Wonderful Years*, p. 100.

46. From 1889 to 1891, Simpson repeatedly publicized the intention of opening a home for the insane. See *The Christian Alliance* (January 1889): 8 (hereafter, *CA*); *CAMW* (November 21, 1890): 306; *CMAW* (January 1891): 6; *CMAW* (August 7, 1891): 82. We are not aware that the intention was ever fulfilled.

47. *WWW* (January 1882): 44.

48. *WWW* (June 1882): 218.

49. See *CAMW* (April 15, 1892): 242-243; *CAMW* (May 13, 1892): 306; *CAMW* (July 15, 1892): 40.

50. In *WWW* (March 1883): 61, he criticizes a medical missionary for saying medical missions is a part of the church's task, and affirms that our real task is to get people to trust in Christ as their healer.

51. *CAMW* (March 27, 1891): 194.

52. See description of this program in *CMAW* (April 16, 1897): 376.

53. Magnuson, *Salvation in the Slums*, p. 98; *CAMW* (February 13, 1891): 108; *CAFMW* (March 30, 1894): 351-352.

54. Magnuson, *Salvation in the Slums*, p. 236 n. 33.

55. *CAMW* (April 28, 1893): 261. See also *CAMW* (December 22, 1893): 387; *CMAW* (February 3, 1900): 79; *CMAW* (March 3, 1900): 142; *CMAW* (May 3, 1902): 241-242.

56. See *CMAW* (November 19, 1904): 392; Magnuson, *Salvation in the Slums*, p. 99. When famine conditions in India eased, the Alliance phased out its homes for orphanages and its industrial programs. See *CMAW* (February 15, 1908): 332; cf. *The Thirteenth Annual Report of the Christian and Missionary Alliance*, May 24, 1910, p. 11.

57. *CMAW* (March 6, 1891): 146.

58. *CMAW* (June 20, 1903): 37. See also *CMAW* (April 18, 1903): 221.

59. *CMAW* (June 13, 1903): 15.

60. See *CMAW* (November 25, 1899): 405-407, 419; *CMAW* (February 3, 1900): 67, 73, 79; *CMAW* (March 10, 1900): 152; *CMAW* (March 31, 1900): 195-197; *AW* (April 6, 1912): 10. In 1918, Alliance personnel were released for relief work in Palestine. See *AW* (March 30, 1918): 401.

61. *AW* (April 6, 1912): 10.

62. *CAFMW* (April 24, 1896): 406.

63. *CMAW* (December 26, 1903): 53.

64. See *CMAW* (April 28, 1906): 249; *CMAW* (May 5, 1906): 265.

65. *AW* (April 5, 1913).

66. See Magnuson, *Salvation in the Slums*, p. 17.

67. *Christian and Missionary Alliance Annual Report*, 1910 (for the year 1909), p. 117.

68. See A.B. Simpson, comp., *Michele Nardi, the Italian Evangelist, His Life and Work* (New York: Published by Mrs. B.P. Nardi, 1916), p. 3, 22, 24, 28-30, 33, 51, 143.

69. See *CMAW* (April 23, 1904): 313.

70. See *CMAW* (January 22, 1897): 89; and *CMAW* (April 11, 1903): 205 for tributes in Simpson's magazine when they died.

71. See A.B. Simpson, *From the Uttermost to the Uttermost: The Life Story of Josephus Pulis* (New York: Christian Alliance Pub. Co., 1914), p. 11, 31, 55.

72. Magnuson, *Salvation in the Slums*, p. 136.

73. *CAFMW* (April 24, 1896): 403.

74. See *CAFMW* (February 2, 1894): 137; *CMAW* (April 9, 1897): 353; *CMAW* (November 11, 1899): 382. In *CAFMW* (January 31, 1896): 110, A.B. Simpson commended the temperance work of the renowned W.C.T.U. leader, Frances Willard.

75. *CMAW* (November 9, 1907): 96.

76. *AW* (November 16, 1912): 97.

77. Ibid. (January 25, 1913): 257.

78. Education for Christian ministry does not concern us in this study, except as general education may be said to be for the purpose of training for ministry.

79. *WWW* (January 1882): 23, 44.

80. *WWW* (January 1885): 32.

81. *WWW* "Report of the Christian Convention at Old Orchard, Inc., held July 31 to August 9, 1887": 84.

82. *CAMW* (August 7, 1891): 82; *CAMW* (September 25, 1891): 194; *CAFMW* (February 9, 1894): 144.

83. *CAFMW* (December 7, 1894): 542.

84. D.W. Cartmel, *Mission Policy and Program of A.B. Simpson* (unpublished M.A. thesis, Hartford Seminary Foundation, 1962), p. 156-157. For reference to High School and College work at Nyack, see *AW* (June 15, 1912): 165; *AW* (December 21, 1912): 187; *AW* (March 17, 1914): 354; *The Thirteenth Annual Report of the Christian and Missionary Alliance*, May 24, 1910, p. 89.

85. *Thirteenth Annual Report*, p. 157.

86. *CMAW* (June 6, 1908): 157.

87. See p. 13, 19.

88. A.B. Simpson, *Larger Outlooks on Missionary Lands* (New York: Christian Alliance Pub. Co., 1893), p. 579, 356. In *CAFMW* (March 6, 1896):

229, he opposed the establishment of Christian Schools in Manitoba, Canada, on the basis that the public schools were not sectarian.

89. Simpson, *Larger Outlooks*, p. 579.

90. *AW* (December 21, 1912): 178.

91. See Magnuson, *Salvation in the Slums*, p. 122. For reports of Alliance work among blacks in the United States, see *CMAW* (May 2, 1898): 228; *CMAW* (July 6, 1898): 13; *CMAW* (September 23, 1899): 265.

92. *CAFMW* (January 24, 1896): 86.

93. See *CMAW* (January 13, 1906): 35; *CMAW* (October 27, 1906): 257; *CMAW* (May 2, 1908): 83-84; *CMAW* (June 6, 1908): 157.

94. See *CAMW* (March 27, 1891): 195; *CMAW* (June 24, 1899): 61; *CMAW* (July 2, 1904): 66-67; *CMAW* (June 9, 1906): 354.

95. *CAFMW* (January 3, 1896): 13.

96. *CMAW* (April 15, 1911): 40. He said, "With Great Britain and America united for peace, the world would have to behave itself!"

97. *AW* (March 7, 1914): 354.

98. *CMAW* (March 2, 1898): 204. cf. *CMAW* (April 27, 1898): 393 and *CMAW* (May 4, 1898): 411. He opposed the pacifist position of the Quakers. See *CMAW* (May 4, 1898): 420-421.

99. *CAFMW* (April 17, 1896): 373.

100. *CMAW* (May 4, 1898): 420-421. See also *CMAW* (April 27, 1898): 396. For a somewhat similar statement concerning the Japanese-Chinese War, see *CAFMW* (November 1894): 410-411. Earlier still, he had condemned France in regard to the Franco-Prussian War. See *WWW* (May 1885): 129.

101. *CMAW* (August 3, 1898): 108.

102. *CMAW* (November 12, 1898): 444. Simpson adds, "We are not pleading for war," but "it may be the day has come for the renewed chastening of France, as well as Spain, and the using of Great Britain as the instrument of God's judgment on another Roman Catholic country...."

103. *CMAW* (March 18, 1905): 161.

104. *CMAW* (September 9, 1905): 561. For his harsh words for Italy in the Italian-Turkish conflict, see *CMAW* (November 18, 1911): 98.

105. *AW* (November 20, 1915): 113. Earlier in 1915, it was stated in the same periodical that Belgium, England, France, Germany, and Russia were "all suffering for national sins." See *AW* (August 28, 1915): 339.

106. *AW* (April 28, 1917): 49; *AW* (January 5, 1918): 209. Cf. *AW* (January 6, 1917): 264; *AW* (April 17, 1917): 7; *AW* (April 28, 1917): 50-52; *AW* (May 25, 1918): 116.

107. Simpson, *Practical Christianity*, p. 135-136.

108. Ibid., p. 139.

109. Ibid., p. 132-134.

110. Ibid., cf. *CAFMW* (July 20, 1894): 51; *CAMW* (October 7, 1892): 248. *CMAW* (August 17, 1908): 332. In *AW* (October 7, 1911): 3, he declares that the solution to labour problems is the return of Christ. In A.B. Simpson, *Christ and the Bible*, Vol. XVII (New York: Christian Alliance Pub. Co., 1904), p. 240, he speaks of "letting them (i.e. the governments of the world) see that Christ's kingdom is not of this world, nor in antagonism to any human authority." Simpson criticizes governments, and on at least one occasion, indicates that revolution is not necessarily wrong, *AW* (April 28, 1917): 50, but that is as far as he goes.

111. *CAFMW* (July 24, 1896): 94.

112. *WWW* (February 1885): 64.

113. A.B. Simpson, *The Old Faith and the New Gospels* (New York: Alliance Press Co., 1911), p. 7. Cf. *AW* (May 4, 1912): 65; *AW* (May 18, 1912): 98.

114. Simpson, *Practical Christianity*, p. 75. Cf. *AW* (November 25, 1911): 118.

115. He insisted that liberals were seldom effective with the "lowest classes," because they lacked both the message and the spiritual empowerment which were required. See *AW* (May 20, 1911): 120. For Simpson's endorsement of a negative review of C.M. Sheldon's book *In His Steps*, see *CMAW* (August 26, 1899): 201.

116. See Simpson, *The Old Faith and the New Gospels*, p. 127; *CAFMW* (May 22, 1896): 492; *CMAW* (March 2, 1898): 204.

117. *CAMW* (May 1, 1891): 283. For criticisms of the Salvation Army by Simpson on other grounds, see *WWW* (July 1882): 283; *WWW* (January 1883): 1.

118. *CMAW* (October 20, 1900): 225; *CAMW* (April 22, 1892): 257; *AW* (September 7, 1912): 369.

119. *CMAW* (June 25, 1897): 612. Cf. *CMAW* (November 10, 1897): 472.

120. Magnuson, *Salvation in the Slums*, p. 18.

121. *CMAW* (March 9, 1907): 111-112, 118.

122. *CAMW* (October 20, 1893): 243. Apparently in the same year, he did say, "A certain amount of educational work seems to be necessary (in south China), as the native schools compel their pupils to learn and practice heathenism." However, he wished such schools to become the responsibility of national Christians as swiftly as possible. See his *Larger Outlooks on Missionary Lands*, p. 356. Cf. p. 187, 578, 579.

123. D.W. Cartmel, *Mission Policy and Program*, p. 154; *CMAW* (March 14, 1908): 400, tells of Fuller's coming to the U.S.A. to confer concerning the "orphanage, educational and industrial work." *CMAW* (February 15, 1908): 332, reports that "gradual discontinuance of regular orphanage work in India was authorized."

124. *First Annual Report of the Christian and Missionary Alliance*, 1897-8, p. 84, 85. On p. 13, it is stated, "We have not forgotten the claims of the fatherless and the orphan." See also *The Fourteenth Annual Report of the Christian and Missionary Alliance*, 1910, p. 99.

125. D.W. Cartmel, *Mission Policy and Program*, p. 124.

126. See *The Twenty-first Annual Report of the Christian and Missionary Alliance*, 1917, p. 19.

JOHN V. DAHMS

John V. Dahms, B.A., B.D., Th.M. and Th.D. received his graduate degrees from Emmanuel College of the University of Toronto. He served as a pastor in Ontario before becoming Professor of New Testament at Canadian Theological Seminary in 1971. Dr. Dahms has written a number of articles in scholarly journals and popular periodicals.

REDISCOVERING THE MUSIC OF A.B. SIMPSON

by

Eugene Rivard

INTRODUCTION

"ALBERT B. SIMPSON'S HYMNS ARE UNSINGABLE!"
is an opinion shared by many members of the Christian and
Missionary Alliance today. Forty-five of his songs are included
in the present *Hymns of the Christian Life* but are rarely used in
congregational singing. Why have they fallen into disuse?
Were they always considered "unfit" to sing? Is the Alliance
losing a legacy of its founder, or is it merely allowing sub-
standard hymnody to die a natural death?

A contemporary Alliance church-goer might well wonder if
Simpson's hymns were regarded with the same general disdain
during his lifetime. If this were the case, it would be difficult to
understand why any were included in the following edition of
the society's hymnal. Were they retained solely for the depth,
intensity and call for Christian commitment in their lyrics?

The hymns do effectively reflect the distinctive theology of
Simpson and the Alliance: the Spirit-filled deeper life, world
evangelization, and the gospel of Christ as Saviour, Sanctifier,
Healer and Coming King. This is no coincidence, since the
songs were often the poetic essence of a poignant writing or an
impassioned sermon. Moreover, the early publications of the
Alliance and the writing of Simpson's contemporaries indicate

75

that his songs were held in great favor. Not only were they eagerly received, but they became dear to the hearts of those who sang them and carried them throughout the world.

THE GOSPEL SONG

The "gospel song" was the form of music most closely associated with the revivals and evangelistic meetings of the late nineteenth and early twentieth centuries. It is, therefore, not surprising that A.B. Simpson employed it (and with great success) as his own musical medium. The gospel song differs from the traditional church anthem in its focus on the individual, its lively rhythms and tuneful, easily-remembered refrains. In addition, unlike the hymn, it is intensely personal and immediate in nature, and is often written in the first person as a testimony.

Since Simpson was, above all, an evangelist, he stressed the need of the individual to respond to the will of God and saw the gospel song as an ideal means of calling sinners to repentance, educating them in sound doctrine, deepening their life in the Spirit and challenging them to live in a Christ-like manner. He also considered the gospel song as the best means of expressing his own love for Jesus Christ in music.

"What ministry today has been more honored than gospel song?" he wrote. "How God has shown in a Bliss, Sankey or a Phillips, the honor He still will put on this simple taste to draw millions by the power of the consecrated melody of the gospel!"[1] A.W. Tozer wrote of early Simpson meetings where the "popular" gospel song was used:

> ...they joined in mass singing of old time church favorites and the more recent Gospel Songs, composed by Sankey, Bliss, Crosby and others of the gospel musicians of the day. Popular? Sure, it was popular and it was frowned upon by many of the sterile scribes of the synagogues, but to Mr. Simpson, the word "popular" carried no terrors. It meant "of the people" and it was people he was interested in...so the singing went on and the crowds loved it and kept coming back week after week to enjoy it.[2]

76

Despite his preference for the gospel song (for largely pragmatic reasons), Simpson never disparaged traditional hymnody because his Scottish Presbyterian upbringing had given him a deep appreciation for its richness. Indeed, in his preface to the first edition of *Hymns of the Christian Life* (1891), he cautioned against going to the extreme of "relegating all the old hymns to the dusty past."[3] The first Alliance hymnal included many such hymns, with Simpson's gospel songs serving as a contemporary supplement to them.

THE MUSIC OF THE SIMPSON SONGS

Simpson's musical background was not extensive. Although he attempted to learn the violin as a youth, he was unsuccessful and never learned more than to pick out a melody on the piano with one finger. Others provided the harmony. In spite of this, he composed many of the melodies for his own hymns, an unusual accomplishment for hymn-writers of the day. Of the forty hymns that bear his name in the first *Hymns of the Christian Life*, he is credited with the music for thirty-two. In the huge 1908 edition of the hymnal (the last he was to produce), he is credited with the music for 117 of his 166 songs, while in the 1978 edition, 23 of the 45 songs by Simpson have been set to his melodies.

Always a poet, he began writing hymns while a pastor at the Chestnut Street Presbyterian Church in Louisville, Kentucky, from 1873 to 1879. He made no pretense of being a composer of stature, as his unpolished melodies readily confirm. They reveal, rather, an intense involvement with other business, as well as an urgency that did not allow for careful revision. Later in his career, Simpson relegated the melody writing to others, including his daughter, Margaret. By that time, the first hymn tunes had become so closely associated with the Alliance that they could never be changed. Often his daughter was called at the spur of the moment to help him with a song. Long after his death, she recalled some of the songwriting methods her father had used:

...he used to call me often and say, 'I have a message for

77

you for my sermon tomorrow. Meet me at the piano soon.'...there we labored together till he was satisfied it carried his inspiration. Sometimes he would say, 'Here, take this. I can't do a thing with it, but this is what I want.' And where it was crescendo [loud], he would demonstrate it by singing out loudly enough to be heard down the hill, with obvious punctuations and emphasis. When you grasped his idea, he would glow with ecstasy and say, 'You've got it, there, that's fine.'[4]

Several songwriters were used to set his texts to music. John Burke, Minister of Music at the New York Gospel Tabernacle from 1889-1891, is credited with many melodies for Simpson's words, including his best-known lyric, "Yesterday, Today, Forever." Others included the Salvationist Captain Russell Kelso Carter, co-editor of the first Alliance hymnal and an associate of Simpson in the conventions and at the Gospel Tabernacle; James Kirk, a member of the "Ohio Quartet" which sang at the Old Orchard (Maine) missionary conventions; Louise Shepherd, soloist at Old Orchard and member of the Missionary Training Institute faculty from 1897-1899; May Agnew Stephens, pianist and songleader of the Gospel Tabernacle; Winfred Macomber, Missionary Training Institute graduate and missionary to the Congo; and George Stebbins, associate of Moody and Sankey, who was commissioned to set some of Simpson's poetry to music for the 1936 hymnal.

Musical Difficulties

There is no doubt that some of the music to which Simpson's hymns were set, whether written by himself or others, was difficult to sing. The early Alliance overlooked these problems and probably developed their own traditional ways of rendering the songs. Later generations were not as generous.

Perhaps the most widely quoted critic of Simpson's hymns was A.W. Tozer, who wrote, "...it is in the music that his songs suffer the most. A few of his compositions can be sung, but the most of them can be negotiated by none except trained singers."[5] While Dr. Tozer's credentials as a music critic have been questioned, it is true that some of the tunes present irksome rhythmical and melodic problems.

For a hymn to be sung well by a congregation, several musical factors need to be considered. First, the range cannot be too great, as the average church-goer cannot generally sustain high pitches for long. Second, the rhythms of the melody must match the rhythms of the words. The phrases must be balanced, and stressed syllables fall on the stressed beats (ex. "O *God* our *help* in *a*ges *past*"). The words cannot have too many syllables if they are to lend themselves well to simple melodies. Third, the melody must be tuneful with few large jumps, easily remembered without being trite. Fourth, the hymn cannot be too long, and finally, the music must express the mood of the text. Hymn-writers are well aware of the intense amount of work needed to fulfill these requirements. Furthermore (in common evangelical performance practice), all four parts are usually sung, making good harmony another musical consideration. If the music has problems in any of these areas, the congregation will have difficulty singing, no matter how profound the words may be.

The music of some of Simpson's hymns fell short in one or more of these areas. Attempts were made to revise and reharmonize much of the original music of his songs in the 1936, 1962 and 1978 Alliance hymnals, but some of the tunes still require complete rewriting to become more acceptable to today's musical tastes. Only the Simpson hymns in the latest (1978) hymnal were considered in the analysis that follows, because the others are not widely used today. All numbers shown are from this hymnal. Not all have great difficulties. "Thy Kingdom Come" (472), "I Take, He Undertakes" (290), and "Step by Step" (349) are as "singable" as any of the tunes of other 19th Century songwriters. Other Simpson tunes, while not great music, can prove, with repeated use, to be as acceptable as that of any gospel song. Alterations as simple as lowering the key have saved some songs from oblivion. "I Take, He Undertakes," among others, has been lowered since its original appearance in 1891.

Rhythmic and metrical problems mar some of Simpson's hymns. Gospel songs characteristically contain a great number of words in a verse and have a quick tempo, making it imperative that the syllables match the rhythm of the tune. "The Joy of the Lord" (280) is one of the most popular and triumphant hymns in the Alliance tradition, but many congregations will trip when they get to the middle of the third verse — "like the nightingale's notes it can sing in the darkness." This beautiful imagery is lost when "the" receives a stressed beat rather than the more open and important syllable "night" in "nightingale."

Consequently, the emphasis ends up on the wrong syllables and the words "it can" are jammed into two "hurry up" sixteenth notes at the end of the measure. Today's congregations have less patience with this kind of flaw, and after an embarrassing stumble or two, may relegate an otherwise triumphant, joyous song to the "unsingable" list.

"Launch Out" (259) challenges believers to experience the supernatural provision of God if they will only step out in His name. However, many congregations will find it difficult to sing the words in measure three: "boundless and fathomless" because the musical rhythm (♩ ♩.♪ ♪♪ ♩) does not logically follow the speech rhythm (♩ ♪♪ ♩ ♪♪) of the words. As a result, the instrumentalist will be playing something other than that which the congregation is singing, and unless practiced, the congregation will stumble. Even such small problems may cause a congregation to quickly judge a hymn "unsingable."

"I Will Say Yes to Jesus" (217) expresses unreserved consecration to Christ, but the first verse is very difficult to sing because of its rhythmic discrepancies. The opening two measures are in fine rhythmic agreement, but when the words "oft it was no before" are sung, it is obvious that "oft" should have been placed on a strong beat rather than "it," and that perhaps "oft it was no" should have matched the rhythm of "I will say yes" in the first measure. This discrepancy not only causes a "hitch," but is followed too quickly by the next phrase, giving the congregation and songleader no chance to recover. In fact, the entire first verse allows the singer no opportunity to recover because it is so filled with words that the singer can hardly take a breath. Moreover, the syncopated rhythm of the melody on "ever" of "whatever" at the verse's end, constitutes an unexpected and illogical break in the rhythmic pattern and provides yet another stumbling block. A loyal congregation with a strong songleader could sing this song effectively with much repetition, but most will not try a second time.

Rhythmic problems and forgettable melodies certainly characterize Simpson's lesser-known hymns, but his well-known ones present some phrasing problems as well. "Search Me O God" (239) is a beautiful hymn of consecration, but the chorus has two measures extra. The entire song consists of a pattern of balanced four measure phrases, but ends on an unbalanced phrase of six measures that requires an unusual hold on the word "away" of "cannot pass away." Such lack of balance invariably makes the congregation feel ill at ease because they can sense the lack of synchronization between the lyric and the melody. "Christ in Me" (166) is a tremendous statement of love for Jesus Christ and a testimony to the joy and hope that Christ is to us, but the melody on the refrain rambles without a clear musical or poetic phrase, and seems to end twice before the final measure.

Here it must be mentioned that although Simpson's gospel songs contain potentially life-changing truth, they are often too long. Most of the hymns in an average hymnal take three minutes or less to sing. Some of Simpson's compositions take five minutes or more, thereby straining an untrained voice, especially when the songleader urges the people to "sing out" all the way through. The songleader must therefore lead judiciously, leaving out the refrain at the end of one or more verses or using other creative means to avoid vocal strain on the part of the congregation.

The final consideration in this condensed musical critique concerns the style of Simpson's music. Simpson wrote almost all of his in march style, as did most contemporary gospel song writers. Simpson found this style well-suited to the intention of the missionary society, viz. to march throughout the world with the "banner of Christ held high." In an age of nationalism and imperialism, the imagery of war, battle and victory was easily understood and spiritualized. Titles like "I Have Overcome," "Be True," "Go and Tell," "Go Forward," "Fill Up The Ranks," "Jesus Giveth Us the Victory," "March On," "Christ is Conqueror," "Hallelujah," "Burn On," "Launch Out," "To The Regions Beyond," and "Send the Gospel Faster," were set to suitably aggressive music. Even the hymns that told of the person of Christ or the Deeper Life were set to melodies with march-like beats. "Himself," "The Joy of the Lord," "Jesus Only," "I Will Say Yes to Jesus," "I Want To Be Holy," were all written to stimulate rather than to soothe.

A.W. Tozer attributed most of this aggressive style to Simpson's close musical associate, R. Kelso Carter. He wrote that Carter's tunes, "while marked with traces of superior gift, were nevertheless too militant and boisterous for the average Christian to enjoy."[6] John Burke could be accused of the same thing. He is responsible for the most disastrous combination of music and words in the present hymnal, "A Missionary Cry," which is a theme song of the Alliance. Although the lyrics express the deepest and most solemn desire of Simpson's heart, the melody is in a major key and is as lively and happy as any Disneyland march. The song begins with the words,

"A hundred thousand souls a day
are passing one by one away"

but by the time the singer reaches the refrain

"they're passing to their doom"

it sounds more like joyous proclamation than solemn reflection. Militant themes and march-like tunes have gone out of fashion and do not appear in the works of today's peace-conscious song-writers, all of which suggests that the melodies of a bygone era may be a hindrance to using Simpson's compositions effectively in the church of the late twentieth century.

THE WORDS OF SIMPSON'S GOSPEL SONGS

Despite musical and stylistic problems associated with A.B. Simpson's gospel songs, many Alliance members grew up singing them and found them uplifting. One of these was A.W. Tozer, who at the end of his critique of Simpson's music, writes:

> After saying all this, I would yet confess that hardly a day goes by that I do not kneel and sing in a shaky baritone comfortably off key, the songs of Simpson. They feed my heart and express my longing, and I can find no other's songs that do this in as full a measure.[7]

One can catch the vision of A.B. Simpson, his honesty, depth and fervor for Christ in the words of his hymns. "The essence of Simpson's hymns is not in the music but in the words," Tozer wrote, "the awful longing, the tender love, radiant trust, hope and worship and triumph which they express."[8]

Most of Simpson's hymn texts are actually outlines of sermons he had preached, or condensed thoughts from articles he had written. His congregation would sing these hymns before or after he preached the sermons which inspired them, thereby reinforcing the points he had made. Simpson was a powerful preacher, eloquent in style and delivery, and he used poetry well in his sermons. His poetry grew out of a writing style that often began in point form, much like a sermon. He would make an opening statement and begin to expound upon it, ever building in intensity, expanding and developing a thought or scriptural truth until it "overflowed" into a more concentrated and expressive means of communication: poetic verse. The verse he chose would be the logical culmination of the thought. The pamphlet "Himself"[9] is an example of this style of writing as well as the "Joyful Life" chapter of his book, A Larger Christian Life.[10] "The Joy of the Lord" is the distillation of this chapter [actually a sermon] and verses from the hymn are quoted throughout it.

Simpson's hymns expressed the deepest desires of his heart. May Agnew Stephens wrote about this in her memorial tribute:

> He was a prolific writer of hymns but none were [sic] mechanical. They all came from a hidden fire and bore a definite message. And none ever satisfied him unless they expressed the full scope of the fourfold gospel. Especially the hope of the return of our Lord he felt must be added to every hymn of salvation or service, if at all possible, and he often commented on the failure of many a gospel song to carry its message to the highest point — the coming of Christ.[11]

Simpson had not always used music extensively in his services. He first became convinced of the effectiveness of using music as an evangelistic tool in 1894, when he was pastor of the Chestnut Street Presbyterian Church in Louisville, Kentucky, a city still divided from the American Civil War. He joined with other local pastors in inviting evangelist Major Daniel Whittle and gospel singer Phillip Bliss to hold a campaign in their city. The singing of Bliss "convinced Mr. Simpson of the wisdom of giving a large place to the ministry of song, and in all his subsequent work, not only chorus and congregational singing, but solos were special features."[12]

Bliss influenced evangelist D.L. Moody in the same way: "...according to their mutual friend, D.W. Whittle, Bliss crystallized Moody's sense of the power of singing in gospel work."[13] Gospel music was meant to stir people, convict them of sin, show them the beauty of Jesus, invite them to receive Him as Savior and praise Him with full voice. Many people were moved more by the music than the preaching, and those whom the preaching convicted, the music moved to action.

As far as subject matter is concerned, the most distinctive of Simpson's hymns treat the Fourfold Gospel, the deeper Spirit-filled life, divine healing and world missions.

The Fourfold Gospel is encapsulated effectively in the hymn "Jesus Only." This hymn is instructive as well as devotional, and was used to teach the new Alliance that Jesus is Savior, Sanctifier, Healer and Coming King. "Jesus Only" reveals Simpson's deep personal love for Christ as well. The title may have been derived from the opening statement delivered at his first sermon in the Chestnut Street Church in December, 1873.

> In coming among you, I am not ashamed to own this as the aim of ministry and to take these words as the motto and keynote of my future preaching: 'Jesus only.'[14]

This same hymn was printed in its entirety on the front cover of the special memorial issue of the *Alliance Weekly* shortly after his death in 1919. "Jesus Only" truly was the motto of A.B. Simpson's life.

1. Jesus only is our message,
   Jesus all our theme shall be.
   We will lift up Jesus ever,
   Jesus only will we see.

2. Jesus only is our Saviour,
   all our guilt He bore away.
   All our righteousness He gives us,
   all our strength from day to day.

3. Jesus is our Sanctifier,
   cleansing us from self and sin.
   And with all His Spirit's fulness,
   filling all our hearts within.

4. Jesus only is our Healer,
   all our sicknesses He bears
   and His risen life and fulness,
   all His members still may share.

5. Jesus only is our power,
   He the gift of Pentecost.
   Jesus, breathe Thy power upon us,
   fill us with the Holy Ghost.

6. And for Jesus we are waiting,
   listening for the Advent call;
   But 'twill still be Jesus only,
   Jesus ever, all in all.

Refrain:
   Jesus only, Jesus ever,
   Jesus all in all we sing;
   Saviour, Sanctifier and Healer,
   Glorious Lord and Coming King.

"Jesus Only" was included in the very first Alliance hymnal in 1891 and remains one of the most distinctive songs of the denomination.

"Himself" is the other Simpson hymn that encompasses the theology of the Christian and Missionary Alliance. Although Simpson wrote many books and articles, and preached fervently on each truth contained in "Himself" and "Jesus Only," it was through singing that the Alliance affirmed, memorized and endeared them to their hearts. The tract "Himself" contained the entire song at its conclusion. Both song and tract were broadly distributed and Simpson reported in an editorial on October 6, 1893, that on his recent world tour, "the hymn 'Himself' was met with by its author in almost all of the countries he visited, and was being sung in the languages and homes of those heathen people."[15] A further testimony to this hymn's popularity can be seen in an incident recalled by May Agnew Stephens:

> At the Old Orchard Convention many years ago, the convention soloist sang a number of times from manuscript: 'Once it was the blessing, now it is the Lord,' etc. In the audiences sat a clever pirate, pencil in hand, and before the convention was over, it had been taken down and printed unknown to Dr. Simpson and was being sold; and it was with some difficulty rescued from its unlawful promoter.[16]

Its message is direct and appealing:

85

1. Once it was the blessing, now it is the Lord;
   Once it was the feeling, now it is His Word;
   Once His gift I wanted, now the Giver own;
   Once I sought for healing, now Himself alone.

2. Once 'twas painful trying, now 'tis perfect trust;
   Once a half salvation, now the uttermost!
   Once 'twas ceaseless holding, now He holds me fast;
   Once 'twas constant drifting, now my anchor's cast.

After three more verses, the refrain echoes the same sentiments as "Jesus Only":

All in all forever, Jesus will I sing,
Everything in Jesus, and Jesus everything.

Lyrics of a general and inoffensive style certainly do not
characterize Simpson's songs. He assumed that those who sang
his songs desired the deeper Spirit-filled life as much as he, and
that by singing them, the singers would be able to testify to
that desire. Who could sing the words to "Burn On!" without
meaning them?

1. O fire of God begin in me,
   Burn out the dross of self and sin.
   Burn off my fetters, set me free,
   And make my heart a heav'n within.

3. Burn in, O fire of God, burn in,
   Till all my soul Christ's image bears
   And every power and pulse within,
   His holy heavenly nature wears.

"Breathing Out and Breathing In" uses the graphic imagery of
the Holy Spirit as the very life-sustaining air we breath,
necessary for existence:

1. Jesus breathe Thy Spirit on me,
   teach me how to breathe Thee in
   Help me pour into Thy bosom
   all my life of self and sin.
   I am breathing out my own life,
   that I may be filled with Thine,
   Letting go my strength and weakness,
   breathing in Thy life divine.

These are not vague or superficial requests. One of the distinctives of Simpson hymns is that they require action, not mere intellectual assent. "I Will Say yes to Jesus" is no hymn for the uncommitted Christian:

1. I will say "yes" to Jesus
   oft it was "no" before,
   As He knocked at my heart's proud entrance
   And I firmly barred the door.
   But I've made a complete surrender
   and given Him right of way,
   And henceforth it is always "yes"
   Whatever He may say.

2. I will say "yes" to Jesus
   to all that He commands
   I will hasten to do His bidding
   with willing heart and hands,
   I will listen to hear His whispers
   and learn His will each day,
   And always gladly answer "yes"
   Whatever He may say.

Other hymns appearing in the early hymnals had an urgency that told of Simpson's own burning desire to deepen his life in Christ, growing and making himself available for God's service. "Anywhere Everywhere," "I Want To Be Holy" and "Search Me, O God" are hymns requiring action and deep commitment.

Many of Simpson's hymns were written to encourage believers already living the deeper life. "Burn On" was one of the several hymns written especially for the Nyack Missionary Training Institute graduates, calling on the "fire of God" to cleanse and prepare them for service. "Be True" was the first of these graduation hymns, written for the 1894 class in the "call and answer" style:

1. We are going forth from the school of Jesus,
   we have sat at His blessed feet;
   We have drunk from truth's celestial fountain,
   we have tasted its honey sweet.
   We are witnesses for our blessed Master
   in a world where friends are few;
   And He sends us forth with the watchword holy,
   whatsoever it costs, be true.

Refrain:
Be true (We'll be true) Be true (We'll be true)
Let the holy watchword ring,
Be true (We'll be true) Be true (We'll be true)
Be true to your glorious King.
Be true (We'll be true) Be true (We'll be true)
Whether friends be false or few.
Whatsoever betide ever at His side
Let Him always find you true.

Simpson's songs of healing are no less lacking in intensity or commitment. He desired to help other Christians to realize the same truth he had experienced, and was sorrowed at the rejection of this truth by some and the inability of others to step out and claim Christ's healing by faith. The hymn with the most pathos in this regard is "Stretch Forth Thy Hand." It is a hymn that exhorts believers to exercise faith, to reach out and touch Jesus as the sick did in His day:

1. When Christ of old with healing power
   Went forth through all the suffering land
   His word so oft was wont to be
   "Stretch forth thy hand, stretch forth thy hand."

   And though the palsied arm might shrink
   And tremble at the strange command
   The healing touch was only felt
   While stretching forth the withered hand.

Refrain:
O suffering one, stretch forth your hand
Upon His promise take your stand
At His command stretch forth your hand
And Christ shall make you whole.

Although many of Simpson's hymns are testimonial in nature, he intended them to be instructive as well. "Step by Step," "Only Wait," "The Joy of the Lord," "Power From on High" and "My Grace is Sufficient for Thee" are all examples of songs of faith meant to instruct believers in their walk with Christ. Though the words of exhortation could be fiery, they could also be tender.

Simpson believed the Christian had been saved to live life in obedience to God, an obedience that would issue in the spreading of the gospel to the world. He deeply desired the Lord's second coming and was convinced that Jesus would not come again until the world had first heard the gospel (Mark 13:10). His greatest ambition was to spread that gospel so that the Lord would return. The first and sixth verse of "Go And Tell Them" (1978 hymnal) carries this message:

1. Send the Gospel of salvation
   To a world of dying men,
   Tell it out to every nation
   Till the Lord shall come again.

6. Give the gospel as a witness
   To a world of sinful men,
   Till the Bride shall be completed,
   And the Lord shall come again.

The third verse of "A Missionary Cry" expresses his vision with the same urgency:

The Master's coming draweth near;
The Son of Man will soon appear;
His Kingdom is at hand.
But ere that glorious day can be,
The gospel of the kingdom we
Must preach in every land,
Must preach in every land.

He wrote missionary songs to inspire those at home and to encourage those abroad. Hymns about exotic places like "The Dark Soudan," "Beautiful Japan," "In the Land of the Congo" endeavored to impart his vision for the millions who were without a Saviour in those foreign lands. "Go and Tell Them," "Who Will Go?," "To the Regions Beyond," "Send the Gospel Faster" were sung with great zeal by the early Alliance. In February, 1889, writing on the subject of missions, Simpson declared:

One hundred thousand souls are dying without Christ every twenty-four hours in heathen lands. What are we doing to save them? American Christians are giving on an average, one cent a week for missions sand sending one Christian in every ten thousand to save them.[17]

A short while later, this declaration became a hymn, "A Missionary Cry":

1. One hundred thousand souls a day
   Are passing one by one away,
   In Christless guilt and gloom.

5. ...O Church of Christ what wilt thou say
   When in the awful judgment day
   They charge thee with their doom?

"A Missionary Cry" was possibly the first hymn Simpson ever wrote.[18] He wrote it while still in Louisville, but its first publication was delayed until 1891, when his new *Hymns of the Christian Life* was published. He wrote it with the intention of stirring believers to action, rather than soothing their consciences and his intention was fulfilled. Many a farewell service included "A Missionary Cry" as part of the program. At one such service in August, 1891, Simpson spoke after the hymn had been sung:

> The hymn that has been sung is my heart's desire and thought for everyone of you to realize: that with every breath I draw, a soul unsaved is passing into the presence of God and accusing someone of neglecting its salvation. There is no subject that so overawes me and overshadows me with its solemnity as this.[19]

One night, while still a young pastor, he had a vivid dream of a desperate and lost people, mostly Chinese, mutely wringing their hands and looking imploringly to him for the hope of salvation. This dream so moved him that he sought to go to China as a missionary. Although unable to go, he nevertheless carried to his death the vision of evangelizing the unsaved of the Orient. The hymn, "A Macedonian Cry," was inspired by that dream:

1. A cry is ever sounding upon my burdened ear
   A cry of pain and anguish, a cry of woe and fear.
   It is the voice of myriads, who grope in heathen night
   It is the cry of Jesus to rise and send them light.

Refrain:
O hear the pleading message from every land and nation

O haste and send the answer, ye heralds of salvation
'Come over, come over,' I can hear it ever more
'Come over, come over, come over and help us.'

Simpson made the emotional pitch of his missionary songs intentionally high. The 1897 hymnal contained many such missionary songs, but none was so moving as "Only a Little Baby Girl." This song was the direct result of an experience he had had on a trip to China in 1893. He actually saw the body of a baby girl floating in the river near some houseboats, ignored by the people nearby. When he asked why no one had tried to save the girl, he was confronted with the Oriental philosophy of "fate." It was her "fate" to drown, and no one wanted to "interfere." Had she been a boy, they might have tried to prevent the death, but since she was only a girl, she was abandoned to drown.

Shaken by this and other similar experiences in "heathen" countries, Simpson was stirred to write an account in the June 23, 1893, *Christian Alliance Weekly*, and later, a poem in the August 25th edition. The poem was set to music and appeared in the 1897 hymnal. Verses 1 through 5 describe the hopelessness of the situation, and verse 6 concludes with an especially heart-rending challenge:

Only a little baby girl dead by the river side;
Only a little Chinese child drowned in the floating tide;
But it has brought a vision vast, dark as the nations' woe;
Oh, has it left one willing heart, answering "I will go?"

How many answered that call? One who did was missionary Alice Landis. She recalled the pathetic hymn when she encountered the same cruelty and death in China in 1901. Her experiences were much the same as Simpson's, and she quoted the song in an impassioned report in the November 30th, 1901 *Christian Alliance Weekly*.

HYMNS OF THE CHRISTIAN LIFE

There have been seven editions of *Hymns of the Christian Life* since the first in 1891, each distinct in purpose and content.

91

The preface of the first hymnal states its purpose:

The musical taste of our day is in a state of transition. Beyond controversy, the people will have new tunes and hymns that move in a more spirited time than those our fathers sang....Between the Scotch Psalter and the Salvation Army Song Book, there is a wide stretch of territory in which the careful explorer *will* find much that is good, and possessing that rare quality, endurance.... with the belief that a book has been at last prepared that is fully suited for a modern church hymnal, and at the same time adapted to the needs of the prayer meeting, and general gospel work, we present *Hymns of the Christian Life* for the service of our common Lord and Saviour, praying His blessing upon it for His name's sake.[20]

The publishers and editors were A.B. Simpson and R. Kelso Carter.

Hymn requests were solicited from members throughout the country before the first Alliance hymnal was compiled. With "cautious optimism" Simpson announced its release in August, 1891: "We have received the first copies of our new hymnal, and we are sure that our readers will agree with us that it is at least cheap. It is as large as most of the church hymnals which cost a dollar or more, and yet it is offered at the low price of fifty cents."[21] By September, 1891, it had been introduced at the Old Orchard Missionary Convention, and the review was more confident: "We are gratified to find that all who have examined it are much pleased with *Hymns of the Christian Life*, and it is beginning to be circulated somewhat widely."[22]

In the May 18, 1892 magazine, Simpson reported "highest approval" of the new hymnal, and in December 22, 1893, eighteen months after its release, he announced that "they [the office] were receiving testimonies from all directions of the high appreciation with which many of the hymns have been received."[23] Simpson noted at the same time that "a good many" of the hymns were being republished in Great Britain and he trusted that God would send them "over the world as messages of His grace and Love."[24]

The formal introduction of each of these new hymnals usually took place at the Old Orchard conventions in August, and they were well received by all reports. The new hymns by the founder were especially popular, being sung by both special musicians and congregation. Simpson wrote the following about the 1897 convention:

> One of the most delightful additions to the Convention was the introduction of our hymn book, which was received with universal favor and gave a pronounced inspiration to the service of song, which was better than at any previous conference.[25]

The early Alliance identified strongly with its hymnody and its distinctive hymnal. No other hymnal was so tailored to the theology of the Alliance as was *Hymns of the Christian Life*. Several smaller, more specialized Alliance songbooks have been compiled, but *Hymns of the Christian Life* still represents the main body of Alliance hymnody. The first hymnal contained 454 hymns and was subtitled, "New and Standard Songs for the sanctuary, Sunday schools, prayer meetings, mission work and revival services." It included forty Simpson hymns, the greater part of which dealt with sanctification, joy and peace. This hymnal did not include a section specifically identified as "Missions," although "A Missionary Cry" and "Who Will Go?" were included, as was "Trust," one of Simpson's first Missionary Institute graduation songs.

The second hymnal, *Hymns of the Christian Life #2* was published in 1897. Sixty-eight of its 336 hymns credit Simpson with either words or music. None of these sixty-eight was carried over from the first hymnal, and nineteen were classified "Christian Work and Missionary" hymns. The missionary zeal of that particular stage of Alliance growth is represented by the significant inclusion of ninety-four songs in the "Christian Work and Missionary" category. Here was the first appearance of "The Dark Soudan," "Beautiful Japan," "The Land of the Congo," and the plaintive "Only a Little Baby Girl."

Seven years later, in 1904, Simpson announced that the need for a new hymnal had been fulfilled, and that this latest hymnal had an "unusual number of new pieces" with a "richer blessing to the household of faith than even the previous numbers, which have been so widely used."[26] The subtitle for *Hymns of the Christian Life #3* read: "For church worship, conventions, evangelistic services, prayer meetings, missionary meetings, revival services, rescue mission work and Sunday school."

Simpson had composed the music or written the lyrics to 67 of its 270 hymns. Most of these were new, and only four had appeared in either of the first hymnals. (See appendix.) More than half of them fell into the categories of "Deeper Christian Life" or "Christian Work and Missions." Simpson proudly wrote that "no other book contains so many mission hymns,"[27] and it was the first to contain the well-known hymn, "To the Regions Beyond." Margaret Simpson's name appears more often in this hymnal as well; she is credited with the music for thirty-four of the sixty-seven Simpson hymns.

The fourth hymnal, *Hymns of the Christian Life #1, 2 and 3*, was published in 1908, and remains the "magnum opus" of Alliance hymnals, containing 946 selections. These were compiled from the first, second and third editions, although four new Simpson songs were included. In an editorial comment in the August 1, 1908 *Weekly*, Simpson wrote of the new hymnal:

> It is being rapidly adopted in the various states, districts and branches as the permanent hymnal of the Alliance work, so that every member should have a copy, and there is little prospect of any change for many years to come.[28]

The long subtitle of *Hymns #3* was retained, but the largest section of hymns (164) was devoted to "Salvation and Invitation." The 1908 hymnal contained 166 of Simpson's songs. Of these, most had to do with salvation and invitation, Christian work and missions, trial, trust and comfort, deeper life and the Lord's coming. Seven of his hymns appeared for the first time, including "Launch Out," which was retained in the following three editions.

This 1908 hymnal was the standard denominational hymnal until 1936, when the fifth edition was published. David J. Fant, one of the editors of the hymnal, recalled that "a new singing era had been introduced by Billy Sunday and Homer Rodeheaver,"[29] [because of their revival and crusade songs] and in response to this change, the Alliance Board of Managers asked him to prepare a replacement for *Hymns of the Christian Life #1, 2 and 3*, containing some of this type of music. Neither the 1936 edition nor the succeeding hymnals included an identifying number in their title. The 1936 hymnal contained 504 hymns, 59 of which were Simpson's. Five of these were poems which had been posthumously set to music. (See appendix.) The subtitle of the 1936 revision was less pretentious than the last two: "A Book of Worship in Song, emphasizing Evangelism, Missions and the Deeper Life." Several Simpson hymn tunes had been re-written, adapted or arranged. The "Evangelism" section, listed under "Evening Service" was the largest category, containing 130 hymns, 30 by Simpson. Only nine of Simpson's mission hymns were included among the considerably decreased total number of missionary songs.

For twenty-six years, the 1936 hymnal was the official song-book of the Alliance. In 1962, the sixth hymnal was published. Much more sophisticated than the earlier editions, this one included cross-referenced indexes and reference guides. There were 566 hymns, 50 of which were Simpson's. Harmonic changes were again made in an attempt to appeal to con-temporary worshippers, and only nine of his hymns remained unchanged, with original words and music. Twenty-three Simpson hymns appear under the categories "Consecration, Sanctification and the Deeper Life," "Divine Healing," and the "Overcoming Life," but only seven of his missionary hymns are included. The 1962 edition used some Simpson hymns from earlier hymnals which the 1936 edition did not include. As well, a new hymn, "Jesus Interceding," with music by J. Buchanan MacMillan was published; it was a poem which had never been set to music in Simpson's lifetime.

The most recent *Hymns of the Christian Life* is the seventh hymnal by that title, and was published in 1978. It contains 612 hymns, 45 of which are attributed to A.B. Simpson. This hymnal includes greatly expanded indexes, scripture readings and worship aids, making it the most sophisticated Alliance hymnal to date. Four Simpson hymns appear in the 1978 edition which were not included in the 1962 hymnal, and ten which were in the 1962 edition were not selected for the present one. Ten of his hymns fall into the "Deeper Life" category, six each into the categories "Divine Healing," the "Overcoming Life," and "Missions," and the rest are evenly distributed. Of the forty Simpson hymns which were printed in the very first hymnal, fourteen remain in the 1978 edition. Of these fourteen, only "Himself" and "I Will Say Yes to Jesus" still appear with the original, unrevised music.

In all of the seven Alliance hymnals, Simpson receives credit 181 times for either words or music or both. Many others of his hymns were published in Alliance magazines and elsewhere during his lifetime, but were not selected for the hymnals.

Probably the last hymn he wrote before his death was one entitled "The Upward Calling," and it appeared as a tribute in the 1945 (Nyack) *Missionarian*. It was set to music by his daughter, Margaret, but was never distributed. The words depict clearly the Christian's final meeting with Jesus, coming from a man who had looked forward to that meeting all of his life.

1. A voice is calling me, a hand has grasped me;
   By cords unseen my soul is upward drawn;
   My heart has answered to that upward calling;
   I clasp the hand that lifts and leads me on.

4. And in my heart I hear the Spirit's whisper;
   "The bridegroom cometh, hasten to prepare;"
   And with my vessels filled and lamps all burning;
   I'm going to meet Him in the air.

THE EFFECT OF HIS MUSIC

Did the hymns of A.B. Simpson truly inspire people, or did those who sang them do so merely out of courtesy to a prominent spiritual leader? May Agnew Stephens wrote:

If it were possible to marshal together all the people to whom Dr. Simpson's hymns have been an inspiration and a blessing, what a mighty host they would be! All around the world they have carried their sweet fragrance; into the jungles of Africa and India, China, Japan, Palestine, Europe, South America and the islands of the sea.[30]

A.W. Tozer emphatically stated that the songs of Simpson "became a powerful factor toward the success of the Christian and Missionary Alliance."[31] Yes, he did inspire people with his music.

He wrote hymns of instructions, hymns of challenge, hymns of testimony and of great longing. He wrote hymns of the Fourfold Gospel, hymns that called for a filling of the Holy Spirit, hymns of healing and of missions. He wrote hymns that delighted in the beauty of the person of Jesus Christ. He presented a call to holiness, urged people to replace the self life with the Christ-life, showed the hopelessness of the lost world and encouraged believers to sing of the hope of Christ's return. He wrote hymns of Christ's sufficiency and the scope of His love, writing not merely for one denomination, nor for his own sphere of influence, but for the universal priesthood of all believers. He wrote of his vision, and continually directed attention to Christ. He wanted the faithful to sing about their faith and to sing heartily.

Are Simpson's hymns really unsingable by today's voices, unfit for a contemporary service? Perhaps. The gospel song itself may be unsuitable for today's worshipper, out of style and out of favor. If such is the case, the great majority of evangelical hymnody is obsolete. A more interesting question might be, "Would Simpson himself frequently use his original hymns one hundred years later?" Perhaps not. To such a question, he might respond with this statement from the preface of his first hymnal: "The musical taste of our day is in a state of transition. Beyond controversy, the people *will* have new tunes and hymns that move in a more spirited time than our fathers sang...."[32] We may need to rewrite the music to some of Simpson's hymns. Tunes have been changed before: almost none of the hymns of Isaac Watts and Charles Wesley are sung to their original obscure melodies. But more likely, we need new and fresh hymns, hymns which flow from a vision shared with the founder of our denomination. Were Dr. Simpson alive today, I believe he would be calling for new songs, songs that would stir this generation.

The early Christian and Missionary Alliance sang their theology. They shared the vision their founder expressed through his preaching, writing and music. Today's Alliance congregations are not able to listen to A.B. Simpson's preaching and few will study his writings, but in a day when this denomination needs to remember its distinctives, Alliance constituents can see his view of Christ and share his concern for a lost world through his songs.

Until we see the works of new Alliance hymn writers, we can sing of Christ as Saviour, Sanctifier, Healer and Coming King in the hymns of A.B. Simpson. We can read the words in our devotions. We can take "Jesus Only" as our theme. We can sing of world missions, the consecrated Christian life, and the power of the Holy Spirit in the yielded heart. It may be that our singing will help us to share the life-changing vision of the founder of the Christian and Missionary Alliance.

END NOTES

1. A.B. Simpson, *Wholly Sanctified* (New York: Christian Alliance Publishing Co., 1893; Harrisburg, PA: Christian Publications, 1982), p. 58.

2. A.W. Tozer, *Wingspread: Albert B. Simpson, A Study in Spiritual Altitude* (Harrisburg, PA: Christian Publications, 1943), p. 53.

3. R. Kelso Carter and A.B. Simpson, comps., *Hymns of the Christian Life* (New York: Alliance Press, 1891), preface.

4. Margaret Simpson Buckman, "The Hymns of Dr. Simpson," *Missionarian* (1945): 17.

5. Tozer, *Wingspread*, p. 118.

6. Ibid., p. 117.

7. Ibid., p. 119.

8. Ibid.

9. A.B. Simpson, *Himself* (Harrisburg, PA: Christian Publications, n.d.).

10. A.B. Simpson, *A Larger Christian Life* (New York: Christian Alliance Publishing Co., 1890; Harrisburg, PA: Christian Publications, n.d.).

11. May Agnew Stephens, "Dr. Simpson's Ministry in Song," *The Alliance Weekly* 53 (December 20, 1919): 206.

12. A.E. Thompson, *A.B. Simpson, His Life and Work* (Harrisburg, PA: Christian Publications, 1960), p. 56.

13. J.C. Pollock, *Moody, a Biographical Portrait* (New York: MacMillan Co., 1963), p. 77.

14. Thompson, *A.B. Simpson*, p. 53.

15. A.B. Simpson, "Editorials," *The Christian Alliance and Missionary Weekly* 11 (October 6, 1893): 209. (Hereafter cited as CAMW).

16. Stephens, "Dr. Simpson's Ministry," p. 206.

17. A.B. Simpson, "Editorials," *CAMW* 2 (February 1889): 17.

18. David J. Fant, "Genealogy of a Hymnal," *The Alliance Witness* 113 (April 5, 1978): 9.

19. A.B. Simpson, "Editorials," *CAMW* 7 (August 28, 1891): 141.

20. Carter and Simpson, *Hymns*, preface.

21. A.B. Simpson, "Editorials," *CAMW* 7 (August 7, 1891): 82.

22. Simpson, "Editorials," *CAMW* 7 (September 18, 1891): 178.

23. Simpson, "Editorials," *CAMW* 11 (December 22, 1893): 385.

24. Ibid.

25. Simpson, "Editorials," *The Christian and Missionary Alliance Weekly* 19 (August 11, 1897): 156 (Hereafter cited as *CMAW*).

26. A.B. Simpson, May Agnew Stevens and Margaret M. Simpson, comps., *Hymns of the Christian Life*, 3rd ed. (New York: Alliance Press Co., 1904), p. 27.

27. Simpson, "Editorials," *CMAW* 34 (June 3, 1905): 350.

28. Simpson, "Editorials," *CMAW* 30 (August 1, 1908): 296.

29. Fant, "Genealogy," p. 10.

30. Stephens, "Dr. Simpson's Ministry," p. 206.

31. Tozer, *Wingspread*, p. 119.

32. Carter and Simpson, *Hymns*, preface.

APPENDIX

		Hymns #1 1891	Hymns #2 1897	Hymns #3 1904	Hymns #4 1908	Hymns #5 1936	Hymns #6 1962	Hymns #7 1978
1	ABIDING AND CONFIDING	X			X	X	X	X
2	ALL THE WAY TO CALVARY			X	X			
3	A MACEDONIAN CRY		X		X		X	
4	A MISSIONARY CRY	X			X	X		X
5	ANYWHERE, EVERYWHERE		X		X			
6	A SINNER SAVED BY GRACE			X	X	X		
7	AWAY ACROSS THE OCEAN		X		X			
8	BALM IN GILEAD		X		X	X		X
9	BEAUTIFUL JAPAN		X		X			
10	BERACHAH SONGS	X			X			
11	BE STILL			X	X		X	
12	BE TRUE		X		X	X	X	X
13	BLESSED BE THE GLORIOUS TIDINGS					X	X	X
14	BLESSED BE THE GREAT ATONEMENT	X			X			
15	BREATHING OUT AND BREATHING IN		X		X			X
16	BURN ON				X	X	X	X	X
17	CAST NOT AWAY YOUR CONFIDENCE			X	X			
18	CEASE YOUR THINKING		X		X			
19	CHRIST IS ALL IN ALL TO ME			X	X			
20	CHRIST IS CONQUEROR, HALLELUJAH			X	X			
21	CHRIST IN ME	X			X	X	X	X
22	COME AND TAKE			X	X	X		
23	COME BACK TO GOD		X		X			
24	COME SEVENFOLD HOLY SPIRIT	X			X		X	X
25	COME TO JESUS NOW		X		X	X	X	
26	COME TO THE THRONE OF GRACE		X		X			
27	COME WITH US AND WE WILL DO THEE GOOD	X			X			

		Hymns #1 1891	Hymns #2 1897	Hymns #3 1904	Hymns #4 1908	Hymns #5 1936	Hymns #6 1962	Hymns #7 1978
28	DAYS OF HEAVEN					X	X	X
29	DE MASSA OB DE SHEEPFOL'		X		X			
30	DYING WITHOUT JESUS		X		X			
31	EVEN AS HE		X		X	X	X	X
32	EVEN SO		X		X			
33	EVERLASTING LOVE	X			X			
34	FELLOWSHIP			X	X			
35	FILL THE CENSER		X		X			
36	FILL UP THE RANKS		X		X	X	X	
37	FULFILLMENT			X	X			
38	GIDEON'S BAND		X		X			
39	GO AND TELL		X	X	X	X	X	X
40	GOD'S BEST		X		X			
41	GO FORWARD		X		X			
42	GOD IS LOVE			X	X			
43	GOD IS MY HOME		X		X			
44	GOD'S TRANSCENDENT LOVE			X	X			
45	HASTING ON HIS COMING			X	X			
46	HEALING IN HIS WINGS		X		X	X	X	X
47	HEALING IN JESUS	X			X	X	X	X
48	HE BORE OUR SORROWS	X			X			
49	HE DIED FOR ME			X	X			
50	HE IS ABLE			X	X			
51	HE IS COMING BACK AGAIN			X	X			
52	HE IS COMING FOR ME		X					
53	HE KNOWS			X	X			
54	HELP ALONG		X		X			
55	HIDDEN AWAY WITH JESUS			X	X			
56	HIMSELF	X		X	X	X	X	X
57	HIMSELF HE COULD NOT SAVE			X	X			
58	HOLD THE ROPES		X		X			

	1891 Hymns #1	1897 Hymns #2	1904 Hymns #3	1908 Hymns #4	1936 Hymns #5	1962 Hymns #6	1978 Hymns #7
59 I ALWAYS WILL REMEMBER THEE		X		X			
60 I AM CRUCIFIED WITH CHRIST			X	X	X		
61 I AM ENTERING IN		X		X			
62 I BELIEVE IN GOD THE FATHER				X			
63 I BELONG TO HIM			X	X	X		
64 I HAVE GIVEN MYSELF AWAY		X					
65 I HAVE LEARNED THE SECRET	X						
66 I HAVE OVERCOME		X		X	X	X	X
67 I LOVE HIM SO		X		X			
68 I'M LIVING IN HEAVEN TODAY					X		
69 I'M SAVED AND I KNOW IT			X	X			
70 IS IT FOR ME?		X		X			
71 IS IT RIGHT WITH GOD?		X		X			
72 I TAKE, HE UNDERTAKES	X			X	X	X	X
73 IT IS DONE	X			X			
74 IT MEANS JUST WHAT IT SAYS		X		X			
75 IT SEEMS TOO GOOD TO BE TRUE			X	X			
76 I WANT TO BE HOLY				X	X	X	X
77 I WILL SAY YES TO JESUS	X			X	X	X	X
78 JESUS GIVETH US THE VICTORY				X	X	X	X
79 JESUS INTERCEDING						X	
80 JESUS IS ABLE				X	X	X	X
81 JESUS IS COMING AGAIN			X	X			
82 JESUS IS TENDERLY PLEADING		X		X			
83 JESUS KNOWS OUR EVERY CARE				X			
84 JESUS ONLY	X			X	X	X	X
85 JESUS THE ROCK OF AGES	X			X			
86 JUST BEYOND THE GOLDEN GATE		X					
87 KADESH BARNEA	X			X			
88 KEEP SWEET		X		X	X		
89 LAUNCH OUT				X	X	X	X

		1891 Hymns #1	1897 Hymns #2	1904 Hymns #3	1908 Hymns #4	1936 Hymns #5	1962 Hymns #6	1978 Hymns #7
90	LEST WE FORGET			X	X			
91	LET NOT YOUR HEART BE TROUBLED			X	X			
92	LET US GO			X	X			
93	LET US REJOICE			X	X			
94	LIVING IN THE GLORY			X	X	X	X	X
95	MARCH ON			X	X			
96	MUST JESUS BEAR THE CROSS ALONE?			X				
97	MY BELOVED	X			X			
98	MY BELOVED IS MINE	X			X			
99	MY GRACE IS SUFFICIENT FOR THEE		X		X	X	X	X
100	MY HOLY GUEST		X		X			
101	MY TRUST			X	X	X	X	X
102	NO MORE SORROW	X			X	X	X	
103	NOTHING IS TOO HARD FOR JESUS		X	X	X	X	X	X
104	NOT I BUT CHRIST (music only)	X			X	X	X	X
105	NOT I BUT CHRIST (words only)		X		X			
106	NOT MY WILL			X	X			
107	O COMFORTER, GENTLE AND TENDER		X		X	X	X	X
108	O CROSS OF CHRIST			X	X			
109	OH THE GLAD HOMECOMING	X			X	X		
110	O LORD IN ME THY MIGHTY POWER EXERT		X					
111	O LOVE DIVINE					X	X	X
112	ONLY A LITTLE BABY GIRL		X		X			
113	ONLY BELIEVE IT AND LEAVE IT			X	X			
114	ONLY WAIT		X		X			X
115	O SETTLE IT ALL WITH JESUS	X		X				
116	OVER LIFE'S PATHWAY I JOURNEY			X				
117	PASS IT ON		X		X			
118	PLOD		X		X			
119	POWER FROM ON HIGH		X		X	X	X	X
120	RECKON		X		X			

		Hymns #1 1891	Hymns #2 1897	Hymns #3 1904	Hymns #4 1908	Hymns #5 1936	Hymns #6 1962	Hymns #7 1978
121	REDEEM THE TIME			X	X	X	X	X
122	RISEN WITH CHRIST				X		X	
123	SAVING AND SERVING			X	X	X	X	X
124	SAY, IS IT ALL FOR JESUS?		X					
125	SEARCH ME O GOD		X		X	X	X	X
126	SEEKING THE LOST		X		X			
127	SEND THE GOSPEL FASTER			X	X	X		
128	SHINE ON			X	X			
129	SOMEBODY			X	X			
130	SOME SWEET MORN		X		X			
131	SPEAK TO THE ROCK	X			X	X		
132	STEP BY STEP			X	X	X	X	X
133	STRETCH FORTH THY HAND				X	X		X	X
134	TAKE IT AND LEAVE IT THERE				X	X	X	
135	TARRY FOR THE POWER				X	X		
136	THE BRANCH OF HEALING	X			X	X	X	X
137	THE COMFORTER HAS COME		X		X			
138	THE DARK SOUDAN		X		X			
139	THE DAYS OF HEAVEN	X			X			
140	THE DOOR OF HOPE	X						
141	THE EVERLASTING ARMS	X			X	X	X	X
142	THE FIRST AND THE LAST	X			X	X		
143	THE FOUNTAIN OF LIFE	X			X	X	X	
144	THE HEART OF GOD			X	X			
145	THE JOY OF THE LORD	X			X	X	X	X
146	THE LAND OF THE CONGO		X		X			
147	THE LAST HANDFUL			X	X			
148	THE LOST SOUL		X	ı	X			
149	THE MORNING STAR			X	X			
150	THE NAMES OF JESUS			X	X			
151	THE OTHER SHEEP			X	X			

		1891 Hymns #1	1897 Hymns #2	1904 Hymns #3	1908 Hymns #4	1936 Hymns #5	1962 Hymns #6	1978 Hymns #7
152	THE PEACE OF GOD		X		X			
153	THE POTTER AND THE CLAY			X	X			
154	THE REGIONS BEYOND			X	X	X	X	X
155	THE RIGHT SIDE		X		X			
156	THE RISEN ONE			X	X			
157	THE SHEPHERD TRUE		X		X			
158	THE SUMMERLAND OF LOVE	X			X			
159	THE WONDROUS RIVER		X		X			
160	THERE'S A SECRET					X	X	X
161	THERE IS A NAME TO JESUS GIVEN						X	
162	THERE IS JOY IN HEAVEN			X	X	X		
163	THERE IS NOTHING TO DO BUT COME		X		X			
164	THIS SAME JESUS			X	X			
165	THROUGH DEATH TO LIFE	X			X			
166	THY KINGDOM COME		X		X	X	X	X
167	THY LOVE IS SUNSHINE			X	X			
168	TIMNATH SERAH		X		X			
169	TRUST	X			X			
170	TRUST AND REST		X		X			
171	UNTO THE COMING OF THE LORD			X	X			
172	WAITING ON THE LORD	X			X			
173	WE LOVE HIM, BECAUSE HE FIRST LOVED US	X			X			
174	WHAT WILL YOU DO WITH JESUS?		X		X	X	X	X
175	WHAT WOULD JESUS DO?	X			X			
176	WHEN JESUS COMES			X	X			
177	WHEN SHADOWS FLEE AWAY			X	X	X		
178	WHO WILL GO?	X						
179	WILL YOU MEET ME IN THE AIR?			X	X			
180	YES, HE'LL COME AGAIN (Star of Hope)		X		X	X	X	
181	YESTERDAY, TODAY FOREVER	X		X	X	X	X	X

EUGENE RIVARD

Eugene Rivard holds a B.Sc. from St. Cloud State University and a M.Mus. from Northwestern University. He served for several years as a high school band director in the United States and Canada before coming to Canadian Bible College, where he is Assistant Professor of Music and Chairman of the Department of Music. Mr. Rivard plays second trumpet with the Regina Symphony Orchestra and is otherwise active as a solo trumpet player. He is also a member of the Hymn Society of America and serves as a worship leader and chairman of the music committee at Rosewood Park Alliance Church.

THE DOCTRINE OF SANCTIFICATION IN THE THOUGHT OF A.B. SIMPSON

by

Samuel J. Stoesz

Albert Benjamin Simpson described the society which he founded as "an organization to promote a deeper spiritual life among Christians of all denominations, and a more aggressive missionary work in neglected fields at home and abroad." This quotation appeared in the entry on "The Christian and Missionary Alliance" in the *Schaff-Herzog Encyclopedia* in 1907.[1] During the first hundred years of the C&MA's history, there have been many changes. For example, no longer is the C&MA an interdenominational missionary society; no longer is the work at home served by branches or auxiliaries, but by regular churches. Despite these changes, however, the Alliance continues to promote both missions and the necessity of a deeper spiritual life for the Christian.

SIMPSON'S SCOTTISH PRESBYTERIAN BACKGROUND

Simpson was raised in a staunch Scottish Presbyterian home, his grandfather having emigrated from Moreyshire, Scotland, to Prince Edward Island in 1775. Both his father and mother and his wife's father and mother were of Scottish ancestry.

In the background of the Scottish ancestry were the effects of the English reformation, which were mainly political. The Anglican church, with its church-state alignment, was forced toward religious tolerance of the Puritans and the Presbyterian and Congregational parties under Oliver Cromwell. The Scots, having contributed heavily to the formation of the Westminster Confession of Faith for the Presbyterian church (1647), soon were disillusioned by the political dominance of government over the church in England. In Scotland, a century earlier, under the leadership of John Knox, they had formed a church separate from the state, capturing many of the pious forms of Puritanism and the wholesome effects of Pietism present in the English reformation movement. But in Scotland, there was also much suffering caused by Roman Catholic tyranny and the political fortunes of kings and feudal lords who vied for authority. The Scottish Presbyterians survived by raw courage and the use of a covenant bond that was signed by blood pricked from their hands. In common language, they became known as "Covenanters."

Religion was rigorous and exacting among the Scottish Covenanters and the concept of sanctification had its own particular context. Puritan virtues of reverence, chastity, sobriety, frugality, industry, and honesty gained their fullest expression among the Scottish Presbyterians. To them, the Church of Scotland was central to both social life and industry. Great stress was laid on doctrine and its demand for discipline and obedience. As far as sanctification is concerned, the Presbyterians of Simpson's day followed the teaching of John Calvin who taught that sanctification comes with a life of repentance in which the believer exercises piety as he recognizes that he is by nature a sinner. By continuously renouncing this sinful nature and striving after godliness, the believer experiences progressive sanctification, which provides assurance of election to salvation.[2]

By age twelve, Albert Simpson, who grew up in Chatham, Ontario, had learned by rote the Westminster Shorter Catechism. Though he sought personal salvation earnestly, it did not come easily, for the Calvinist teaching on salvation was severe, declaring that God's sovereignty alone could save helpless, hopeless sinners in prevenient grace. However, in the Simpson home were the writings of the Puritans Richard Baxter, Philip Doddridge, and Walter Marshall. While reading Marshall's book, *The Gospel Mystery of Sanctification*,[3] fifteen-year-old Albert understood the simplicity of the gospel and received assurance of faith. Herbert T. Stevens observes that this book contained "all that Keswick later reminted in present-day language."[4] Yet, it would be another sixteen years before Simpson would come to know Christ as His own sanctifier, an experience he described as the watershed of his ministry.

After finishing his theological training at Knox College in Toronto, Simpson, at age twenty-one, entered the ministry. In spite of his youth, he was an instant success: during eight years of ministry at Knox Presbyterian Church in Hamilton, Ontario, he saw 750 persons added to the membership. About the time he moved to Louisville, Kentucky, to become minister at the Chestnut Street Presbyterian Church, he became aware of strange stirrings in England. Dwight L. Moody was enjoying a successful evangelistic ministry (1872-73) following his unusual experience of being filled with the Holy Spirit in 1871. By 1874, these meetings were being followed by conferences on "the higher Christian life," later known as the Keswick movement.

THE DOCTRINE OF SANCTIFICATION IN THE KESWICK MOVEMENT

The conferences on "the higher Christian life" began when W. E. Boardman and Robert Pearsall Smith visited England in 1874. Boardman had published a book titled *The Higher Christian Life*[5] in 1858. As a Presbyterian minister, leader in the Sunday School Union, and chaplain in the United States Christian

Commission during the Civil War, he held extensive meetings on the subject of the book he had written. Now of retiral age, he went to England out of interest in the Moody meetings and to rest from his strenuous ministry. Robert Pearsall Smith, his friend of thirty years, accompanied him. Smith was a wealthy glassmaker in Philadelphia where Boardman had pastored. Though of Quaker background, both Smith and his wife (Hannah Whitall Smith, author of the well-known classic, *The Christian's Secret of a Happy Life*[6], published in 1870) had joined the Presbyterian church.

In 1873, prior to the "higher Christian life" conferences, a series of articles which had been written in America and published in a London weekly, stirred considerable interest because they claimed to be addressing a neglected part of gospel preaching. The writer observed that in the Epistles the mention of Christ offering Himself for the sanctifying of the believer occurs more often than the matter of Christ offering Himself for the justification of the believer. He asserted that this was more than judicial pardon and imputed righteousness and that the Bible also taught a victorious life over sin as well as pardon for sins.[7] Though not identified, the author appears to have been W.E. Boardman.

When Boardman and Smith began to teach these truths in the YMCA in England, there was an unusual, immediate response. To begin with, Samuel Morley, the member of parliament for Bristol, sponsored a series of breakfasts for ministers in London. Then, in 1874 and 1875, breakfasts with groups of 30 to 40 were conducted until about 2,400 pastors had been introduced to the teaching of the higher Christian life. A large meeting of 1,000 ministers was held at Oxford in 1874. Ministers came from France, Belgium, Norway, Sweden, Holland, Switzerland, and Germany, as well as from England.

The breakfasts were followed by conferences. The conferences were opened to the Christian public, and 6,000 attended the one at Brighton in 1875. Although spearheaded under the leadership of Smith at Brighton, the conferences were later organized at Keswick by Rev. Canon Battersby, an Anglican bishop, and became known as Keswick conferences. When Smith failed to appear for one of the early scheduled conferences, Moody became the main speaker.

SANCTIFICATION AND SIMPSON'S
CRISIS EXPERIENCE

News of the conferences did not escape Simpson. Faced with a serious problem in Louisville, he became hungry in his spirit and deeply restless over the need of his own heart. When he arrived in Louisville in 1873, he found that the end of the Civil War had not brought an end to bitter disagreements among Christians over the issues that had started the war. Baptists, Presbyterians, and Methodists were divided, and animosity ran so deep as to divert people from the claims of the gospel.

A different conflict was raging in Simpson's heart as he struggled with his intense nature and strong self-will. The peculiar temptations of pride and discouragement brought him constant humiliation. He tried to minister to his people the deeper things of the Spirit, but his preaching had a hollow ring to it and his heart yearned for the reality of a Spirit-filled life.

Upon hearing of a Christian workers' conference sponsored by Moody in Chicago, Simpson determined to attend. At a pre-conference meeting, he heard an earnest Christian with a shining face testify: "I came here expecting Mr. Moody to help me. But last night I saw Jesus, and I got such a look at Jesus that I am never going to need anything as long as I live."[8] As the brother concluded with a big "hallelujah," conviction smote Simpson's heart. He was overcome with the conviction that he needed to take a look at Jesus and that he must go directly to Him.

Without attending the conference or hearing Moody, Simpson returned home that evening. Arriving in Louisville in the early morning, he went immediately to his study and locked the door to seek the face of God. During the vigil, he took from his library shelf "an old musty book," *The Higher Christian Life.* As he poured over the volume, a new light began to break. He saw the Lord Jesus revealed as a living, bright reality, as one who offered His own all-sufficient presence. Christ had not saved him merely from future peril and then left him to fight the battle of life, but the Christ who had justified him was waiting to sanctify him. Through the Holy Spirit, Christ had come to enter his spirit and to substitute His strength, holiness, joy, love, faith, and power for the helplessness and emptiness that had so troubled him. As Simpson threw himself at the feet of such a glorious Master, he claimed the promise, "I will dwell in you and walk in you." Across the threshold of his heart came a presence as real as the Christ who had come to John on Patmos. "From that moment," asserted Simpson, "a new secret [became] the charm, glory, and strength of his life and testimony."[9]

Soon Simpson understood how to meet the need in Louisville: he approached the ministerial association with the challenge to unite in prayer and to sponsor the Major Daniel Whittle and Philip P. Bliss team for united evangelistic meetings. Major Whittle, formerly in the United States army, had joined Moody's evangelistic association. In his ministry, he incorporated the gospel of the "higher Christian life." Prayer meetings and the exchange of pulpits within the city prepared the way for powerful meetings in which several thousand were converted. (It is of interest to note that during the campaign, a Baptist church sponsored Robert Pearsall Smith in afternoon meetings.) These meetings opened Simpson's eyes to the power and effectiveness of the gospel when preached and sung under the anointing of the Spirit of God.

Simpson's experience in the Whittle/Bliss meetings changed the shape of his ministry at Chestnut Street church. He continued public services at the Library Hall where the Whittle/Bliss meetings were held and eventually built Broadway Tabernacle, a large auditorium accommodating about two thousand people. This eliminated pew rents and provided a neutral place for people who shied away from formal churches. As hundreds were converted, Simpson also became convinced of the need to promote missions and the fulfillment of the Great Commission (Matthew 28:18-20). But these new dimensions in Simpson's ministry were the direct result of the sacred experience in the study and the doctrine of sanctification as he had come to understand it.

SANCTIFICATION TRUTH EXTENDED TO MISSIONS AND DIVINE HEALING

Simpson's move to Thirteenth Street Presbyterian Church in New York City in 1879 was motivated by a desire to reach the immigrant masses that were flooding the city and to publish a missionary magazine of cross-denominational interest. His determined zeal literally outran his health and stamina. While ministering to a large and prestigious church, he also edited a missionary magazine that was gaining the notice of the evangelical denominations and carried on an aggressive evangelistic ministry in the ghettos of New York.

Not blessed with a rugged physique, Simpson suffered several incapacitating breakdowns in health. Facing death, according to a medical diagnosis, he became interested in the doctrine of divine healing. This came about through the ministry of Charles Cullis, an Episcopalian physician in Boston who ministered in a camp meeting at Old Orchard, Maine, where Simpson had gone for rest and quiet. Simpson experienced this miracle of healing as he knelt alone with an open Bible at a pine log. He returned to his ministry with more vigor than ever.

Simpson's healing experience added a new dimension to his understanding of the higher Christian life. He now realized that the Christ who had dwelt on earth physically and had ascended in physical resurrection life would mediate his own life to the body as well as to the soul, just as he had done for the church in the healings recounted in the book of Acts. For Simpson, Jesus Christ had become the same yesterday, today, and forever (Hebrews 13:8).

Thus, the blend of sanctification, of evangelism and missions, and of divine healing served to empower and to enlarge Simpson's motivation for ministry. Neither the experience of sanctification nor that of divine healing was the main focus; rather, they were the potential resources available for the believer who would dare to live from the throne of Christ's glory. Though the divine laws and principles in divine healing were at times difficult to discern, Simpson found that the dynamic bridging of the physical and spiritual generated a new power for life and service.

Simpson believed that the doctrine of divine healing had a profound bearing on the spiritual life.[10] Man has a twofold nature, material and spiritual, and both have been affected by the fall.[11] Though it is not immortal life that is promised to mortal bodies, there is a close relationship between the soul and the body as evidenced by 3 John 2, Ephesians 5:30, Romans 8:11, and 2 Corinthians 4:10-11.[12] Furthermore, healing is not restricted to emergency incidents of occasional need, but more directly it is living from the throne where a physical Christ in resurrection power mediates life and health and strength to believers. As Simpson put it: "The doctrine of Christ's healing power is so closely linked with the necessity of holiness, and the deeper truths and experiences of the spiritual life, that it tends, in a preeminent degree, to promote purity and earnestness."[13]

Because Simpson was not one to make exclusive claims on doctrinal truth, this new expansiveness of faith went through a crucible of trial. But the implications of the doctrine of divine healing in relation to divine providence in suffering, and particularly to sanctification, became a question of debate. Nevertheless, the divine healing movement grew rapidly in England, Europe, and America. Hundreds of evangelical leaders gave affirmation, if not open proclamation, to it, including A.J. Gordon of Clarendon Street Baptist Church in Boston, C.H. Spurgeon of the Metropolitan Tabernacle in London, and R.A. Torrey of Moody Bible Institute in Chicago.

SIMPSON'S DOCTRINE OF
SANCTIFICATION TESTED

During the International Conference for Holiness and Healing held in London in 1885, a number of divergent views of sanctification were expressed. W.E. Boardman was the prime mover and moderator of this conference, and Mrs. Elizabeth Baxter, who operated the Bethshan healing home in London, served as cohost. (In his semi-retired years, Boardman had moved to London and had become associated with Mrs. Baxter.) The conference attracted about twenty-five hundred people from England, Europe, and America, many of whom were leaders in the holiness and healing movement.

One of the various positions on holiness articulated at this conference was eradicationism, the belief that a person's carnal nature comes from an inherited fallenness that needs to be expurgated by a second definite work of grace. Boardman explained this position as that of the self-perfectionist who "reckons himself perfect in himself because Christ has perfected him by the Holy Spirit; so that, like a lump of gold freed from its dross by the refiner, he is absolutely pure in himself."[14]

Another position put forth at the conference was one that

114

Simpson labeled "suppressionism." Its adherents held that the carnal nature was not eradicated but that it needed to be suppressed by walking after the Spirit. According to Ernest Sandeen, this emphasis became a reaction to the Keswick movement and with particular design was promulgated by those who initiated the prophetic conferences that began at Niagara-on-the-Lake, Ontario, apparently in 1876. George C. Needham and James Inglis, initiators of the conference, were of the Plymouth Brethren. Their chief concern was "the ancient heresy of a sentimental higher life."[15]

The chief theologian of the suppressionist school, J.N. Darby of Great Britain, visited America seven times between 1862 and 1877, and had a profound influence in evangelical circles. As Sandeen observes, Darby's doctrine of the church was apparently the catalytic agent for the rest of his beliefs.[16] For Darby, the reformed churches in Britain and America had lost their spirituality through institutionalism. They were of the earth, earthy. They had absorbed naturalism and humanism because they had identified themselves with world systems, and so, had become adulterous and decadent. The true church was wholly spiritual and was born from above, existing in the heavenlies and outside of history. The age of grace which coincided with "the church" was parenthetical within God's dispensational scheme for an earthly kingdom. Similarly, the spiritual nature of the believer was in tension with his earthly or carnal nature. Only as he lived in the heavenlies and put down the flesh by the Holy Spirit would he attain true spiritual life.

In 1878, the Niagara conference formulated a creed that contained the following statement on holiness:

> We believe that we are called with a holy calling to walk, not after the flesh, but after the Spirit, and so to live in the Spirit that we should not fulfill the lusts of the flesh; but the flesh being still in us to the end of our earthly pilgrimage needs to be kept constantly in subjection to Christ, or it will surely manifest its presence to the dishonor of His name.[17]

To a large extent, the prophetic conference movement absorbed the Keswick movement in America. While the entrenched leadership of the prophetic conference movement

115

represented Darby's theology, those attracted to the conferences were unaware of the initial interests of its progenitors. The upheaval caused by liberalism and the contagious interest in prophecy that developed largely absorbed this interdenominational movement. It attracted evangelically conservative leaders in both Europe and America. But, as Sandeen so clearly demonstrates, dispensational theology and American fundamentalism became allied through the prophetic conference movement and the Northfield conferences conducted by D.L. Moody. Apparently this produced the emphasis on suppressionism at the Bethshan Conference in 1885.

THE BETHSHAN DECLARATION
OF CHRIST HIMSELF

The International Conference for Holiness and Healing in 1885 was also called the "Bethshan Conference" because of its association with Mrs. Baxter's Bethshan Home. Apparently it was also a part of the Mildmay Conferences held each Spring at a campground near London. It was, in effect, an open forum on holiness that had grown out of the Keswick movement. Simpson attended in 1884, and became interested in the association of holiness with healing promoted by Boardman at the 1885 conference.

On three occasions, Simpson addressed the conference and also listened to the various speakers' views on holiness. He then asked for a special privilege and preached an impromptu sermon which has come to be known by the title "Himself." He emphasized that the Christian's need was not blessing or healing or sanctification but Christ Himself. The question was not what people thought of Bethshan or about divine healing, but what they thought of Christ. He described his own experience of how he had prayed long and arduously for sanctification and that he sometimes thought he had obtained it. He related that on one occasion he felt something and, with desperate grip, held on for fear of losing it, but it went with the next sensation and mood. The Lord seemed to say so tenderly, "My child, just take me, and let me be in you the constant supply of all this, myself."

In regard to divine healing, Simpson reminisced:

And so I thought the healing would be an *it*, too, that the
Lord would take me like the old run-down clock, wind me
up, and set me going like a machine. It is not thus at all. I
found it was Himself coming in instead and giving me
what I needed at the moment. I wanted to have great
stock, so that I could feel rich; a great store laid up for
many years, so that I would not be dependent on Him the
next day; but He never gave me such store. I never had
more holiness and healing at one time than I needed for
that hour.[18]

For Simpson, Christ was for the whole person, for the body
as well as for the soul. To separate the body from the soul
would be to disfigure Christ and the nature of His fullness.
This truth applies not only in regard to divine healing, but also
in regard to sanctification and to the second coming of Christ.
Christ will come again in His body. He who came in the incar-
nation, who in bodily ministry fulfilled all that the law pre-
figured, who by a physical act took our sins in His own body on
the tree, who arose physically and ascended bodily, is mediating
His life to the believer by sending the Holy Spirit. The life
Christ had lived on earth is now available on earth by the Holy
Spirit. Through the fall Satan usurped rule over creation
through man, now creation is to be wrested from his power and
Christians are to become instruments to serve Christ to whom
all power in heaven and on earth is given.

In a series of sermons, Simpson used 1 Thessalonians 5:23-24
as the text to expound sanctification: "And the very God of
peace sanctify you wholly; and I pray God your whole spirit,
soul and body be preserved blameless unto the coming of our
Lord Jesus Christ. Faithful is he that calleth you who also will
do it." In 1890, these sermons were published as a book titled
Wholly Sanctified.[19] In this work, Simpson makes the following
assertions:

1. It is useless to look for sanctification until we have been
   reconciled and know justification as a fact in our relationship to God. Sanctification and peace with God begins
   with justification through the vicarious atonement of
   Christ.

117

2. "Sanctification is the pathway to a deeper peace, even the 'peace of God which passeth all understanding.'... Sanctification brings the soul into harmony with God and the laws of its own being, and there must be peace, and there can be in no other way."[20]

3. The deeper meaning of the passage is that sanctification is the work of God Himself and it expresses emphatically that it is Christ's own direct personality that is the author of the believer's sanctification. This comes, not by human struggle, but through Christ's prerogative.

Thus, for Simpson, divine holiness is not human self-improvement or perfection, but the inflow into man's being (i.e., body, soul, and spirit) of "the life and purity of the infinite, eternal and Holy One, bringing His own perfection and working out in us His own will. How easy, how spontaneous, how delightful this heavenly way of holiness!"[21]

Though the Word of God does not promise the mortal body immortality, it does promise power to fulfill God's purpose and will in the here and now. The body is not intrinsically evil, as eradication and suppression theories of holiness seem to suggest, for creation has yet to experience fully a re-creation. "A consecrated body is one that recognizes itself as the property of God and recognizes Him as the Guardian and Keeper of all its interests and needs."[22] The body is a channel for Christ's life and a weapon for His work. (Simpson titled his devotional messages on the cross, the resurrection, and the coming glory *Echoes of the New Creation*, 1903.)[23]

Repeatedly, Simpson emphasized that this holistic impartation of divine life for the body and life for the spirit, represented Christ's own direct personality to sanctify the believer. There was a physical as well as a spiritual side to the gospel. Man's worth anthropologically is found in identification with Christ and the goal of life is to become more like Him, who manifested the Father in bodily form for man's redemption (Colossians 2:9). Simpson often reiterated that a whole Christ was for the whole man to reach the whole world.

SANCTIFICATION AND THE
MISSIONARY DIMENSION

Clearly, Simpson's focus on the cosmic work of Christ and the identification of the believer with Christ, have important implications for the missionary task. The higher Christian life and missions directly complement each other, since Christ does not indwell or fill the believer merely to grant good feelings or experiences, but rather to enable the believer to live for Christ and His kingdom. This is no mere theological abstraction, for as Christ had invested His life for the need of the world, so will the believer who identifies with Him.

This kind of commitment and identification causes believers to go, give, and pray with the realization of Christ's power and enabling. They will go to any field to which the Holy Spirit directs them unless by the same constraint and direction they should support missions at home by praying, giving, and sending. To use giving as an illustration, 2 Corinthians 8:2-5 shows clearly that the Macedonians had been given power to give beyond their natural ability. It logically follows, then, that missionaries will be given power to minister overseas beyond their natural ability. To Simpson, realism of involvement attended a vision of ministry that hardly recognized a distinction between the physical and the spiritual or between the missionary and the sender. It was all of one ministry: "Christ in you, the hope of glory" (Colossians 1:27).

In the final analysis, the purpose of Christ's enthronement in glorification is to make His life available by the Holy Spirit so that Christians will be workers for Him and witnesses to Him: "But you will receive power when the Holy Spirit comes on you; and you will be my witnesses in Jerusalem, and in all Judea and Samaria, and to the ends of the earth" (Acts 1:8).

Simpson published a transdenominational missionary magazine (1880-1881) to counter the neglect of missions in the churches. He was particularly fascinated by geography and ethnology, and his description of various nations was the best of its kind in missionary journalism. He had a special ability to see the application of the gospel to the social and economic as well as the spiritual needs of various peoples.

Simpson's New York Gospel Tabernacle, organized in 1882,

employed a congregational polity and soon became a people movement for evangelism and missions. In 1884, it began to hold annual conventions emphasizing the deeper life (or the higher Christian life),[24] and missions featuring speakers from different denominations. The convention programs described in Simpson's missionary magazine caught the attention of many evangelicals. Soon requests for conventions came from different places, and five were held in 1885 — in Brooklyn, Buffalo, Philadelphia, Pittsburgh, and Detroit.

On the subject of conventions, George P. Pardington, an Alliance historian and theologian, observed: "It is the simple truth to say that the Alliance was born and has grown to maturity in the atmosphere of conventions."[25]

These early conventions lasted usually eight to ten days. The schedule of events for a typical day looked something like this: prayer at 6:30, workers' meeting at 8:00, quiet hour service at 9:00, messages on deeper truth and life at 10:00, children's meeting at 1:30, missionary addresses at 2:00, preaching or addresses on spiritual themes at 3:00, inquiry meeting at 5:00, young people's meeting at 7:00, and an evening service at 8:00.

As many as thirty-five different people spoke at one convention. They came from England and Europe and from many denominations. Conventions were held in Baptist, Anglican, Methodist, Congregational, and Presbyterian churches, as well as in public auditoriums and YMCAs. Their main aims were to deepen the commitment of Christians through experiencing the Spirit-filled life and to promote missions.

The Fourfold Gospel — Christ as Saviour, Sanctifier, Healer, and Coming King originated with Simpson, and became a slogan for the conventions. Simpson saw this not as a doctrinal platform for a church, but as a rallying theme with which evangelicals could identify. The message was simple enough, dynamic enough, and broad enough to represent the heart of the gospel trans-denominationally, without interfering with other distinctive doctrines of evangelical churches. Doctrinal controversy was of little concern in the conventions.

By 1887, seven ordained men from five denominations began to form a working relationship — two Presbyterians, two Baptists, one Anglican, one Mennonite, and one Methodist. The C&MA was never a part of the "come-out" movements typical of fundamentalism. Its orientation and motivation never did fit that mold. Time and again, Simpson explained that the C&MA was not a "come-out" movement and that he and his co-workers did not intend to start a church or a denomination.

Two organizations were formed in 1887 as an interdenominational movement. The Evangelical Missionary Alliance was to serve as a mission agency for the training and sending of missionaries and the Christian Alliance was to form auxiliaries at home to support and promote the Fourfold Gospel and support missions by praying, sending, and giving. Thus, the C&MA began with the doctrine of sanctification providing a strong impulse.

ENDNOTES

1. *The New Schaff-Herzog Encyclopedia* reprint ed. (Grand Rapids: Zondervan Pub. Co., 1977), 3:41.

2. John Calvin, *Institutes of the Christian Religion*, ed. John T. McNeil; trans. Ford Lewis Battles, Vol. 1 (Philadelphia: Westminster Press, 1960), p. 609-610.

3. Walter Marshall, *The Gospel Mystery of Sanctification*, reprint ed., (London: Oliphants Ltd., 1954).

4. Herbert T. Stevens, ed., *Keswick's Authentic Voice* (Grand Rapids: Zondervan Pub. Co., 1959), foreword.

5. W.E. Boardman, *The Higher Christian Life* (Boston: Henry Hoyt, 1858).

6. Hannah Whitall Smith, *The Christian's Secret of a Happy Life* (Westwood, N.J.: Fleming H. Revell, 1870).

7. Arthur T. Pierson, *The Story of Keswick* (London: Marshall Bros., n.d.), p. 37-38.

8. A.B. Simpson, "A Personal Witness" (*Alliance Weekly*, Oct. 2, 1915): 11.

9. Ibid.

10. A.B. Simpson, *The Gospel of Healing*, rev. ed. (New York: Christian Alliance Pub. Co., 1915), p. 8.

11. Ibid., p. 9

12. Ibid., p. 25-27.

13. Ibid., p. 72.

14. W.E. Boardman, *The Higher Christian Life*, rev. ed. (1871), p. 61-62.

15. Ernest R. Sandeen, *The Roots of Fundamentalism* (Chicago: University of Chicago Press, 1970), p. 177.

16. Ibid., p. 66.

17. Ibid., p. 276.

18. *The Word, the Work and the World* (July/August, 1885): 208.

19. A.B. Simpson, *Wholly Sanctified* (New York: Christian Alliance Pub. Co., 1890).

20. Ibid. reprint ed. (Harrisburg: Christian Publications, 1925), p. 9-10.

21. Ibid., p. 10-11.

22. Ibid., p. 87.

23. A.B. Simpson, *Echoes of the New Creation* (New York: Christian Alliance Pub. Co., 1903; reprint ed., Harrisburg, PA: Christian Publications, n.d.).

24. It is of interest to note the similarities and differences between Boardman's stress in *The Higher Christian Life*, first published in 1858 and revised in 1871; Hannah Whitall Smith's emphasis in *The Christian's Secret of a Happy Life*, published in 1870; and Simpson's major themes in his writings to 1890: *The Fullness of Jesus* (New York: Christian Alliance Pub. Co., 1886); *The Christ Life* (New York: Christian Alliance Pub. Co., 1888); and *A Larger Christian Life* (New York: Christian Alliance Pub. Co., 1890). All the books reflect the early Keswick emphasis — they are christological more than pneumatological and emphasize the transition from a self-centered life to a released Spirit-filled life, but differ in the practical concerns and needs the authors address. Smith stressed personal experience of inward rest and outward victory in wholesome daily living. Boardman emphasized sanctification as a vehicle for a more effective ministry, particularly for the clergy in the churches. He believed that the doctrine had always been part of Reformation theology, but that its implications had not been recognized by leaders in the church. Simpson concentrated on the neglected forces in the churches where the higher life needed to be caught as well as taught. The Christ life was designed for a people movement of committed, Spirit-filled Christians who realized the urgency of evangelism and missions in the light of Christ's sufficiency,

122

power, and authority to accomplish the task. For Simpson, the book of the Acts demonstrated the primacy of missions in the light of Christ's availability and power to complete the Great Commission.

25. George P. Pardington, *Twenty-five Wonderful Years* (New York: Christian Alliance Pub. Co., 1914), p. 78.

SAMUEL J. STOESZ

Samuel J. Stoesz studied at St. Paul Bible College, Bethel College and Wheaton College, before doing graduate work at Fuller Theological Seminary, and at Northern Baptist Theological Seminary, where he earned a Th.D. He has pastored several churches and served as managing editor at Christian Publications. In addition, he taught Bible and Theology at Nyack College for five years, was Academic Dean at Canadian Bible College for six years, and co-founded Canadian Theological Seminary. Dr. Stoesz is currently Professor of Pastoral Studies at the Seminary. He has done considerable research into the origins of the Alliance, and specializes in the period from A.B. Simpson's death in 1919 to the present. He has written *Understanding My Church*, and has contributed research to a history to commemorate the centennial of the Christian and Missionary Alliance in 1987.

A.B. SIMPSON:
FORERUNNER AND CRITIC OF
THE PENTECOSTAL MOVEMENT

by

Charles Nienkirchen

In the writing of history, a historian sometimes realizes intuitively that an anecdote is worth a thousand words. The following two reports, which pertain to A.B. Simpson's perception of Pentecostalism, are sufficient to impress upon the mind of the reader, the weighty issues at stake in historical interpretation.

In 1907, concerned about the mushrooming influence of Pentecostalism in Alliance circles, Simpson, according to A.W. Tozer, sent his longtime trusted friend and associate, Dr. Henry Wilson, an Episcopalian clergyman, to visit the Alliance church in Alliance, Ohio. Wilson's mission was to secure a first-hand report of the Pentecostal phenomena that had inundated the congregation.[1] Wilson was allegedly unimpressed by what he observed and returned with an ambivalent evaluation: "I am not able to approve the movement though I am willing to concede that there is probably something of God in it somewhere."[2] Simpson later made public his own evaluation of the Pentecostal movement. In it he denounced the "evidence doctrine" which required speaking in tongues as the initial sign of the baptism of the Holy Spirit.[3] His opposition to this distinctive tenet of Pentecostalism set the stage for numerous individuals and congregations with Pentecostal sympathies to withdraw from the Alliance and align themselves with the Pentecostal movement.[4]

A second incident, drawn from the annals of Pentecostal history, suggests an evolution in Simpson's attitude towards Pentecostalism. David McDowell, a one-time student of Simpson's at the Nyack Missionary Training Institute, who in 1907, received the Pentecostal baptism at the Rocky Springs camp meeting in Pennsylvania, returned to Nyack in 1912, where he was able to have a private conversation with Dr. Simpson. In the context of discussing Pentecostalism, McDowell recollected Simpson as having said: "David, I did what I thought was best, but I am afraid I missed it."[5]

These accounts, which have become enshrined in Alliance and Pentecostal tradition, reflect the conflicting assessments of A.B. Simpson's position toward the burgeoning Pentecostal movement in the early twentieth century.

PENTECOSTAL INDEBTEDNESS TO SIMPSON
AND THE ALLIANCE

Those Pentecostal pioneers who were contemporaries of Simpson acknowledged that his ministry and writings had a significant spiritual impact on their age. In many respects, they saw their own experience of being filled with the Holy Spirit with the accompanying phenomenon of tongues, as the full recovery of the same apostolic truth to which Simpson was committed.

Rev. Charles Parham, a patriarch of modern Pentecostalism, who had been successively a Congregationalist, Methodist and holiness preacher prior to his Pentecostal experience in 1901, made a trip to several places in the eastern United States in 1900, including "Dr. Simpson's work in Nyack," where spiritual truths were being "restored." He made the following assessment of what he had seen:

> I returned home fully convinced that while many had obtained real experience in sanctification and the anointing that abideth, there still remained a great outpouring of power for the Christians who were to close this age.[6]

Howard Goss, a Pentecostal contemporary of Parham, believed that Parham's teaching on the second work of grace and sanctification differed little from that of A.B. Simpson.[7]

Agnes Ozman was the first of Parham's students to receive the baptism of the Holy Spirit. The event took place on January 1, 1901, at Bethel Bible College in Topeka, Kansas; during the next three days, Ms. Ozman spoke and wrote only in Chinese. She, too, counted Simpson among her spiritual teachers. Her personal pilgrimage, which had included in adolescence an experience of Methodist entire sanctification, later entailed a sojourn of study at Nyack. She recalled those days with fondness:

> Our teachers were A.B. Simpson, Farr, Funk, Wilson and Stephen Merritt. The latter had learned much about the workings of the Holy Ghost, and our hearts were blessed as we were admonished to trust Him to use us.... At the Christian Mission Alliance Bible School, we were privileged to bid farewell to many dear hearts who laid their lives down going to Africa, China, India and Jerusalem.[8]

Other prominent Pentecostal personalities were also influenced by Simpson and the Alliance, albeit some more directly than others. Prominent among these was the Norwegian, Thomas B. Barratt, who has been hailed as "the apostle of the Pentecostal Movement in Europe."[9] In his autobiography, Barratt readily acknowledged that "some articles in Dr. A.B. Simpson's Magazine were a great help to [him]."[10] Of particular significance to him was an incident that took place in 1906 while he was staying in the Alliance guest house in New York City. After participating in a communion service conducted by Henry Wilson at the Gospel Tabernacle, he sought for the baptism of the Holy Spirit and was "seized by the Holy Power of God throughout [his] whole being, and it was swept through [his] whole body as well."[11] Five weeks later, Barratt received what he termed the "full Pentecostal experience" with the accompanying evidence of speaking in tongues.[12] In an article published in the periodical *Living Truths*, which Simpson edited anonymously, Barratt claimed that the gift of tongues, which he had received on November 15, was the seal to his "baptism of fire" which he had experienced in the Alliance guest house on October 7.[13] Simpson openly commended Barratt for his "uprightness and sincerity" and encouraged others among his readership to submit for publication articles that would further illuminate the subject of the baptism of the Spirit.[14]

The Alliance also exerted an influence on Pentecostal notables Alice Belle Garrigus and D. Wesley Myland. Garrigus, a Congregationalist from Connecticut, received the Pentecostal baptism in 1906 at the end of an Alliance camp meeting held at Old Orchard, Maine, largely through the influence of Minnie Draper, who had been both converted in the Alliance and trained at Nyack. Garrigus went on to become the founder of the Pentecostal Assemblies of Newfoundland.[15] D. Wesley Myland, originally a Methodist minister and pastor of the Alliance congregation in Columbus, Ohio, before becoming a spokesman for the Pentecostal movement, came into the truth of divine healing through the Christian and Missionary Alliance. He recalled attending an Alliance convention at Linnwood, Ohio in 1888. Here he met John Salmon, a Canadian associate of Simpson's who served as vice-president of the Christian Alliance for twenty-five years. Salmon, on this occasion, anointed Myland with oil and Myland was healed of paralysis.[16] He recalled travelling with Simpson to Columbus, Ohio in 1900.[17] Six years later at a convention in Columbus, Myland received the baptism of the Spirit with tongues as well as a healing from acute burns and blood poisoning.[18] He later established the Gibeah Bible School near Indianapolis.

Second generation Pentecostal historians have realized, as did their forefathers, that twentieth-century Pentecostalism stands on the shoulders of those spiritual giants of the late nineteenth century who aroused large numbers of people in America and Western Europe to the possibility of heightened levels of Christian experience through Spirit-baptism. Their examination of the roots of Pentecostalism has brought about a generous recognition on the part of Pentecostals of the significant contribution made by Simpson and the Alliance to the genesis and development of the Pentecostal movement during its infancy and adolescence.

Donald Gee, the astute British Pentecostal leader and theologian, credits Simpson with originating the slogan, "Four-fold Gospel," observing that Pentecostals adapted it for their own purposes by substituting the baptism of the Holy Spirit for sanctification.[19] Gee bemoans the lack of attention given to

128

holy living in the Pentecostal assemblies and prefers to have "a fivefold gospel [including] sanctification [to] a fourfold gospel without it."[20]

Out of Simpson's Missionary Training Institute came such adept Pentecostal pastors and administrators as John W. Welsh, an early Assemblies of God general superintendent, and Noel Perkins, who served as the foreign missions director for the Assemblies of God during the period, 1927-1959. Two other graduates, William I. Evans and Frank M. Boyd, of the classes of 1910 and 1911 respectively, became deans of Bethel Bible Training School in Newark, New Jersey, and Central Bible Institute in Springfield, respectively. Nyack alumni also constituted the largest representation of any one school serving in the Assemblies of God missionary force during the early 1920s.[21] On the Canadian scene, R.E. Sternall, the first pastor of the influential Pentecostal assembly in Kitchener, Ontario, received the Pentecostal baptism at Nyack, in 1911.[22]

Since so many graduates of Nyack transferred their allegiance from the Alliance to the Assemblies of God, the three-year Bible institute model perfected by A.B. Simpson and D.L. Moody, in which the atmosphere of the school was geared more to spiritual development than to academic performance, became the dominant strategy for the preparation of Pentecostal leadership.[23] The indebtedness of the Assemblies of God to Simpson's school at Nyack is not overstated by Gary McGee, a theology professor at the Assemblies of God graduate school in Springfield, Missouri, who concludes that

> the Assemblies of God has a marvelous heritage, and part of it is traced back to the ministry of A.B. Simpson, the Alliance and the school at Nyack. Through these means, the Spirit of the Lord prepared a surprising number of leaders to guide the Assemblies of God in its early years. In addition, these leaders, both men and women, brought with them sound Bible teaching on salvation, the deeper life of the Spirit, divine healing, the second coming of Christ and the imperative of world evangelization.[24]

The legacy of Simpson and the Alliance to early Pentecostalism went far beyond the domain of education. According to Carl Brumback, an Assemblies of God historian, the Pente-

129

costal movement owes the Christian and Missionary Alliance a seven-fold debt:[25] (1) doctrines borrowed from the Alliance;[26] (2) the hymns of Simpson; (3) the books of Simpson, Pardington, Tozer and others; (4) the terminology "Gospel Tabernacle" which, when supplemented with "Full," became a popular name for churches among Pentecostals; (5) the polity of the early Alliance Society, after which the Assemblies of God was styled; (6) a worldwide missionary vision; and (7) numerous leaders converted and trained in Alliance circles.[27]

A.B. Simpson's life and teaching embodied several of the streams of spiritual awakening that flowed through the second half of the nineteenth century and ultimately emptied into the river of Pentecostalism.[28] He was simultaneously a revivalist preacher, a holiness prophet of the "deeper" or "higher Christian life," a promoter of world missions, an eschatological speculator, and a theological synthesizer. It is therefore not surprising that his theology, spirituality, ministry and polity became an inspiration to many in the Pentecostal movement who had sat by and drunk from the same spiritual streams in which Simpson himself had been refreshed.

SIMPSON AS A FORERUNNER OF PENTECOSTALISM

It can easily be seen from his writings that Simpson was a forerunner of the modern Pentecostal movement. Several themes surface as points of ideological continuity between Simpson and the early Pentecostals, and these serve to explain the latter's willing affirmation of him as one of their most esteemed spiritual mentors. Of special importance in this regard are Simpson's view of church history, understanding of spiritual gifts, interpretation of the book of Acts and doctrine of the baptism of the Holy Spirit.

Simpson believed that the most significant feature of church history from the Protestant Reformation to his own time was the progressive recovery of certain essential biblical truths. These truths had been part of the first-century apostolic gospel but had been obscured and lost in subsequent centuries. John Calvin began the process by recovering the doctrine of divine

130

sovereignty to counteract the medieval papacy's pretensions to universal authority. In the eighteenth century, the Wesleys, George Whitefield and John Fletcher sensitized the church to the necessity of the new birth and the work of the Holy Spirit as a corrective to the formalism of the established churches. The nineteenth century witnessed the recovery of a number of spiritual truths: Charles Finney and his followers brought a new awareness of a "deeper Christian life as an antidote to the worldliness and compromising spirit of the times." The ministry of faith was exemplified in the lives of August Francke and George Muller; the teachings of Johann Blumhardt, Dorothea Trudel, W.E. Boardman, Charles Cullis, A.J. Gordon and others, restored the credibility of divine healing; and conferences on prophecy, held towards the end of the century, brought a reawakening of interest in premillenialism as a paradigm for understanding biblical eschatology.[29]

In reflecting on the significance of history as it pertains to the church's role in the world, Simpson elucidated his view of the ultimate meaning of the historical process:

> ...from age to age God speaks the special message most needed so that there is always some portion of Divine truth which might properly be called present truth, God's message to the times.[30]

The responsibility for announcing the divine plan for a specific time falls to the "prophet," whom Simpson described as being "not so much a teacher of the written Word as a messenger of the very thing that God would say at the time to the generation to which he speaks or the community to whom he bears witness." The prophetic ministry, though embracing the task of teaching, remains unique in the sense that it calls for an "immediate power and unction of the Holy Spirit" to enable the prophet to discern "the mind of his Master" and dispense it "to his fellowmen at the divine direction."[31] Simpson himself frequently ministered in this capacity, on occasions even receiving dreams which he regarded as divinely sent, to confirm new directions to be undertaken.[32]

Like many of his Pentecostal contemporaries, Simpson expected the present age to conclude with the days of the "latter rain," when there would be a "special outpouring of the Holy Spirit upon the world" resulting in the conversion of "great multitudes." Whereas the day of Pentecost had marked the coming of the "early rain," Simpson interpreted the "latter rain" as falling in his own time. To support this contention, he pointed to the success of the revivalists of Europe and America in the later decades of the nineteenth century and to the large strides taken by Protestant missionary organizations around the world. These successes indicated to Simpson that the "bride" (church) was being prepared for the soon coming of the "bridegroom" (Christ).[33]

Simpson, in his various publications, frequently alluded to the significance of the prophecy recorded in Joel 2 for eschatology. The "latter rain" which had already begun to "sprinkle" in his own time would continue to intensify as the second advent neared, reaching proportions never before witnessed in church history.[34] If the "early rain" had come at Pentecost accompanied by supernatural manifestations of the Spirit such as tongues, miracles and prophecy, Simpson reasoned that one could rightly expect these "wonderful manifestations" to be part and parcel of the "latter rain."[35] Believers must therefore pray for "a special manifestation of the supernatural power of God," since this had typified the great revivals of the past.[36] Moreover, for the church to attain "full maturity" before Christ's coming, it must be "adorned with all the gifts and graces of her divine ministry."[37] For the Spirit to complete His work of preparing the church for Christ's appearance, believers must not fear Him, but rather seek to understand fully His person and work. Only then would they be "ready to cooperate with Him and receive all His gifts and graces."[38]

A logical corollary of both Simpson's belief that the church had been progressively recovering neglected biblical truths and his doctrine of the "latter rain," was his categorical rejection of cessationism. Cessationism, promoted by churchmen of varying theological stripes, argued that the supernatural gifts of the Spirit had necessarily ceased with the end of the apostolic age. Simpson found cessationism particularly objectionable because of his campaign to advance the cause of divine healing through association with a contemporary interdenominational, international healing movement.[39] Moreover, he saw no biblical grounds for making any essential distinctions between the apostolic and later ages since the Pentecostal promise of Joel 2

and 1 Corinthians 12 affirm the continued presence of supernatural gifts of the Holy Spirit in the church until the second
advent.[40] He exposed the cessationist theory as "one of the lies
the devil [had] sugar-coated, candied and crystallized in the
form of a theological maxim."[41] Such a delusion could not be
endorsed by any serious Christian because "the dear Master
never contemplated or proposed any post-apostolic gulf of
impotence and failure."[42]

Simpson concluded that "unbelief and sin" rather than divine
volition had caused the decline in the use of spiritual gifts after
the death of the apostles.[43] Citing the church fathers Irenaeus
and Tertullian, Simpson posited that the supernatural gifts of
the Spirit had continued on in the postapostolic church as late
as the fifth century, wherever "faith and holiness" were
retained in some measure.[44] For Simpson, the recovery of
divine healing logically implied the continuation of "all the
charismata of the Pentecostal Church," including the gift of
tongues, which had always been present in the history of the
church.[45] Every generation of Christians needed "a living
Christ" to perform miracles that authenticated the gospel in the
face of unbelievers. The need for signs and wonders had
certainly not diminished:

> We are in the age of miracles, the age of Christ, the age
> which lies between two Advents...the age of Power, the
> age which, above all other ages of time, should be
> intensely alive....Until he [Christ] comes again, the world
> will never cease to need the touch of His Power and
> Presence in the form of supernatural spiritual manifesta-
> tions.[46]

Simpson insisted that just as the preaching of the gospel in the
book of Acts had been "sealed...with signs and wonders" so the
church had "a right to expect such manifestations in every new
stage of Christian work today."...[47] He had nothing but biting
criticism for those churches in which supernatural gifts of the
Holy Spirit were absent, calling them "religious club[s] bound
together by social affinities," and only "moderately exercised
and occupied in respectable forms of benevolence and useful-
ness."[48] Satirically he declared that in such churches, biblical
"exegesis" in reality meant "exit Jesus."[49]

More seriously, Simpson warned that a church devoid of the

133

supernatural powers of the Holy Spirit would be defenseless against the false miracles of Satan in the end times.[50] At the same time, he was painfully aware of the antisupernaturalistic spirit of the age in which he lived. The growing popularity of Darwinism and the "higher criticism" of the Bible revealed the "increasing rationalism" and "unbelief" of the age. The contemporary worldview no longer had room for the supernatural and maintained that laws of secondary causation and natural development govern all areas of life.[51]

Unfortunately, this doctrine of natural "development," which Simpson punned as "devilment,"[52] had managed successfully to invade the church. Even the clergy, to their shame, frequently seemed to want to eliminate the supernatural from both the Scriptures and the church. They preferred to search for alternate explanations for supernatural phenomena, rather than to affirm and open themselves to the supernatural working of God.[53] As history progressed toward its climax, Simpson envisioned a steadily mounting confrontation between the "manifestations of divine power" and a society gripped by rationalism and materialism.[54] Consequently, he delivered a clarion summons to the "ministers of the Lord" to "claim" and "exercise" the "gifts and offices" given to them, in the power of the Holy Spirit. They must never accommodate themselves placidly to the anti-supernaturalistic sentiments of the age, but rather seek more discernment in spiritual matters and thereby awaken the church from its slumber.[55]

Simpson's interpretation of the book of Acts was not essentially different from that of the modern Pentecostal movement, which sees in Acts a depiction of normal church life as God intended it to be throughout all ages of church history. He was, as were Pentecostals, fully prepared to use the standard of spiritual life portrayed in Acts as the existential norm by which to measure the shortcomings of the church in his own time. He believed that the entire book expounds the supernatural quality of the Christian life that invariably becomes evident when the church remains open to the fullness of the Holy Spirit. He insisted that the church would inevitably substitute a "conventional formalism" for genuine Christian work, if it neglected to release the power of the Spirit in apostolic fashion.[56]

Simpson's writings indicate that he clearly anticipated the

Pentecostal hermeneutical practice of deriving doctrinal truth from the narrative accounts of Acts. This exegetical method was essential to his theology of the ministry of the Holy Spirit in the life of the believer. An exegesis of history could serve as an adequate theological basis for a two-step model of Christian initiation. Notwithstanding his rejection of the "evidence doctrine," Simpson made full use of some of the classical proof-texts of Pentecostalism (Acts 2, 8, 19) to substantiate his claim that regeneration and the baptism of the Holy Spirit were two distinct experiences in the life of the believer.

For him, as for Pentecostals, the Acts of the Apostles consistently demonstrates that the reception of the Holy Spirit in fullness occurs subsequent to conversion. Just as the apostles had waited in the upper room to receive the "baptism of power," so all believers must follow the apostolic examples of tarrying. The apostles needed to wait not only from the stand-point of the eschatological fulfillment of the divine purpose on the Feast of Pentecost, according to the Hebrew calendar, but also out of psychological necessity. They needed to "search their hearts [and] deepen the hunger and the longing which were necessary for them to appreciate the blessing...."[57] The historical precedent was thereby established for converts who had "accepted Jesus" to be instructed immediately upon their conversion as to how to receive the Holy Spirit. Prescribing a pastoral methodology, Simpson advised:

> ...so still we should lead the convert to the altar of consecration, and never leave him until he has been sealed and sanctified by the same Spirit....[58]

Observing the experience of the Samaritans described in Acts 8, Simpson commented that after embracing the "testimony of Jesus" through the evangelistic ministry of Philip, they subsequently received a "personal baptism of the Holy Ghost" at the hands of the apostolic delegation from Jerusalem.[59] The same two-step pattern can also be seen in the case of the Ephesian disciples (Acts 19). For Simpson, these disciples of John the Baptist represented "a great majority of professing Christians" in his own time who had been converted, but who "[had] not received the Holy Ghost" and "[made] no claim to sanctification."[60] The question posed by Paul to the Ephesians, "Have ye received the Holy Ghost since ye believed?" could legitimately be asked of many of Simpson's contemporaries who knew only the "ministry of repentance."[61]

From the biographical data given on Apollos in Acts 18, Simpson derived "Lessons in the Higher Christian Life." He suggested that Apollos typified the impoverished condition of "hundreds and thousands of ministers and Christians" who had never progressed beyond repentance and conversion.[62] Only after being led into the deeper Christian life by Aquila and Priscilla, did Apollos receive a "new theology," a "new experience" and a "new equipment" for Christian work.[63]

In this context, Simpson castigated the established church for its "intellectual self-sufficiency" and overdependence upon "colleges and books," all of which were impotent to convey the reality of life lived in the fullness of the Holy Spirit. A "cold and worldly church" invariably had an over-abundance of Apollos' followers but a tragic lack of truly "anointed messengers" capable of leading others into "a life of consecration and full salvation."[64] From the experience of Apollos, Simpson drew pointed conclusions concerning the indispensability of the baptism of the Holy Spirit to the life of the church:

> The general lesson from the life of Apollos is the necessity of a real spiritual experience of the deeper things of God and a baptism of the Holy Ghost, if we would be used effectually in the work of God.... The church today is suffering from too much intellectural culture and too little spiritual unction. No class of men more than the class represented by Apollos need the baptism of the Holy Ghost. The more brain we have, the more spiritual power we need to preserve the true balance of humility and heavenly mindedness.[65]

In his work, *Forward Movements of the Last Half Century* (1905),[66] Arthur T. Pierson, a Presbyterian minister, calls the "Pentecostal movement," with its emphasis on receiving the Pentecostal gift of the Spirit for "sanctifying, enduring and filling," the most important of the "spiritual movements" of the later nineteenth century.[67] Simpson was but one of many within the world of nineteenth-century evangelical Protestantism who had come to reject the historicist interpretation of Pentecost because it limited the significance of the event solely to the introduction of the "new dispensation of the Holy Spirit."

Simpson and his allies regarded Pentecost rather as a normative experience to be appropriated personally, like the sacrifice of Christ for the forgiveness of sins, by every believer. They saw the Pentecostal gift of the Spirit not as the automatic result of conversion, but as the rightful inheritance of those who sought for it. In an editorial of 1906, Simpson stated the baptism of the Holy Spirit to be the "greatest thought that God [was] projecting upon the hearts of Christians," during what he perceived as a time of "increasing revival."[68]

Historians have made various attempts at contextualizing Simpson's theology of the baptism of the Holy Spirit as a second experience in the believer's life distinct from and subsequent to conversion. Though crediting Simpson with being a relatively independent thinker, Harold Hunter alleges that his views resemble those of R.A. Torrey, C.I. Scofield and A.J. Gordon.[69] Donald Wheelock attributes Simpson's use of the phrase "higher Christian life" to Asa Mahan and William E. Boardman, both of whom exerted a formative influence upon him, and both of whom promoted Oberlin perfectionism in the tradition of Charles Finney.[70] William Menzies identifies Simpson as a mediator of the Keswick-type concept of Christocentric sanctification (as opposed to the Wesleyan eradicationist view of holiness).[71] Curiously, Edith Waldvogel identifies Simpson, along with A.J. Gordon and A.T. Pierson, as "Reformed evangelicals" who dissociated themselves from the Wesleyan holiness movement by "[denying] that sanctification was instantaneous...and [contending] that sanctification was not the baptism with the Holy Spirit."[72] In fact, the eclectic character of Simpson's views on this subject makes definitive classification according to the categories of contemporary holiness movements virtually impossible.

The entire corpus of his writings, however, testifies uniformly to his understanding of the baptism of the Holy Spirit (also termed "second blessing," "crisis sanctification," "the anointing," "the sealing," "receiving the Holy Spirit," "the indwelling of Christ") as an experience in the life of the believer subsequent to, and distinct from, regeneration. He had had this experience himself in 1874, during his second pastorate in Louisville, Kentucky, when, as he wrote:

> Just at that time God poured out His Spirit upon my own heart. It was then that I received for the first time the new

light of the indwelling Christ and the baptism of the Holy Ghost and it became a fire in my bones.[73]

Though he sought this experience initially as a result of reading W.E. Boardman's *The Higher Christian Life* (1858), Simpson's convictions regarding the baptism of the Holy Spirit were firmly anchored in Scripture.[74] Paramount for the believer is the example of Christ. As an infant, Christ had been born of the Spirit, but "not baptized with the Spirit until His thirtieth year" when He underwent water baptism in the Jordan River at the hands of John the Baptist.[75] This enduement with power, bringing to an end Christ's "quiet years in Nazareth" was experientially necessary to His earthly ministry, which Simpson interpreted as being accomplished in the power of Spirit-filled humanity.[76]

The same is also true of Christ's disciples who, prior to Pentecost, "were undoubtedly saved men and women," but as a result of their baptism of the Spirit at Pentecost, "there came to them an entirely new experience involving not only power for service, but power for holiness and righteousness in their own lives."[77] Simpson overlooked the significance of the events in Judas' house (Acts 9:11-19), and chose Romans 7-8 instead as the biblical proof for Paul's crisis experience subsequent to his conversion, suggesting Arabia rather than Damascus as the site where this occurred.[78]

Simpson laid much of the blame for the loss of this important truth at the feet of the Protestant reformers. Luther, though he rediscovered justification, nevertheless "failed to go on to the deeper teachings of the Christian life," thereby consigning Germany to a "cold and lifeless rationalism and all its attendant evils."[79] In contrast, the religious life of England and America was decisively shaped by the likes of Wesley, Baxter, Whitfield, Moody and Gordon, who knew well, and preached concerning, the ministry of the Holy Spirit.[80]

Simpson employed a variety of images to reinforce the significance of the baptism of the Holy Spirit in the spiritual life. He likened it to an initiation into "the second year or chapter of [one's] spiritual history," the climax of salvation, or crossing the Jordan River and entering the promised land.[81] This special visitation of the Spirit only comes about as a result of "deep and intense desire," waiting upon God in sustained prayer, and consecrating oneself unreservedly to the service of the Lord.[82] Waiting for the Spirit could not be short-circuited. It was, to Simpson, "a discipline of self-crucifixion and stillness" without which there would be no "deep and full" reception of the Spirit.[83]

Most significantly, the baptism of the Holy Spirit was for Simpson the occasion at which the Spirit, who is present with the believer at regeneration, becomes fully resident "within the converted heart," transforming it into "the temple of the Holy Ghost."[84] This crisis not only meets the "deeper need of sanctification" but also holds the secret of holiness and happiness.[85] In this experience, the Holy Spirit becomes both "refiner" and "energizer."[86] Out of this experience flows the power to manifest holy character, supernatural gifts and divine healing, the capacity to receive divine guidance and endure suffering in the service of Christ, as well as the authority for governing the church.[87] The power of the Spirit is given above all for a life of "the most strenuous service" and only secondarily for spiritual enjoyment.[88] Since it is this experience that transforms the "real...honest...constant church member" into one "possessed by the indwelling God," Simpson stressed that no person in the church, regardless of role, could claim exemption from the need to be baptized with the Holy Spirit:

> The mother needs it in the nursery, the Sunday School teacher in his class, the preacher in his pulpit, the soul winner in his dealings with the inquirer, and the saint in his ministry of prayer in the secret closet.[89]

The commitment to a two-step pattern of Christian initiation based on the experience of Christ, the apostles and early church, dictated Simpson's firm opposition to any doctrine of progressive sanctification that would undermine the importance of a Spirit-baptism subsequent to conversion. He called "Progressivists" (who minimize the necessity of a post-regeneration baptism of the Spirit), the religious equivalent of "evolutionists" who explain the earth's history as a process of natural development in which direct divine intervention plays no role.[90] Even if following almost immediately after conversion, the baptism of the Spirit is nonetheless distinct from regeneration:

> We are willing, however, to concede that the baptism of

139

the Holy Ghost may be received at the very same time a soul is converted. We have known a sinner to be converted, sanctified and saved (sic.) all within a single hour, and yet each experience was different in its nature and was received in proper order and by a definite faith for that particular blessing.[91]

There was, in Simpson's words, no need for a "long interval" between conversion and the baptism of the Holy Spirit. In the early church, the two experiences were either "contemporaneous or close together."[92] Far from being a terminal point in the believer's experience, the baptism of the Spirit as taught by Simpson, introduces Christians into a life of repeated baptisms that take them ever deeper into the incomprehensible fullness of God. In the Spirit-filled journey, there are "Pentecosts and second Pentecosts...great freshlets and flood-tides" that punctuate the ongoing process of constantly receiving divine life "breath by breath and moment by moment."[93] In the liturgical year, Simpson saw the days following the commemoration of Easter as the most appropriate season for seeking "a deeper filling, a mightier baptism" of the Holy Spirit, through a personal reenactment of the apostles' waiting for the first Pentecost.[94] Under no illusions about the limitations of "crisis experiences," he warned against the perilous consequences of backsliding after being baptized in the Spirit. Without the continual cultivation of a separated and consecrated life, it is all too possible to regress from "even...the very...deepest and highest experiences of the Holy Ghost."[95]

In summary, it has been demonstrated that in large measure, Simpson promoted several themes that later became conceptual cornerstones on which the modern Pentecostal movement was built. However, he criticized Pentecostals for their secondary theological distinctives and experiential excesses, even though they accentuated certain gifts of the Spirit, the restoration of which Simpson had taught his own followers to expect as part of the endtime "latter rain."[96]

SIMPSON AS A CRITIC OF PENTECOSTALISM

A recent study by an Alliance pastor, Ernest G. Wilson, calls the incursion of Pentecostalism into the ranks of the Alliance during the first decade of this century the "most serious crisis" and "the greatest problem" in C&MA history. Wilson also claims that the Alliance, as a result of "unhappy experiences with Pentecostal people," changed doctrinal camps in practice if not in theory, by diminishing its "active relationships" with "Pentecostal, charismatic or holiness groups" in favor of strengthening both its relationships with "'Baptistic groups' and...emphasis on 'Baptistic' doctrinal concepts."[97] Simpson forged his response to Pentecostalism amid the stress of having to deal with diametrically opposite assessments of the movement among the members of the Alliance: many (some leaders included) had received the Pentecostal experience and had evident Pentecostal sympathies, while others were suspicious of, and strongly opposed to, the movement.[98] Ironically, events at the Azusa Street mission in Los Angeles in the Spring of 1906, coincided with a pre-Council gathering of Alliance leaders at Nyack, New York, in May of the same year, at which the "baptism of the Holy Spirit" was solidly endorsed as "a definite second blessing" and "a distinct experience" subsequent to conversion.[99]

Simpson developed his critique of Pentecostalism within the context of his wholehearted affirmation of the continued presence within the church of all the gifts of the Spirit. In a series of sermons preached in 1898, and later published in a volume entitled *The Apostolic Church*, he systematically expounded the nature and purpose of each of the *charismata* listed in 1 Corinthians 12.[100] From 1 Corinthians 12:7, Simpson deduced that every believer "ought to have some special manifestation of the Holy Ghost and some gift for Christian service." The Holy Spirit gives gifts to each believer according to his sovereign purpose.[101] These supernatural spiritual gifts are essential consequences of the baptism of the Holy Spirit.[102] The diversity of these supernatural powers makes them all equally necessary to the health of the church. In its public meetings, the church is to welcome all manifestations of the Spirit, including prophecy and tongues, provided that the "order...reverence and decorum due to the house of God" are not violated.[103] Since the "gifts of power" were, for Simpson, "the jewels upon the robes of the Bride," he found it inconceivable that they could be either discredited or excluded from the church's life.[104]

The gift of tongues surfaced as a major point of contention in the Pentecostal controversy. Simpson showed an enlightened understanding of its function in Christian experience. In his opinion, tongues serve to elevate "the soul above the ordinary modes and expressions of reason and utterance."[105] Used properly, tongues are

> ...an expression of lofty spiritual feeling and the intense moving of the heart, the subject of this gift, by the divine Spirit leading [the speaker] to express the state of spiritual elevation by which he was moved in some utterance, which, while not always intelligible, yet always left the impression of divine presence and power.[106]

Simpson did not, however, embrace the popular notion that the gift of tongues has been given for the purpose of missionary work, and that those missionaries who possessed it would have minimal need for language study.[107] He understood tongues to be, rather, a sign of "supernatural presence in the heart of the speaker."[108] The revival of the gift in the late nineteenth century generated "much confusion," but a "genuine movement of the Holy Ghost" had accompanied "many undoubted manifestations" of it.[109] From the reports that he had received on the phenomenon, he concluded that tongues are a mixture of "known languages" and "unintelligible and incoherent speech."[110]

Simpson was not reluctant to grant the gift of tongues its rightful status as "one of the special manifestations of the Holy Ghost in the apostolic church" that could be expected to reappear at any time in the church's history.[111] At the same time, he hastened to delineate the inherent limitations of the gift as compared to other manifestations of the Spirit. It is a "showy gift," the "least honored" of all the supernatural powers with which the church was endued.[112] When exercised by the vain and ambitious, it is prone to abuse and thus, to a large extent, had been withdrawn in the early post-apostolic age.[113] Simpson could also point to the destruction of the ministry of the promising Scottish preacher, Edward Irving, as a more recent example of the dangers of a preoccupation with tongues. History held a stern warning for all who would pretentiously seek after the gift.[114] In view of the attention that was currently being lavished on the supernatural gifts of the Spirit, Simpson thought it more constructive to promote the "practical and useful" benefits of love over the "sensational" gifts of power.[115]

Simpson's criticisms of the Pentecostal movement centered on the "evidence doctrine," which he saw as offensive to sound biblical doctrine and injurious to the unity of the Alliance. He charged that Pentecostals, in teaching that tongues were the initial evidence of the baptism of the Holy Spirit, had fallen prey to one of the "evils of the apostolic age" (against which Paul had written).[116] Simpson considered the unwarranted exaltation of tongues by Pentecostals to be responsible for transforming what had begun as a "genuine movement of the Holy Spirit" into a movement fraught with "extravagance," "excess," "serious error," "wildfire" and "fanaticism."[117] Furthermore, in preaching the "evidence doctrine," Pentecostals were displaying themselves to be both "narrow" and "uncharitable" to their Christian brethren.[118]

The Pentecostal insistence on tongues led Simpson to refine further his understanding of the relationship between Spirit-baptism and supernatural gifts. In the face of the Pentecostal overemphasis on manifestations of the Spirit, Simpson increasingly deemphasized the baptism of the Holy Spirit as a source of power for service, accentuating instead its role in bringing "union with Christ, cleansing from sin and equipment for our practical Christian life."[119] He maintained that the gifts of the Spirit do not have a bearing on one's conversion and growth in holiness. For him, to make the presence of spiritual gifts a necessary indicator of having received the Holy Spirit, was nothing less than a "pernicious error."[120]

From 1907 onwards, Simpson's publications were liberally seasoned with anti-Pentecostal articles by various of his associates. Each had the same intent: to refute the "evidence doctrine" as well as excessive Pentecostal practices with respect to spiritual gifts.[121] One of the most important of these was an anonymous article entitled "True and False Fire," most likely written by Simpson himself.[122]

Those both outside and inside the Alliance who had received Spirit-baptism with tongues, frequently viewed Simpson as negatively disposed to the Pentecostal experience because of his unyielding opposition to the "evidence doctrine." One such person was Frank Bartelman, an itinerant evangelist and eye-witness of the events at the Azusa Street mission in Los Angeles, who zealously promoted Pentecostalism in Alliance circles during his trips to the eastern United States in 1907 and 1908. He reported that at an all-night meeting held at Simpson's Gospel Tabernacle in October, 1907,

> ...a young girl came under the power and her spirit was caught up to the throne. She sang a melody, without words, that seemed to come from within the veil, it was so heavenly. It seemed to come from another world. I have never heard its equal before or since. A.B. Simpson was there himself that night and was tremendously impressed by it.[123]

With special reference to Simpson, Bartelman contended: "He had been much opposed to the 'Pentecostal' work. Doubtless God gave it as a witness for him. Several were slain under the power."[124] Nine years later, W.W. Simpson, an Alliance missionary to China, who had withdrawn from the Alliance in 1914 over the issue of the Pentecostal experience, made a similar evaluation. In a letter to A.B. Simpson dated October 17, 1916, he challenged the Alliance founder and "many others in the Alliance" to stop

> ...fighting against God in turning down the teaching that the Lord baptizes people in the Holy Spirit now just as He did on the day of Pentecost.... And if you will only humble yourself to seek the Lord for this mighty baptism, you'll get it and then you'll *know* what I am talking about.[125]

Simpson responded to this uncomplimentary image projected on him by stating repeatedly that he and the Alliance rejected only the exclusivist doctrine of tongues, and not the validity of the Pentecostal experience itself. The Alliance had always affirmed the legitimacy of all the gifts of the Spirit.[126] To see the Society in any other light amounted to a "gross misrepresentation."[127] Simpson complained that Pentecostals had falsely accused the "wise and conservative people" of the Alliance of being opponents of the work of the Holy Spirit.[128] Far from denouncing the Pentecostal baptism, he pointed out to his critics that many Alliance workers, at home and abroad, as a result of their new "baptism," had grown in personal piety and devotion to service within the Alliance.[129]

As further evidence of the freedom to be found in the Alliance, Simpson alluded to the ten-day Old Orchard Convention held in the Summer of 1907. He insisted that, though the teaching provided was "careful and, in some respects, conservative," every opportunity had been given for seeking and receiving the fullness of the Holy Spirit with all the accompanying gifts and graces: "No restraint whatever was put upon true seekers after truth and life."[130] On another occasion, to dispel rumors of his anti-Pentecostalism, Simpson even published the complete correspondence between Kay Knight and the Alliance Executive Committee in India to confirm that she had resigned from the mission over "questions of missionary polity" and not at all because of her recent Pentecostal experience.[131]

Simpson's pastoral concerns led him to fear that Pentecostal abuses of spiritual gifts would seriously jeopardize the efforts of the Alliance to sustain a climate of true spiritual liberty. Invariably, many sought the Pentecostal baptism with tongues only because they felt they were not truly baptized until they had it. On the other hand, the unbiblical practices of Pentecostals became "scarecrows" to sincere Christians whose fear of "certain manifestations" inhibited them from seeking the real blessing of God.[132]

Simpson preached that discernment and sanity would have to prevail within the church to counteract effectively the Pentecostal obsession with spiritual manifestations and particularly tongues. If these qualities were not present in the church, "rational Christians" would "be turned away" from the authentic manifestations of divine power out of fear of the counterfeit.[133] One could expect that "delusions and counterfeits," if left undiscerned, would follow closely on the heels of the genuine, and thus undermine any spirit of revival.[134] In the earlier revival of divine healing, the devil had tried to thwart the recovery of truth by raising up Spiritualism and Christian Science as his own substitutes. Simpson urged his workers to be on guard against the work of the same diabolical forces of deception present in the Pentecostal movement.[135]

Commendably, Simpson, in the midst of heated controversy, continued to affirm the desirability of exercising supernatural gifts within the Alliance. He considered the risks involved to be worthwhile, for he knew that he could not solve the problem of excesses by suppressing all spiritual manifestations. He advised that "the only way to meet error [is] to go all the way with truth."[136] Thus, his strategy, difficult as it was to carry out, was to strike a middle road between the two extremes of credulity and fanatical excess on the one hand, and ultra-conservatism, which refused to recognize added blessings of God, on the other. Expectancy and discernment needed to triumph over fear and reaction if revival was to flourish.

Simpson prized, above all, the unity of the Alliance, a unity based on a "common experience" and "precious revelation" of Jesus as "Savior, Sanctifier, Healer and Coming Lord," and on a common commitment to the task of world evangelization. Within these mutually agreed upon perimeters, there was ample allowance for diversity of belief, expression and experience. To him, it was unrealistic to expect "that all the teachers of sanctification could agree about phases and phrases."[137] The preservation of unity was vital to the ongoing success of the Alliance and dogmatism of experience was just as much an enemy of this unity as was dogmatism of creed. The Alliance would remain united only as long as Alliance workers could see Christ in one another.[138] The disagreements over the "latter rain" and the baptism of the Holy Spirit were not to be resolved by any ecclesiastical authority, but were to remain matters of personal conviction and liberty. Additional doctrinal statements would only bring more bondage than freedom.[139]

The Pentecostal "evidence doctrine" tore at the fabric of Alliance unity. When some of those of Pentecostal persuasion within the Alliance expressed desire to establish a new organization, Simpson insisted that there was no need for this since the Alliance embraced "all the Scriptural manifestations of the Holy Ghost."[140] Those who advocated schism were invariably those who had come to regard themselves as "more highly gifted spiritually than others."[141] Simpson had a different perspective on some of their activity. He accused certain of those pursuing a "special baptism of the Holy Ghost" of "smallness...meanness...gossiping, criticizing, back-biting, slandering and condemning other Christians."[142] They were luring Alliance supporters away from branch meetings and regular services to participate in "partisan movements and meetings."[143] The "fanaticism" and "strife" engendered by the Pentecostal movement resulted in the tragic "division" and virtual "dismemberment" of some Alliance branches. Practically, this translated into reduced financial support for the cause of Alliance world missions, a development that grieved Simpson greatly.[144] Fortunately, Alliance regional conventions remained characterized by love, wisdom and unity rather than sectarian strife. By 1908, Simpson could claim that the crisis had passed and that there was still room in the Alliance for anyone seeking "all the heights and depths of the Holy Spirit's grace and power."[145]

Fearful of more Pentecostal encroachments on the Alliance constituency, Simpson decided to tighten the lines of supervision. He urged those branches desiring "special services and larger blessing" to consult with a "state or district superintendent" in order to obtain a "wise evangelist or authorized leader." He knew that there were all too many "unknown and ...unwise shepherds" who would exploit sincere spiritual seekers for their own gain and cause further losses to the Alliance.[146] Simpson counseled his troops not to "run after men or women who seem to have supernatural gifts and powers," convinced that an individual's ministry would be accredited on the basis of its "long-suffering love," not its "power, light or mystery."[147]

Simpson did not hold that the Pentecostal movement warranted a wholesale condemnation despite its evident shortcomings. Where the movement had had strong and wise leadership, it had indeed born impressive spiritual fruit that could not be gainsaid.[148] In his report to the 1908 Alliance Council, however, he lucidly enumerated the negative effects that Pentecostalism had had on the Alliance. The "evidence doctrine" had spawned a preoccupation with special manifestations rather than with God, and had tended to reduce evangelistic concern. Those who claimed the Pentecostal experience had often lit sectarian fires that had consumed Alliance branches and substantially reduced missionary contributions. Some inexperienced persons had been sent to foreign countries under the naive assumption that they would receive the gift of tongues as a substitute for language study. Lastly, Simpson noted the prevalence of a "prophetic authority" within the movement that smacked of "the Romish confessional" or "spiritualism."[149] Notwithstanding the movement's evident drawbacks, Simpson remained open, yet cautious to Pentecostalism — an appropriate response to a mixed blessing.[150]

Above all, he was grateful that the largest Alliance gatherings and branches had weathered the storm in a spirit of unity and order, without compromising spiritual power and liberty.

EPILOGUE: THE CASE OF THE
FORGOTTEN DIARY

In his biography of Simpson, published in 1943, A.W. Tozer, on the subject of Simpson's attitude to Pentecostals, asserted:

> The simple fact is that Mr. Simpson was miles out ahead of these people in his spiritual experience. He did not need anything they had. He had found a blessed secret far above anything these perfervid seekers after wonders could ever think or conceive.[151]

The contents of a long-overlooked diary kept by Simpson from 1907-1916 call into question the accuracy of Tozer's evaluation.[152] For the most part, the spasmodic entries in the diary disclose Simpson's personal response to the revival and outpouring of the Spirit, as well as the Pentecostal movement which absorbed his attention during this period.

Simpson's assessment of the manifestations of tongues at the close of the 1907 Council was that some were "certainly genuine" while others were "peculiar" and "eccentric." Nothing had happened, however, to make him "question the reality of the gifts." Instead, he pledged himself to "hold quietly to the divine order for the gifts of the Spirit in 1 Corinthians 12-14."[153] The unprecedented events at the Council, far from unnerving Simpson, encouraged him in the ensuing months to make "a new claim for a Mighty Baptism of the Holy Ghost in His complete Pentecostal fullness embracing all the gifts and graces of the Spirit."[154] Realizing that he had been previously baptized with the Holy Spirit in Louisville over thirty years before, he was now seeking God for a "deeper and fuller baptism," assured that the Spirit had confirmed to him to do so through Isaiah 49:8 and Acts 1:5.[155] On September 12, 1907, Simpson recorded that "the Spirit came with a baptism of holy laughter for an hour or more" but that he was still waiting "for all [God had] yet to give and manifest."[156] He admitted that in

148

prior times, he had, out of deference to the "sovereignty" of the Holy Spirit, been "timid" in the seeking of spiritual gifts. Now, however, he was prepared to "fully take all that [was] promised" in the name of Jesus.[157]

After five years of seeking "all the fullness of [divine] power," during which period he had "been open to God for anything He might be pleased to reveal or bestow," Simpson still could not testify in his diary to having received any "extraordinary manifestation of the Spirit in tongues or similar gifts." This apparently perplexed him, given both his intense desire for the full Pentecostal baptism as well as the Pentecostal experiences of "many of [his] friends." Nevertheless, he remained content with the "old touch and spiritual sense" of the divine presence in his life.[158]

The diary concludes with Simpson's agonizing personal plea for the fullness of the Spirit to enable him to transcend besetting financial hardships, external opposition to the work of the Alliance and new limitations imposed by his own diminishing physical strength.[159] He had earlier incisively pinpointed the flaws and frailties of the Pentecostal movement. However, when the dust of the controversy had almost settled, he became sufficiently convinced of the validity of the Pentecostal claim to have recovered the full apostolic experience of Pentecost, and he began to desire the same blessing. His stance had evolved from forerunner of Pentecostalism to critic of the "evidence doctrine" in public while a seeker of the Pentecostal baptism with tongues in private.

ENDNOTES

1. Miss Ivey Campbell was most likely the person who brought back the Pentecostal experience from Los Angeles to Alliance, Ohio. See W.A. Cramer's report, "Pentecost at Cleveland," *Christian and Missionary Alliance Weekly* (hereafter cited as *CMAW*) (April 27, 1907): 201.

2. Quoted in A.W. Tozer, *Wingspread — A.B. Simpson: A Study in Spiritual Altitude* (Harrisburg, Pennsylvania: Christian Publications, 1943), p. 133 (hereafter cited as *Wingspread*). According to Tozer, Wilson's statement became "the crystallized utterance of the Alliance." Alice Belle Garrigus, a Pentecostal pioneer in Newfoundland, mentions that a co-worker of Simpson (maybe Wilson) had

delivered a somewhat different assessment to Simpson: "It is the river of God, but not yet as clear as crystal." "Building According to the Pattern," *Good Tidings* (April, 1935): 4. cf. Simpson's reference to Wilson's trip in his "Editorial," *CMAW* (April 6, 1907), 157. Wilson supposedly reported that there was "a deep spirit of revival" free from "fanaticism and excess," which calls into question the credibility of Tozer's account. Moreover, W.A. Cramer, an Ohio superintendent, stated that "Our state workers and field superintendent, Dr. Henry Wilson from New York, were all in perfect accord with the testimony given by those who received their Pentecost, and expressed themselves in thorough sympathy with the experiences as witnessed in our midst." "Pentecost at Cleveland," *CMAW* (April 27, 1907): 201. Apart from Tozer's report which is unsupported, there is no evidence that Wilson actually visited the church at Alliance, Ohio.

3. See Simpson's report on "Special Revival Movements," prepared for the 1908 Council which was recast in the Alliance in 1963 as the "Seek Not, Forbid Not" position towards the gift of tongues, even though the phrase itself was never used by Simpson. It was largely the creation of A.W. Tozer and adopted by the Board of Managers and constituted a subtle departure from Simpson's posture which was to seek gifts with discernment. See *Board of Managers Minutes* (April, 1963), p. 9; "Where We Stand on the Revived Tongues Movement," *Alliance Witness* (May 1, 1963), 5-6. Cf. Simpson's report in *Christian and Missionary Alliance, 11th Annual Report (1907/1908)*, pp. 9-13.

4. According to Carl Brumback, the following men and women left the Alliance to assume leadership positions in the Assemblies of God: J.W. Welch, Frank M. Boyd, D.W. Kerr, John Coxe, Herbert Cox, John Waggoner, David McDowell, E.F.M. Staudt, William I. Evans, A.G. Ward, G.N. Eldridge, Louis and Josephine Turnbull, R.E. Sternall, C.A. McKinney, G.F. Bender, W.W. Simpson, Noel Perkin, Minnie Draper, Alice Reynolds Flower, D.W. Myland, J.T. Boddy, William Cramer, Joseph Tunmore, Frederick Reel, and J.E. Kistler. *A Sound From Heaven* (Springfield, Missouri: Gospel Publishing House, 1977; original edition, 1961), p. 92 (hereafter cited as *Sound*).

5. McDowell's conversation with Simpson is reported in Carl Brumback, *Sound*, pp. 93-94, who cites as his source, a private interview with McDowell.

6. Quoted by his wife, Sarah E. Parham, in *The Life of Charles F. Parham, Founder of the Apostolic Faith Movement* (New York: Garland Publishing Inc., 1985; original edition, 1930), p. 48. Cf. Vinson Synan, *The Holiness-Pentecostal Movement in the United States* (Grand Rapids, Michigan: Wm. B. Eerdmans Publishing Co., 1971), pp. 100-101, and Robert Mapes Anderson, *Vision of the Disinherited. The Making of American Pentecostalism* (New York: Oxford University Press, 1979), p. 50 (here-

after cited as *Vision*) who identifies the motivation for Parham's tour, which took him to several "other sites of Holiness experimentation," as a quest for the true biblical understanding and experience of the baptism of the Holy Spirit. He returned convinced that no one possessed it.

7. See Ethel E. Goss, *The Winds of God. The Story of the Early Pentecostal Days (1901-1914) in the Life of Howard A. Goss* (New York: Comet Press Books, 1958), pp. 15, 18.

8. Agnes N.O. LaBerge, *What God Hath Wrought. Life and Work of Mrs. Agnes N.O. LaBerge Nee Miss Agnes N. Ozman* (New York: Garland Publishing Inc.: 1985; original edition; n.d.), p. 23. There is a consensus among Pentecostal historians that the outbreak of tongues at Parham's college in Topeka, Kansas in 1901, marks the beginning of the modern Pentecostal movement, even though it did not take on an international profile until the meetings at the Azusa Street mission in Los Angeles (1906-1909). Some instances of tongues predate those at Topeka. For documentation of those occurring prior to 1901, see George H. Williams and Edith Waldvogel, "A History of Speaking in Tongues and Related Gifts," in Michael P. Hamilton (ed.), *The Charismatic Movement* (Grand Rapids, Michigan: Wm. B. Eerdmans Co., 1975), p. 75f (hereafter cited as "History"); cf. Stanley H. Frodsham, *With Signs Following. The Story of the Pentecostal Revival in the Twentieth Century,* revised edition (Springfield, Missouri: Gospel Publishing House, 1946), pp. 9-17. Church of God historian, Charles W. Conn, *Like a Mighty Army. A History of the Church of God, 1886-1976* revised edition (Cleveland, Tennessee: Pathway Press, 1977), p. 18f., esp. p. 25, establishes that over 100 people received the Pentecostal baptism at Camp Creek in Cherokee County, North Carolina in 1896, ten years prior to the Azusa St. events of 1906. He regards this as the cradle of the Pentecostal movement. *Contra* Conn, Harold Hunter suggests "that the Parham-Seymour formula of Spirit-baptism was not known in the 1896 Revival in the Schearer Schoolhouse in Cherokee County, North Carolina." "Spirit-Baptism and the 1896 Revival in Cherokee County, North Carolina," *Pneuma,* 5 (Fall, 1983), 3-17, esp. 17.

9. See Nils Bloch-Hoell's thorough discussion of Barratt's impact on Scandinavia and continental Europe in *The Pentecostal Movement. Its Origin, Development, and Distinctive Character* (London: Allen and Unwin; New York: Humanities Press; Oslo: Universitetsforlaget, 1964), pp. 75-86.

10. T.B. Barratt, *The Work of T.B. Barratt* (New York: Garland Publishing Inc., 1985; original edition, 1927), pp. 107-108. On Sunday, October 14, 1906, Barratt attended a missionary meeting in the Gospel Tabernacle at which Simpson preached and collected an offering of more than 70,000 dollars. He wrote: "I reckon Dr. Simpson to be one of the greatest preachers of our day." Ibid., p. 121.

11. Ibid., pp. 111-114.

12. In the intervening period between the time of the "first mighty out-pouring on [his] soul" on October 7, 1906, and his full reception of the baptism of the Holy Spirit on November 15, Barratt exchanged letters with friends in Los Angeles regarding the nature of the gift of tongues and its relationship to the baptism of the Holy Spirit. The Holiness circles in which he had been moving in New York, apparently offered no teaching on this subject, thus encouraging his contact with the Azusa Street mission and Charles Parham's Apostolic Faith Movement. Ibid., pp. 121-124.

13. See T.B. Barratt, "The Seal of My Pentecost," *Living Truths* (December 1906): 735-738, esp. 736 (hereafter cited as *LT*).

14. A.B. Simpson, "Editorial," *LT* (December 1906), 707.

15. Burton K. Janes, *The Lady Who Came. The Biography of Alice Belle Garrigus, Newfoundland's First Pentecostal Pioneer* (St. John's, Newfoundland: Good Tidings Press: 1982), Vol. 1 (1858-1908), pp. 100-107.

16. Rev. D. Wesley Myland, *The Latter Rain Covenant and Pentecostal Power With Testimony of Healings and Baptism*, second edition (Chicago: Evangel Publishing House, 1911; original edition, 1910), p. 153f., esp. p. 160 (hereafter cited as *Latter Rain*). The formative role of John Salmon in the development of the Canadian Alliance is fully discussed in Lindsay Reynolds, *Footprints: The Beginnings of the Christian and Missionary Alliance in Canada* (Beaverlodge, Alberta: Buena Book Services, 1981) (hereafter cited as *Footprints*), esp. pp. 96, 77. Salmon received the Pentecostal baptism with tongues at the Beulah Park convention in August, 1907, and attended the first Pentecostal convention held in Toronto in 1908. Ibid., pp. 560-561; and Gloria G. Kulbeck, *What God Hath Wrought* (Toronto: Pentecostal Assemblies of Canada, 1958), p. 109.

17. Myland, *Latter Rain*, p. 164.

18. Ibid., p. 171.

19. Donald Gee, *Now That You've Been Baptized in the Spirit* (Springfield, Missouri: Gospel Publishing House, 1972; original edition, 1945, 1930), p. 55 (hereafter cited as *Baptized*). See Gee's reference to the "saintly A.B. Simpson" as having had a ministry in North America which paralleled that of R.A. Torrey, whose preaching of the baptism of the Spirit sowed the seeds of the Pentecostal movement in Germany. *The Pentecostal Movement* revised edition (London: Elim Publishing Co., 1949: original edition, 1941), p. 5.

20. Gee, *Baptized*, p. 55.

21. Gary B. McGee, "Pentecostal Awakenings at Nyack," *Paraclete* 18 (Summer, 1984): p. 27 (hereafter cited as "Awakenings"). McGee notes that five of the main buildings on the campus of Central Bible College in Springfield are named after prominent Pentecostal leaders whose spiritual roots were in the Alliance (Eleanor Bowie, Frank M. Boyd, William I. Evans, J. Rosewell Flower, John W. Welch).

22. See Paul Hawkes, "The Pentecostal Assemblies of Canada Organizational Structure and Growth" (unpublished paper presented to Dr. Roger Nicole, Gordon Divinity School, June, 1965), p. 12; and Roy Clifford Spaetzel, *History of the Kitchener Gospel Temple 1909-1974* (Kitchener, Ontario: Kitchener Gospel Temple, 1974), p. 5.

23. See William W. Menzies' discussion of educational development within the Assemblies of God in *Anointed to Serve. The Story of the Assemblies of God* (Springfield, Missouri: Gospel Publishing House, 1971), pp. 354-355 (hereafter cited as *Anointed*); cf. John T. Nichol, *Pentecostalism*, revised edition (Plainfield, New Jersey: Logos International, 1977), p. 55, who identifies as one of the causes of the early success of Pentecostalism the fact that "...scores of Pentecostal leaders had been nurtured in Simpson's Christian and Missionary Alliance society."

24. McGee, "Awakenings," p. 27-28.

25. Brumback, *Sound*, p. 92.

26. Articles 7-9 (with the exception of article 8 which enunciates the "evidence doctrine") of the Assemblies of God *Statement of Fundamental Truths* are essentially an expanded version of what is compressed into article 7 of the Alliance *Statement of Faith* regarding the ministry of the Holy Spirit in the life of the believer. Compare Menzies, *Anointed*, Appendix A, p. 388, and *Manual of The Christian and Missionary Alliance* (Nyack, New York: The Christian and Missionary Alliance, 1978), pp. 11-12.

27. Other Pentecostal historians who have acknowledged the rich contributions of Simpson and the Alliance to early Pentecostalism include: Steve Durasoff, *Bright Wind of the Spirit. Pentecostalism Today.* (Engelwood Cliffs, New Jersey: Prentice-Hall Inc., 1972), pp. 51, 55; Klaude Kendrick, *The Promise Fulfilled: A History of the Modern Pentecostal Movement* (Springfield, Missouri: Gospel Publishing House, 1961), p. 43: David A. Reed, "Origins and Development of the Theology of Oneness Pentecostalism in the United States" (unpublished Ph.D. dissertation, Boston University, 1978), pp. 22, 37; Vinson Synan, *In the Latter Days. The Outpouring of the Holy Spirit in the Twentieth Century* (Ann Arbor, Michigan: Servant Publications, 1984), pp. 44-45.

28. Dr. George Pardington, in his *Twenty-five Wonderful Years 1889-1914:*

A Popular Sketch of the Christian and Missionary Alliance (New York: Christian Alliance Publishing Co., 1914), which he dedicated to Rev. and Mrs. A.B. Simpson, lists the "providential movements" of the nineteenth century that provided the conditioning context for Simpson and the Alliance as: 1) gospel evangelism conducted by Finney, Moody, Whittle and Bliss; 2) the holiness movement in Europe and America as promoted by George Muller, Horatius Bonar, Frances Havergal, Charles Finney and Dr. and Mrs. Palmer; 3) the healing movement of Dorothea Trudel (Switzerland), Pastor Johann Blumhardt (Germany), Pastor Otto Stockmayer (Switzerland), W.E. Boardman and Mrs. M. Baxter (London), Charles Cullis, Carrie F. Judd and "Father" Allen (United States); 4) the modern missionary movement originating with William Carey, and 5) the rebirth of pre-millenialism associated with James Brooks (St. Louis) and A.J. Gordon (Boston). Many of the roots of Pentecostalism are intertwined with those of the Alliance and are masterfully surveyed in Donald Dayton, "Theological Roots of Pentecostalism," *Pneuma* 1 (Spring, 1980): 3-21.

29. Simpson succinctly articulates this view of church history in *The Present Truth* (South Nyack, New York: Christian Alliance Publishing Co., 1897), pp. 6-7 (hereafter cited as *Truth*). Pentecostal and charismatic writers often set forth a similar thesis. See David Womack, *The Wellsprings of the Pentecostal Movement* (Springfield, Missouri: Gospel Publishing House, 1968), p. 83, who likens the relationship of the holiness movement to Pentecostalism to that of John the Baptist to Jesus Christ. Cf. the essay by the American Presbyterian charismatic theologian, Rodman Williams, "A New Era in History," in J. Rodman Williams, *The Pentecostal Reality* (Plainfield, New Jersey: Logos International, 1972), pp. 46-47; and the writings of the British Anglican and Methodist charismatics, Michael Harper, *As At The Beginning* (Plainfield, New Jersey: Logos International, 1971), p. 22; and Leslie Davison, *Pathway to Power: The Charismatic Movement in Historical Perspective* (Watchung, New Jersey: Charisma Books, 1972), p. 77f.

30. Simpson, *Truth*, p. 28.

31. A.B. Simpson, *The Apostolic Church* (Nyack and New York: Christian Alliance Publishing Co., n.d.), pp. 138-139 (hereafter cited as "Apostolic Church"). Cf. Simpson's article, "Gifts and Grace," *CMAW* (June 29, 1907): 303 (hereafter cited as "Gifts"), in which he distinguished prophecy from the teaching of doctrine on the basis that "the prophetic message has more immediate reference to the particular condition of the hearer and the need of immediate spiritual help." In this sense, Simpson saw all preaching as needing to have a "prophetic" thrust.

32. See Simpson's description of two dreams from which he received significant guidance related to missions and his "life of faith." See "Simpson's Anecdotes," compiled by Emma Beere, in "Simpson's

154

Scrapbook" compiled by C. Donald McKaig, p. 231. A copy is in Canadian Bible College/Canadian Theological Seminary Archives, Regina, Saskatchewan. The precise dating of the dreams remains problematic.

33. A.B. Simpson, *The Gospel of the Kingdom* (New York: Christian Alliance Publishing Co., 1890), p. 214; cf. Simpson, *The Coming One* (New York: Christian Alliance Pub. Co., 1912), pp. 190-191; his meditations for the twenty-fifth and twenty-sixth days of the month in *When the Comforter Came* (Harrisburg, Pennsylvania: Christian Publications, 1911) (hereafter cited as *Comforter*); and his poem, "The Latter Rain" in Simpson, *Songs of the Spirit* (New York: Christian Alliance Publishing Co., 1920), p. 52.

34. See Simpson's editorials in *LT* (September, 1906): 519; *CMAW* (February 4, 1905): 65; (June 8, 1907): 205; (October 19, 1907): 38; cf. "A Great Revival," *CMAW* (September 26, 1908): 431.

35. Simpson, "Editorial," *LT* (December, 1906): 706; "Spiritual Sanity," *LT* (April, 1907): 191.

36. Simpson, "Editorial," *CMAW* (April 8, 1905): 209.

37. Simpson, "Editorial," *LT* (August, 1907): 433.

38. Simpson, "Gifts," 303; "The Ministry of the Spirit," *LT* (August, 1907): 438.

39. In view of Simpson's prominent role, it is unfortunate that Paul Chappell gives only minimal attention to Simpson in his survey of the international healing movement of the nineteenth century, "Origins of the Divine Healing Movement in America," *Spiritus* 1 (Winter, 1985): 5-18. For a more generous assessment of Simpson, see Donald Dayton, "The Rise of the Evangelical Healing Movement in Nineteenth Century America," *Pneuma* 4 (Spring, 1982): 1-18. Prudencio Damboriena makes an interesting observation on the similarities between Simpson and the Pentecostal healing evangelists, Aimee Semple McPherson and Oral Roberts on the understanding and practice of healing, *Tongues As Of Fire: Pentecostalism in Contemporary Christianity* (Cleveland, Ohio: Corpus Books, 1969), pp. 134-135.

40. A.B. Simpson, *The Gospel of Healing*, revised edition (New York: Christian Alliance Publishing Co., 1915; original edition, 1888), p. 51 (hereafter cited as *Healing*).

41. A.B. Simpson, *Earnests of the Coming Age* (New York: Christian Alliance Publishing Co., 1921), p. 118 (hereafter cited as *Earnests*).

42. Simpson, *Healing*, p. 52.

43. Ibid., p. 53.

44. Ibid., p. 54.

45. See Simpson's allusion to the longer ending of Mark 16 as substantiating the permanence of healing and tongues, *Healing*, p. 59.

46. Ibid., pp. 55, 57.

47. A.B. Simpson, *The Christ of the Forty Days* (New York: The Christian Alliance Publishing Co., n.d.), p. 252 (hereafter cited as *Forty Days*).

48. Simpson, *Apostolic Church*, p. 133.

49. Simpson, *Forty Days*, p. 242.

50. Simpson, *Healing*, pp. 54-55.

51. Simpson, *Healing*, pp. 70-71. See Simpson's critique of Darwinism and biblical higher criticism as opponents of a supernatural worldview in *The Old Faith and the New Gospel* (New York: Alliance Press Co., 1911), pp. 9-57.

52. Simpson, *Earnests*, p. 15.

53. A.B. Simpson, *Walking in the Spirit* (Harrisburg, Pennsylvania: Christian Publications, Inc., n.d.), p. 140 (hereafter cited as *Walking*); cf. Simpson, *Apostolic Church*, p. 133.

54. Simpson, *Walking*, p. 140.

55. Simpson, *Healing*, pp. 73-74.

56. Simpson, *Truth*, pp. 7, 148; cf. A.B. Simpson, *The Acts of the Apostles: Christ in the Bible Series*, Vol. 16 (Harrisburg, Pennsylvania: Christian Publications, Inc., n.d.), p. 447 (hereafter cited as *Acts*).

57. Simpson, *Acts*, pp. 23, 24.

58. Ibid., p. 49; cf. Simpson's interpretation of Acts 2:38 as teaching that baptism with the Holy Spirit follows repentance and water baptism. Ibid., pp. 43, 123.

59. Simpson, *Forty Days*, pp. 252-253; *Acts*, pp. 54-55.

60. Simpson, *Acts*, p. 122.

61. Ibid., pp. 123, 120. Simpson's exegesis and application of these texts in Acts does not differ essentially from that of numerous Pentecostal and charismatic writers. For recent examples, see J. Rodman Williams,

156

The Gift of the Holy Spirit Today (Plainfield, New Jersey: Logos International, 1980); Howard M. Ervin, *Conversion-Initiation and the Baptism in the Holy Spirit* (Peabody, Massachusetts: Hendrickson Publishers, Inc., 1984); Roger Stronstadt, *The Charismatic Theology of St. Luke* (Peabody, Massachusetts: Hendrickson Publishers, Inc., 1984); Stanley M. Horton, *The Book of Acts* (Springfield, Missouri: Gospel Publishing House, 1981).

62. A.B. Simpson, *In The School of Christ* (New York: Christian Alliance Publishing House, 1890), p. 211 (hereafter cited as "School"); cf. *Acts*, p. 120.

63. Simpson, *School*, pp. 215-216.

64. Ibid., pp. 214, 217, 218.

65. Ibid., pp. 222, 223.

66. Arthur T. Pierson, *Forward Movements of the Last Half Century* (New York and London: Garland Publishing Inc., 1984; original edition, 1905), p. 137.

67. Ibid.

68. Simpson, "Editorial," *LT* (March, 1906): 129.

69. Harold D. Hunter, *Spirit-Baptism, A Pentecostal Alternative* (Lanham, Maryland: University of America Press, 1983), p. 189.

70. Donald R. Wheelock, "Spirit Baptism in American Pentecostal Thought" (unpublished Ph.D. dissertation, Emory University, 1983), p. 51f., esp. p. 56.

71. William Menzies, "The Non-Wesleyan Origins of the Pentecostal Movement," Vinson Synan (ed.), *Aspects of Pentecostal-Charismatic Origins* (Plainfield, New Jersey: Logos International, 1975), p. 87f. With more sophistication, George M. Marsden distinguishes between "Keswick teachers, A.B. Simpson, the Salvation Army, and the Holiness Camp meeting movement" who were all "allies" using similar terminology until the 1890s, but whose differences, by 1900, "were becoming noticeably sharp," *Fundamentalism and American Culture* (New York: Oxford University Press, 1980), pp. 94, 95. The Alliance included in its fellowship, persons who represented all streams of the late nineteenth-century holiness movement. Even "eradicationists" and "suppressionists" were embraced provided they did not militantly engage other views of sanctification held within the Alliance.

72. Edith L. Waldvogel, "The 'Overcoming' Life: A Study in the Reformed Evangelical Contribution to Pentecostalism," *Pneuma* 1 (Spring, 1979): 8-9.

73. *Alliance Weekly* (April 24, 1915): 51. Simpson reflected on the profound significance of that event for his life and ministry in *The Fullness of Jesus* (New York: Christian Alliance Publishing Co., 1890), p. 66; *Acts*, pp. 64-65. On the other hand, he cautioned those seeking the fullness of the Holy Spirit not to discredit past Christian experiences of forgiveness and justification in conversion. There was no better preparation for the deeper life than to be "well saved." "Editorial," *CMAW* (October 19, 1907): 39.

74. See Simpson's reference to "the higher Christian life" in *Alliance Weekly* (November 8, 1919): 98; *Word, Work, and World* (1885): 315.

75. A.B. Simpson, "The Baptism of the Holy Spirit, a Crisis or an Evolution" *LT* (December, 1905): 705 (hereafter cited as "Baptism").

76. Simpson, *Walking*, pp. 7, 64; *The Holy Spirit or Power From on High* (Harrisburg, Pennsylvania: Christian Publications Inc., n.d.), Vol. 2, pp. 14, 15, 20 (hereafter cited as *Power*); *The Gospel of Luke*, Christ in the Bible Series, Vol. 14b (Harrisburg, Pennsylvania: Christian Publications Inc., n.d.), pp. 38-45; *Earnests*, pp. 23-24; *The Names of Jesus* (New York: Christian Alliance Publishing Co., 1892), p. 250 (hereafter cited as *Names*); cf. the meditation for the second day in Simpson, *Comforter*.

77. Simpson, "Baptism," 709.

78. Ibid., p. 715; Simpson, *Romans*, Christ in the Bible Series, Vol. 17 (New York: Christian Alliance Publishing Co., 1904), pp. 149-184. Perhaps Simpson was influenced by George Pardington, a professor at Nyack, who saw the events of Acts 9:17-18 as not "altogether clear" regarding the time of Paul's conversion. If Paul did receive the Spirit subsequent to conversion, then the interval was only three days. See "The Crisis of the Deeper Life," *LT* (September, 1906): 536-537.

79. A.B. Simpson, *The Four-Fold Gospel* (Harrisburg, Pennsylvania: Christian Publications Inc., 1925), p. 28.

80. Ibid., pp. 28-29; *Earnests*, pp. 24-25. For further comment on the imperfections and limited success of the Protestant Reformation, see also Simpson, *The Land of Promise* (New York: Christian Alliance Publishing Co., n.d.), p. 257 (hereafter cited as *Promise*); "Editorial," *Word, Work, and World* (1885), 13.

81. See the meditation for the ninth day in Simpson, *Comforter*; cf. "Baptism," 714; "The Ministry of the Spirit," *LT* (August, 1907): 440.

82. See meditation for the thirtieth day in *Comforter*; *Power*, Vol. 2, pp. 67-76.

83. Simpson, *Forty Days*, p. 233.

84. Simpson, "The Ministry of the Spirit," *LT* (August, 1907): 440: "The regenerated soul has the Holy Spirit with it, but not in it, even as the builder of a house may have constructed it by his own hand, but he has not yet made it his residence and his home"; cf. "Baptism," 707, 710; *Power*, Vol. 2, p. 50f. Simpson distinguished between the Spirit "with us," "in us" and "on us" as referring to the sequential experiences of: 1) converted but yet unsanctified; 2) consecrated and Spirit-baptized; 3) clothed with manifestations of the Spirit for the purpose of Christian service. "Editorial," *CMAW* (October 19, 1907), 39. His conception of the baptism of the Spirit as an "indwelling" subsequent to regeneration is markedly similar to that of the popular charismatic teacher, Derek Prince, *Purposes of Pentecost* (Ft. Lauderdale, Florida: Derek Prince Publications, n.d.), pp. 18f., 106-107.

85. See meditation for the twenty-ninth day in Simpson, *Comforter*.

86. Simpson, *Power*, Vol. 2, p. 24f.

87. On the multiple effects of the baptism of the Spirit, see Simpson, *Walking*, p. 101f.; *Forty Days*, p. 237f.; *Power*, Vol. 2, pp. 77-89; *Apostolic Church*, p. 163; *Acts*, pp. 124, 39.

88. A.B. Simpson, *The Cross of Christ* (New York: Christian Alliance Publishing Co., 1910), p. 130 (hereafter cited as *Cross*).

89. Simpson, *Truth*, p. 138; cf. Simpson, *Fullness*, pp. 65, 66.

90. Simpson, "Baptism," 705, 707; *Earnests*, p. 20; "The Crisis of the Deeper Life," *LT* (September, 1906): 520-521.

91. Simpson, "Baptism," 707.

92. Simpson, "The Crisis of the Deeper Life," *LT* (September, 1906): 523.

93. A.B. Simpson, *A Larger Christian Life* (New York: Christian Alliance Publishing Co., 1890), p. 81; cf. Simpson, *Walking*, p. 133.

94. Simpson, *Cross*, p. 130.

95. Simpson, *Promise*, p. 226f.; *Danger Lines in the Deeper Life* (New York: Christian Alliance Publishing Co., 1898), pp. 7-9.

96. On the universal scene, Simpson expected an unprecedented outpouring of the Spirit in response to "seasons of prayer and fasting." Locally, he noted "a spirit of marked revival in the Missionary Institute and Nyack Seminary" which spread to his Gospel Tabernacle in New York City. See his editorials in *CMAW* (February 25, 1905): 117 and (November 10, 1906): 289.

97. Ernest G. Wilson, "The Christian and Missionary Alliance: Develop-

ments and Modifications of Its Original Objectives" (unpublished Ph.D. dissertation, New York University, 1984), p. 374f.

98. See Anderson, *Vision*, p. 145, who notes that the Alliance suffered defections from both "extreme pro-Pentecostals" and adamant "anti-Pentecostals." Given the growing polarization of attitudes, Simpson was purportedly reluctant to move in either direction for fear of increasing the exodus of people from the Alliance.

99. See the notice sent to Alliance workers in preparation for the May 25-28 Conference, entitled "Respecting Uniformity in the Testimony and Teaching of the Alliance." A copy of the document is in the Canadian Bible College/Canadian Theological Seminary Archives, Regina, Saskatchewan.

100. Simpson, *Apostolic Church*, p. 135f.

101. Simpson, "Gifts," 302; cf. *Power*, Vol. 2, p. 123: "Our ministries are determined, in some measure, by our place in the body, by our environment, by the circumstances and providences amid which we are placed, by leadings, and natural instincts and preferences, and by the gifts both of nature and of grace."

102. Simpson, "The Ministry of the Spirit," *LT* (August, 1907): 440.

103. Simpson, *Apostolic Church*, p. 178f., esp. p. 179.

104. Ibid., p. 151.

105. Simpson, "Gifts," 303.

106. Simpson, *Apostolic Church*, p. 140; cf. Simpson, "Gifts," 303, where he says of tongues that it is "in some sense a real opening of the doors between the earthly and the heavenly."

107. Simpson, *Apostolic Church*, pp. 139, 172, 174-176; cf. Simpson, "The Gift of Tongues," *CAMW* (February 12, 1892): 98; "Queries," *CAFMW* (February 2, 1894): 13; "Editorial," *CMAW* (November 17, 1906): 305; "Editorial," *LT* (December, 1906): 707.

108. Simpson, "The Gift of Tongues," *CAMW* (February 12, 1892): 98.

109. Simpson, *Apostolic Church*, p. 140; "Editorial," *CMAW* (February 2, 1907): 49.

110. Simpson, "Editorial," *CMAW* (September 22, 1906): 177; "Editorial," *LT* (December, 1906): 707.

111. Simpson, "Gifts," 303.

112. Simpson, *Apostolic Church*, p. 148; "Editorial," *LT* (January, 1907): 2. Simpson states that tongues and miracles are "subordinate to the simple and practical ministry of teaching and prophesying."

113. Simpson, *Apostolic Church*, p. 140; "The Gift of Tongues," *CAMW* (February 12, 1892): 98.

114. Simpson, *Apostolic Church*, p. 175.

115. See the meditation for the twenty-fourth day in Simpson, *Comforter;* cf. Simpson, "Spiritual Sanity," *LT* (April, 1907): 194, where he argues for the inferiority of tongues to other more useful gifts.

116. Simpson, "Editorial," *CMAW* (November 17, 1906): 305.

117. *The Christian and Missionary Alliance, 10th Annual Report (1906/07)*, p. 5; cf. Simpson, "Editorial," *CMAW* (February 2, 1907): 49; "Fervor and Fanaticism," *CMAW* (December, 1906): 391.

118. Simpson, "Editorial," *Alliance Weekly* (January, 1912): 258.

119. Simpson, "Editorial," *CMAW* (October 19, 1907): 39. Cf. his editorials in *LT* (February, 1906): 130; (September, 1906): 513, in which he states that power is merely "incidental" to the baptism of the Holy Spirit, which "brings holiness, happiness, healing, and all the fullness of God." Gifts of the Spirit cannot be separated from sanctification without distortion occurring.

120. Simpson, "Gifts," 302; cf. the meditation for the twenty-fourth day in Simpson, *Comforter,* where he describes this doctrine as "extreme" and "most unscriptural."

121. For example, see Rev. J. Hudson Ballard, "Spiritual Gifts With Special Reference to the Gift of Tongues," *LT* (January, 1907): 23-31; Pastor Joseph Smale, "The Gift of Tongues," *LT* (January, 1907): 32-43; A.J. Ramsey, "Speaking With Tongues, An Exegetical Study," *CMAW* (April 4, 1908): 7-17; May Mabbette Anderson, "Deceptive Leadings," *CMAW* (April 11, 1908): 25, 40; William T. MacArthur, "The Phenomenon of Supernatural Utterance," *CMAW* (October 31, 1908): 72-73.

122. See "True and False Fire," *LT* (January, 1907): 44-46. Cf. Simpson's meditation for the twenty-eighth day, entitled "False and True Fire," in *Comforter* as well as his reference to the same in "Editorial," *CMAW* (September 19, 1908): 414. An editorial in *CMAW* (September 7, 1907): 116, refers to Simpson preaching a sermon on "True and False Fire" at the Rocky Springs Park Convention in Lancaster, Pennsylvania.

123. Frank Bartelman, *Azusa Street* (Plainfield, New Jersey: Logos International, 1980; original edition, 1925), p. 112.

124. Ibid.

125. W.W. Simpson to A.B. Simpson, October 17, 1916. A copy of this letter is in Canadian Bible College/Canadian Theological Seminary Archives, Regina, Saskatchewan. See A.B. Simpson's announcement of W.W. Simpson's resignation over the extent to which the Pentecostal experience should be promoted in the Alliance. "Editorial," *Alliance Weekly* (May 30, 1914): 130.

126. Simpson, "Editorial," *CMAW* (April 30, 1910): 78.

127. Simpson, "Editorial," *Alliance Weekly* (January, 1912): 258.

128. Simpson, "Editorial," *CMAW* (September 19, 1908): 414.

129. Ibid.; cf. "Editorial," *Alliance Weekly* (September 6, 1913): 353.

130. Simpson, "Editorial," *CMAW* (August 17, 1907): 73.

131. Simpson, "Editorial," *CMAW* (January, 1909): 291, 296.

132. Simpson, "Side Issues and the Supreme Object of Life," *CMAW* (September 19, 1908): 416.

133. Simpson, "Editorial," *CMAW* (January, 1909): 280.

134. Simpson, "Spiritual Sanity," *LT* (April, 1907): 191.

135. On the need for caution and discernment in assessing spiritual phenomena, see Ibid., p. 191, 194, and Simpson's editorials in *CMAW* (March, 1906): 185; *CMAW* (November 17, 1906): 305; *CMAW* (October 19, 1907): 38.

136. Simpson, "Editorial," *CMAW* (May 4, 1907): 205; "Editorial," *CMAW* (June 12, 1909): 180.

137. Simpson, "Editorial," *LT* (February, 1906): 132; cf. *Christian and Missionary Alliance, 12th Annual Report (1908/09)*, p. 40; Simpson, "Editorial," *CMAW* (August 1, 1908): 296; "Editorial," *CMAW* (September 19, 1908): 414.

138. Simpson, "Editorial," *CMAW* (August 1, 1908): 296.

139. Simpson, "Editorial," *CMAW* (March 28, 1908): 432.

140. Simpson, "Editorials," *CMAW* (July 6, 1907): 313.

162

141. Simpson, "Editorial," *CMAW* (July 13, 1907): 13.

142. Simpson, "Editorial," *CMAW* (September 26, 1908): 430.

143. Simpson, "Editorial," *CMAW* (September 19, 1908): 414.

144. Simpson, "Editorial," *CMAW* (April 4, 1908): 10; "Editorial," *Alliance Weekly* (September 6, 1913): 353.

145. Simpson, "Editorial," *CMAW* (April 4, 1908): 10.

146. Simpson, "Editorial," *CMAW* (October 19, 1907): 37. As a further protective measure, the Alliance eventually adopted a new constitution at the 1912 Council in Boone, Iowa, which featured the "reversion clause." This legislative innovation guaranteed that the property of local branches, schools, and undenominational churches would become the property of the Alliance should the property cease to be used as initially intended, *Christian and Missionary Alliance, 15th Annual Report (1911/12)*, pp. 39-50, esp. p. 49.

147. Simpson, "Editorial," *CMAW* (May 23, 1908): 128.

148. *Christian and Missionary Alliance, 11th Annual Report (1907/08)*, p. 10.

149. Ibid., pp. 11, 12.

150. Prior to the 1908 Council, Simpson had expressed his approval of the five resolutions passed by a conference of German pastors held at Barmen, December 19-20, 1907, which had decided neither to "promote nor oppose" the Pentecostal movement in Europe, but rather to wait on God for a further understanding of truth. "Editorial," *CMAW* (February 29, 1908): 366. He also endorsed the German Pastor Otto Stockmayer's position on tongues expounded in New York City during a trip to America, "Editorial," *CMAW* (February 27, 1909): 364. Stockmayer had been present at Barmen and was a prominent figure in the international healing movement with which Simpson was associated.

151. Tozer, *Wingspread*, p. 133.

152. A copy of the diary is in Canadian Bible College/Canadian Theological Seminary Archives, Regina, Saskatchewan. It was apparently in Tozer's possession at the time he wrote *Wingspread*, but he evidently made no use of it. See John Sawin, "Simpson: The Man and the Movement," first draft (unpublished manuscript, section 1), p. 22, for a description of the diary and confirmation that it was sent to Tozer.

153. Diary entry for May, 1907; cf. Simpson's "Editorial," *CMAW* (June 8, 1907): 205, in which he states that the Council affirmed those

manifestations characterized by the "spirit of power and of a sane mind."

154. Diary entry for August 9, 1907. Prior to the Council of 1907, there were no manifestations of tongues at the Missionary Institute. See Simpson, "Editorial," *CMAW* (June 8, 1907): 205.

155. Ibid.

156. Diary entry for September 12, 1907.

157. Diary entry for August 28, 1907.

158. Diary entry for October 6, 1912. See the suggestions of historians, Williams and Valdvogel, that Mrs. Simpson was "strongly opposed" to speaking in tongues. "History," p. 112, n. 158.

159. Diary entry for May 14, 1916.

CHARLES NIENKIRCHEN

Charles Nienkirchen received a B.Th. from Ontario Bible College, and a B.A. (Honours), M.A. and Ph.D. from the University of Waterloo. He is also a graduate of the Pecos School for Spiritual Directors in Pecos, New Mexico. Dr. Nienkirchen is currently Assistant Professor of Christian History and Thought at Canadian Bible College and Adjunct Professor of Church History at Canadian Theological Seminary. His studies and ministry experience have focused on renewal movements and Christian spirituality. He has directed personal and congregational retreats, and given lectures on the spiritual disciplines and the ministry of the Holy Spirit.

AN OLD MEDIAEVAL MESSAGE:
A TURNING POINT IN THE LIFE OF
A. B. SIMPSON

by

Dwayne Ratzlaff

T his article is a comparative study of spiritual theology; that is, it views A.B. Simpson through the lens of what Richard Lovelace calls "the history and the theology of Christian experience."[1] Prayer is at the heart of Christian experience. This study compares some of the important dynamics of Simpson's understanding of prayer with similar expressions of thought in the rich heritage of Christian spirituality. The writer does not claim that Simpson was influenced by all of the streams represented in this study, nor is it his intention to extract all the sources that informed Simpson's thought on prayer. His purpose is to reveal the similarities between Simpson's understanding of prayer and that of other writers of spiritual theology,[2] and thereby to explore Simpson's testimony to the transformative experience of prayer that influenced profoundly his teaching on progressive sanctification.

The writings of A.B. Simpson are authentic spiritual theology as can be seen from the fact that many of his books are compilations of sermons arranged thematically. Sermons focus by design on a transforming knowledge of God. They do not present theology in the abstract, but expound biblical truth with a view to the spiritual formation of the listeners. This purpose involves the application of truth to human experience.

Simpson, as a preacher, was concerned primarily with the spiritual transformation of his hearers and readers. However, it is wrong to conclude that he did not possess a broad and deep theological awareness. Simpson's principal purpose was to guide people into the fullness of the Christ life, and then into the full expression of His life in the world. Simpson's writings reflected his purpose. It is to a central aspect of his spiritual theology of prayer that we turn now. Simpson records his transformative experience of prayer, precipitated by reading an "old mediaeval message," in his first volume of *The Holy Spirit*.

The Still, Small Voice

"A score of years ago, a friend placed in my hand a little book which became one of the turning points of my life. It was called 'True Peace.' It was an old mediaeval message with but one thought, which was this, that God was waiting in the depths of my being to talk to me if I would only get still enough to hear His voice.

I thought this would be a very easy matter, and so I began to get still. But I had no sooner commenced but a perfect pandemonium of voices reached my ears, a thousand clamoring notes from without and within, until I could hear nothing but their noise and din. Some of them were my own voice, some of them were my own questions, and some of them were my own cares, and some of them were my very prayers. Others were suggestions of the tempter and voices from the world's turmoil. Never before did there seem so many things to be done, to be said, to be thought; and in every direction I was pushed, and pulled, and greeted with noisy acclamations and unspeakable unrest. It seemed necessary for me to listen to some of them, and to answer some of them, but God said, 'Be still, and know that I am God.' Then came the conflict of thoughts for the morrow, and its duties and cares, but God said, 'Be still.' And as I listened and slowly learned to obey and shut my ears to every sound, I found after awhile that when the other voices ceased, or I ceased to hear them, there was a still, small voice in the depths of my being that began to speak with an inexpressible tenderness, power and comfort. As I listened, it became to me the voice of prayer, and the voice of wisdom, and the voice of duty. I did not need to think so hard, or pray so hard, or trust so hard, but that 'still, small voice' of the Holy Spirit in my heart was God's prayer in my secret soul, was God's answer to all my questions, was God's life and strength for soul and body, and became the substance of all knowledge, and all prayer, and all blessing; for it was the living God Himself as my Life and my All.

Beloved, this is our spirit's deepest need. It is thus that we learn to know God; it is thus that we receive spiritual refreshing and nutriment; it is thus that our heart is nourished and fed; it is thus that we receive the Living Bread; it is thus that our very bodies are healed, and the spirit drinks in the life of our risen Lord, and we go forth to life's conflicts and duties like the flower that has drunk in, through the shades of night, the cool and crystal drops of dew. But as the dew never falls on a stormy night, so the dews of His grace never come to the restless soul.

We cannot go through life strong and fresh on express trains, with ten minutes for lunch. We must have quiet hours, secret places of the Most High, times of waiting upon the Lord, when we renew our strength and learn to mount up on wings as eagles, and then come back, to run and not be weary, and to walk and not faint.

The best thing about this stillness is that it gives God a chance to work. 'He that is entered into his rest, he also has ceased from his own works, as God did from His'; and when we cease from our works, God works in us; and when we cease from our thoughts, God's thoughts come into us; when we get still from our restless activity, God worketh in us both to will and do of His good pleasure, and we have but to work it out.

Beloved, let us take His stillness, let us dwell in 'the secret place of the Most High,' let us enter into God and His eternal rest, let us silence the other sounds, and then we can hear 'the still, small voice.'"[3]

It seems an understatement to call Simpson's new experience of prayer profound, for it became one of the "turning points" of his life. He placed this kind of prayer at the center of his spiritual theology. As he listened to the "still, small voice" of the

Holy Spirit in the depths of his being, His voice became the voice of "prayer," "wisdom," and "duty." This listening dimension of prayer, or contemplative prayer, as it is known in spiritual theology, "is our spirit's deepest need." It is through contemplative prayer "that we learn to know God...that we receive spiritual refreshing and nutriment...that our heart is nourished and fed...that we receive the Living Bread...that our bodies are healed, and our spirit drinks in the life of our risen Lord."[4] Clearly, such prayer is the vehicle for divine healing and sanctification. Moreover, it is the fundamental requirement of intercessory prayer that is according to the will of God.

This turning point in Simpson's life came through reading "an old mediaeval message." The message had but one thought, as Simpson describes it, "that God was waiting in the depths of my being to talk to me if I would only get still enough to hear His voice."[5] There is considerable evidence to suggest that this message had a prominent place in his life, as well as in the life of some close associates.

A.E. Thompson, Simpson's biographer, states that this message gleaned from the Quietists "was one of the secrets of his life."[6] Thompson placed the message in a two-fold context. First, the message was a dimension of Simpson's evangelical mysticism. A friend with an intimate knowledge of Simpson described him as 'the last of the great mystics.'[7] He was a mystic after the pattern of the Apostle Paul who offered this summation of the Christian life, 'Christ in you, the hope of glory.' Simpson's message revolved around this mystical union with Christ in His resurrection life. For him, the message was the secret of abiding in Christ.[8]

Henry Wilson, a close friend and associate of Simpson, revealed the preeminence of the "Christ in you" message for Simpson's inner circle of colleagues. In his book, *The Internal Christ*, Wilson expresses the necessity for both the external and internal Christ:

"To the average Protestant, it is the 'Historic Christ'... in all the beauty of His moral character, charming the mind, if not warming the heart of Christendom.... To the devout Catholic, it is the presence of the body of the Crucified Jesus, to be (1) worshipped, and (2) partaken of ...bread and wine. But to both Protestant and Catholic, these two expressions, or manifestations of Jesus, in their practical outcome, mean the 'IMITATIO CHRISTI,' the copying and faithful following of Him thus presented to (1) the eye of the mind; and (2) the eyes of the body, in (a) the written Word of God, and (b) the sacrament of the altar.

But even among Christians who profess to have gone farther than the 'Historic Christ' school, and much farther than those who hold the 'real presence' in the sacrament, the tide of 'devotion,' to use again the word of the schools, hardly rises higher than the teaching of the famous book of à Kempis. There are holiness movements of today headed by noble men of God; led by profound students of the Word; taught by great teachers of entire sanctification and holy living, which at their highest point seldom pass beyond the idea of an external Christ....

Admitting at once the soundness...of the 'Imitation of Christ,' we believe there is a more excellent way of presenting our living Lord to the eyes and heart of Christendom, viz., 'Christ in you, the hope of glory.' We believe that this at once is the highest tide of Christian teaching and the deepest need of human souls today."[9]

Second, according to Thompson, "Dr. Simpson had solved the secret of service when he learned the mystery of prayer."[10] The Apostle Paul commanded the Christian to "pray without ceasing."[11] This directive captured the imagination of those Christians in the history of the Church who had committed their lives to its fulfillment; Simpson was one of them. In *Days of Heaven on Earth*, he writes:

In the consecrated believer, the Holy Spirit is preeminently a Spirit of prayer. If our whole being is committed to Him, and our thoughts are at His bidding, He will occupy every moment in communion and occupy everything as it comes, and we shall pray it out in our spiritual consciousness before we act it out in our lives. We shall, therefore, find ourselves taking up the burdens of life and praying them out in a wordless prayer which we, ourselves, often cannot understand, but which is simply the unfolding of His thought and will within us, and which will be followed by the unfolding of His providence concerning us.[12]

169

His habit of sermon preparation, for example, was "to hush his spirit and literally cease to think. Then in the silence of his soul, he listened for 'the still, small voice.' It was thus he received his messages," although he testified, toward the end of his ministry, to having received "a renewed call both to studious preparation and prayerful reception of his messages."[13]

G.P. Pardington, a close associate of Simpson in the work of the Alliance, considered the message so important as to warrant writing a book with the title, *The Still, Small Voice*. There was a striking similarity between the views of Pardington and Simpson on prayer. Pardington claimed, "Energized prayer is a prayer that is first inwrought by the Holy Spirit and then out-wrought by the same Spirit. In a word, then, the prayer that God answers is first put into our hearts by the Spirit, and then prayed out through our hearts by the Spirit."[14] This was the kind of prayer God answered, the prayer that came from "the still, small voice." Although Simpson did not write a book about his experience, he did write a tract, *The Power of Stillness*, that he distributed widely.[15]

Moreover, there is evidence to suggest that the influence of this "old mediaeval message" permeated the nineteenth century holiness revival in which Simpson was a participant. A.T. Pierson, an associate of Simpson, documents this in his book, *Forward Movements of the Last Half Century*. According to Pierson, one of the spiritual streams that influenced the holiness revival was that of Christian mysticism:

> The Mystics also would deserve a very prominent place in this survey, only that their history reaches back through the ages and demands separate treatment; yet it is not to be overlooked that every great movement in the direction of holier life is inseparable from this great current of thought that is associated with such as Jacob Bohme, St. Theresa, Catherine of Siena, Madame Guyon, Fénelon, Tauler, and William Law.[16]

In a chapter entitled, "The Revival of the Prayer-Spirit," Pierson declares that our greatest need "is to keep in close touch with God; the greatest risk is the loss of the sense of the divine." Also, he pinpoints prayer as the corrective for "the loss of the sense of the divine...."

'Enter into thy closet.' There all is silence, secrecy, solitude, seclusion.... The silence is in order to the hearing of the still, small voice that is drowned in worldly clamor, and which even a human voice may cause to be unheard or indistinct.... The decline of prayer is the decay of piety.[17]

PRAYER OF "STILLNESS"

Simpson gleaned his formative insight into prayer through reading a tract entitled "True Peace." Unfortunately, Simpson did not record the author of the tract. A.E. Thompson informs us that the author was a Quietist. Quietism was a small seventeenth-century movement led by such notable persons as Miguel de Molinos, Madam Guyon, and Francois Fénelon. The movement was known for its teaching on contemplation or stillness.[18] Fénelon (1651-1715) writes these thoughts on the experience of stillness:

The Spirit of Truth will teach you inwardly all that Jesus Christ teaches you outwardly in the Gospel....It is an inward voice, which teaches us as we have need from time to time....It is essential that we get a habit of hearkening to His Voice, of keeping silence within, and listening so as to lose nothing of what He says to us.[19]

As noted above, Simpson called *True Peace* a "mediaeval" message, whereas Thompson attributed the source to the Quietists. The mystery of the book and its authorship was solved by Harry Verploegh in the preface to a book entitled, *A.W. Tozer: An Anthology*. Verploegh wrote,

While A.W. Tozer was pastor of the Southside Alliance Church in Chicago, he once presented me with a small book titled *A Guide to True Peace*, or *The Excellency of Inward and Spiritual Prayer*, selections compiled chiefly from the writings of Fenelon, Guyon and Molinos. According to A.B. Simpson, this same little book, given to him by a friend, became one of the turning points of his life. I have it yet, after perhaps forty years.[20]

171

A Guide to True Peace was compiled anonymously by two Quakers, William Backhouse and James Janson, from the writings of Jeanne de la Motte Guyon (1648-1717), Francois Fénelon (1651-1715), and Miguel de Molinos (1640-1697). In the 1946 edition of the book, a reprint of the 1839 edition, Howard Brinton revealed,

> *The Guide to True Peace* is compiled principally from the *Short Method of Prayer* of Madame Guyon, the *Maxims of the Saints* of Fénelon, and the *Spiritual Guide* of Molinos. The writers of these three mystical classics were the outstanding figures in that seventeenth century movement in France and Italy nicknamed Quietism because of its teaching that God is known only through the prayer of inward silence when all human thought and feeling is quieted.[21]

This "old mediaeval message," as Simpson described it, is similar to what other devotional writers in the history of the Church called contemplative prayer. A consideration of some of these writers will help us to explore further the experience that Simpson described as one of the "turning points" of his life.

In contemplative prayer, the thinking function "is arrested in a simple attention and one-pointedness."[22] "Contemplation" is a mysterious word for many people. The New Testament uses a related word, "gnosis," to translate the Old Testament word "da'ath," which "implies possession of the thing known, an extremely intimate kind of knowledge involving the whole man, not just the mind (Psalm 139:1-6)." The Apostle Paul employs the word "gnosis" in his writings to refer to the "intimate knowledge of God." He considered this knowledge to be a vital element for the full maturity of the Christ life (Ephesians 1:17-19, 3:14-19; Colossians 1:9-10, 2:2-3). The Greek Fathers went one step further, and borrowed the word "theoria," meaning an "intellectual vision of the truth," from the Neoplatonists, and added the meaning of "da'ath, that is, the kind of experiential knowledge that comes through love." For the Greek Fathers, the word "theoria" captures both the "intellectual vision of truth" and the "experiential knowledge that comes through love" as these elements pertain to God. This meaning of "theoria," translated as "contemplatio" in the

172

Latin, came to us as an important dimension of our Christian heritage. In relation to prayer, contemplation is a "stillness" in which the

> ...mind and heart are not actively seeking Him (God), but are beginning to experience—'taste'—what they have been seeking. This places them in a state of repose, tranquility, and profound interior peace. It is not the suspension of all action, but a mingling of very simplified thought and the loving experience of God.[23]

Many writers of spiritual theology acknowledge that contemplation is the deepest form of prayer.

John Cassian (365-435), one of the Desert Fathers, writes in the "Second Conference" of his *Institutes* of a formula for prayer that came to be known as "lectio divina" (sacred reading).[24] There are four aspects to his form of prayer: "lectio," "meditatio," "oratio," and "contemplatio." Lectio (reading) refers to the reception of the word of revelation by whatever vehicle it comes. The reading of the Scriptures is of primary importance in lectio. It is possible also to have received this word through the words of others, through reading, and especially through the liturgy of the Word. It comes by means of homilies, sharing with others, example of others, art or nature. All of life is a vehicle for the reception of a word of revelation.

Meditatio (meditation) naturally follows lectio. Meditatio is a repetition of a word of revelation. It is a single word, a phrase, or a sentence that was quietly repeated over and over again with the use of the lips. The Desert Fathers used the image of the cow to describe the process of meditatio. A cow fills its stomach with food and then settles down quietly and chews it. Through the process of regurgitation, the cow reworks what it has received and moves it lips in the process. In this manner, a cow transforms its food into rich and creamy milk. Similarly, a word of revelation passes from the lips into the mind and then down into the heart through constant repetition. The process effects a loving faith-filled response in the one involved in meditatio. It changes an intellectual assent into a real assent that involves the whole person. Now oratio (prayer) enters the process. The whole person responds affirmatively to the reality.

As meditatio on the word of revelation continues, one's response deepens until the significance of the word of revelation is more fully perceived. The response is one of gratitude, love and prayer. This is oratio. The response continues to grow as one continues to gain nourishment from the word of revelation, a nourishment that comes from illuminating grace. The reality of the word of revelation becomes so real, and God Himself becomes so real, that a word or movement of the heart is no longer adequate. The person has thereby arrived at contemplatio (contemplation), a process whereby the person's whole being says "Yes" to the word of revelation and to God. The entire progression from lectio to contemplatio is a gift from the God of Light. Prayer reaches its deepest level in contemplatio.[25] It was Benedict (480-547), through *The Rule of St. Benedict*, who popularized this form of prayer in the monastic movement.

John Climacus (579-649), in *The Ladder of Divine Ascent*, writes about "stillness" in the context of our union with God. This stillness penetrates "the deep places of the heart." Climacus calls it a "gift of calm from the Holy Spirit."[26] More specifically, "Stillness is worshipping God unceasingly and waiting on Him. Let the remembrance of Jesus be present with your every breath. Then indeed you will appreciate the value of stillness."[27] The "remembrance of Jesus" was an important development in the historical experience of contemplative prayer. It reached fruition in the Jesus Prayer, an unceasing repetition of the phrase, 'Lord Jesus Christ, Son of God, have mercy on me, a sinner.' This prayer lies at the heart of hesychast spirituality. The term "hesychast" comes from *hesychia*, the Greek word for "quietude." The hesychasts were those monks who, from the fourth century onward, devoted their lives to solitude, contemplation, and the Jesus Prayer. Hesychasts used other forms of the prayer, all of which focused on invoking the name and presence of Jesus.[28]

Stillness was central also to the spiritual teaching of George Fox (1624-1691), the founder of the Quakers. In his *Journal* he relates stillness to his belief in the immediate presence and power of the Holy Spirit to teach us the Truth. Fox believed that his own mission was "to direct people to the Spirit that gave forth the Scriptures, by which they might be led into all Truth, and so up to Christ and God...."[29] He believed that the Spirit teaches us directly from the Word. He is our inner Guide.

In following this Guide, the founder of the Quakers became a unique kind of spiritual guide himself. His guidance centered on directing people to the Spirit and cultivating the kind of interior and exterior atmosphere wherein the Spirit was free to teach: "Your teacher is within you; look not forth; it will teach you lying in bed, going abroad, to shun all occasion of sin and evil."[30] In one of his letters, he directs, "Return within, and wait to hear the voice of the Lord there."[31] The most important Quaker discipline is to wait on the Lord.

Similarly, A.B. Simpson considered "stillness" to be a vital means of receiving divine guidance. In an article entitled, "The Secret of Prayer," he writes, "There is a divine and most perfect provision in the economy of grace, by which the Holy Spirit adjusts our spirit into such harmony with God that we can catch His thought and send it back again, not merely as a human desire, but as a divine prayer."[32] He expands on the believer's experience of the direct guidance of the Spirit in *Walking in the Spirit:*

> The Holy Spirit is promised to us as our personal Guide in the path of life....Some persons are so zealous for the word of God that they deny any direct guidance of the Spirit apart from the Word, but if we truly believe the Word itself, we will be forced to accept its distinct statements, that the personal presence of the Holy Spirit is given to the humble and obedient disciple for the needed direction in every step of life.[33]

Simpson believed that "the methods of divine guidance were various." The Spirit guides us through "the Scriptures," "His own direct voice," and "most frequently by intuitions of our sanctified judgment." The Spirit works through our intuitions in this manner:

> The thoughts come as our own...a sort of intuition that it is the right thing to do....It is not so much the Spirit speaking to us as the Spirit speaking with us as part of our very consciousness, so that it is not two minds, but one."[34]

Divine guidance through the prayer of "stillness" is for the mature in Christ. Simpson was aware of the potential danger of this kind of prayer: "There must be real consecration and holy vigilance in such a walk, to guard against our own impressions and inclinations in cases where they are not the intimations of the Spirit's will."[35] Nevertheless, he believed that the provision for Divine guidance was ever present through the indwelling Spirit, and the transformative power of such attentiveness to His voice was profound indeed.

Besides providing divine guidance, contemplative prayer also benefits Christians by deepening their communion with God. According to Simpson,

> ...the deepest kind of prayer is often voiceless. It is communion. It does not ask for anything, but it just pours out its being in holy fellowship and silent communion with God. Sometimes it is an infinite rest to cease all our words and just lie still and rest upon His bosom....There are moments too sacred, too divine for our interpretation. There are joys as well as groans which 'cannot be uttered' ...we should know the depths and heights of silent prayer and divine communion.[36]

The Cloud of Unknowing, an anonymous fourteenth-century classic, suggests that the intention of the "contemplative work of the spirit" is to desire God for who He is, not for what He can do for us; "Lift your heart up to the Lord, with a gentle stirring of love desiring Him for His own sake and not for His gifts."[37] The author describes contemplative prayer as a "work of love" and continues, "But if you strive to fix your love on Him forgetting all else, which is the work of contemplation I have urged you to begin, I am confident that God, in His goodness, will bring you to a deep experience of Himself."[38] By love, the author means a "radical personal commitment to God" which "implies that [one's] will is harmoniously attuned to His in an abiding contentedness and enthusiasm for all He does."[39]

Lest we think that Simpson considered prayer to be "stillness" only, we need to realize that in his spiritual theology of prayer, the "highest ministry of prayer [is] intercession."[40] In other words, for Simpson, while the deepest form of prayer is "stillness," the highest form of prayer is "intercession." It is one's deep attentiveness to the "still, small voice" of the Spirit within that gives direction to intercessory prayer. Simpson testifies:

> ...that 'still, small voice' of the Holy Spirit in my heart was

God's prayer in my secret soul, was God's answer to all my questions, was God's life and strength for soul and body, and became the substance of all knowledge, and all prayer, and all blessing; for it was the living God Himself as my Life and my All.[41]

The Holy Spirit is our "true guardian and monitor" and leads us either to communion or service:

The sensitive spirit grows very quick to discern God's voice. That which would naturally be considered as simple depression of spirits comes to be instantly recognized as a hint that God has something to say to us....Often our physical sensations come to be quick, instinctive interpreters of some inward call; for when we do not quickly listen to God's voice, He knocks more loudly....If we were but more watchful we would find that nothing comes to us at any moment of our lives which has not some divine significance, and which does not lead us in some way to communion or service.[42]

PRAYER OF "RECOLLECTION"

It is one thing to affirm the prayer of "stillness," and quite another to arrive at the experience of "stillness." This reality did not take Simpson long to discover. He decided to practice the "old mediaeval message," but discovered that the beginning of "stillness" brought an onslaught of distractions. He encountered a "pandemonium of voices" and a "thousand clamoring notes from within and without, until [he] could hear nothing but their noise and din."[43] He discovered also the classical response to the problem of distractions through the prayer of "recollection." This discovery became a vital dimension of his spiritual theology. Moreover, he learned that one of the secrets of abiding in Christ was the cultivation of "internal prayer." In *The Christ Life*, Simpson counsels,

Cultivate the habit of always recognizing Him as near, in your heart of hearts....Walking down the street you will

177

find a thousand things to call you from a state of recollection...you have to hold your ears, and your eyes, and live in a little circle...we must cultivate the habit of internal prayer, communing with God in the heart.... This habit of silent prayer, not in words, but in thought, is one of the secrets of abiding. There is an old word the mystics used — 'recollection.' We would call it a recollected spirit.[44]

Many of the writers of spiritual theology support Simpson's discovery that the prayer of "recollection" clears the way for the deeper prayer of "stillness." We gain insight into Simpson's experience of "recollection" as we listen to the mystics who journeyed before him. He acknowledged his discovery as the message of the mystics.

Gregory Palamas (1296-1359), in *The Triads*, suggests that the problem of distractions in prayer is two-fold in nature. First, the senses scatter the mind in all directions. One must learn to "recollect the mind"; that is, one must continue to return the mind to the heart. Second, one's "passionate emotions" distract the mind also. These passions disperse the mind from within itself to seek "sensual delights," and must be brought to calm by directing their "energies toward divine things." For Gregory Palamas, this calm or stillness is achieved through the unceasing remembrance of Jesus.[45]

The Cloud of Unknowing recommends the use of a meaningful prayer word to effect an inner posture of recollection. The author describes interiorization as the "efficacy of one little interior word...surging up from the depths of man's spirit, the expression of his whole being."[46] The seeker must "understand how to work interiorly" in order to prevent the breakdown of the work of contemplative prayer in a seeker's life.[47] This classic was not written for beginners, but for the "mature in Christ," those who are committed to following Christ into the "inmost depths of contemplation."[48] According to the author, the beginner does not know how to work interiorly. This interior work involves knowing how to make words "wholly interior,"[49] and learning how

to gather all your desire into one simple word that the mind can easily retain....A one-syllable word such as 'God' or 'love' is best. But choose one that is meaningful to you. Then fix it in your mind so that it will remain there come what may. This word will be your defense in conflict and in peace. Use it to beat on the cloud of darkness above you and to subdue all distractions, consigning them to the cloud of forgetting beneath you.[50]

John Calvin (1509-1564) noted that Christ encourages us to secret prayer. He perceived this as an invitation from Christ to "descend into our hearts with our whole thought [and Christ] promises us God will be near us in the affection of our hearts, entempled in our bodies."[51] The call to secret prayer suggested to Calvin that "prayer is something secret, lodged chiefly in the hearts, requiring tranquility far from all teeming cares."[52] Calvin was aware of the distractions that hinder prayer. For this reason, he counsels all who pray to unite voice and song:

Voice and song interposed in prayer must spring from one's deepest heart.... And so speaking and singing, must be tied to the heart's affection.... Shifty, slippery, inattentive is the mind toward thinking of God unless exercised by prayerful speech and song.[53]

Johann Arndt (1555-1621) was a 'Lutheran Scholar' who demonstrated in *True Christianity* that the doctrine of "justification by faith" does not prevent good works, but rather, unleashes them in the Christian. Arndt had a deep appreciation for the Catholic mystical tradition. He had a fine grasp of mediaeval mystical classics and integrated them into his Lutheran perspective of union with Christ.[54] In *True Christianity*, Arndt uses expressions evocative of the interior life to refer to the movement into the "house of the heart," where Christ dwells as a living, active presence. Communion with Him there is like a "spiritual Sabbath." The "highest rest of the soul" is in the presence of God. He notes that "the saints of God have always endeavored to live in the wilderness with inner, godly meditation and to be like heavenly minds and to rest in God."[55] A meditative person "is God's friend in that he continually comes before His presence and goes into His holiness without hindrance, and goes about joyously with God."[56] Arndt believed that our encounters with the interior presence of God are inner Sabbaths of the heart. They are occasions of rest, wonder, enjoyment and improvement. The person to whom

God speaks must dwell in the "sacred depths" of the soul.[57] According to Arndt, recollection into the presence of God occurs through meditation, prayer, Scripture and the Lord's Supper. These are the vehicles that guide us into the "sacred depths" of the soul where communion with the indwelling Christ occurs.

William Law (1686-1761) in his classic, *A Serious Call to a Devout and Holy Life*, proposes a pattern of devotion that includes six specific periods of prayer, from early morning to late evening. An important preliminary to prayer for him is finding the correct location. He encourages the pray-er to "consecrate a room or part of a room as a holy place unto God." This location becomes a sacred place to be used for nothing but prayer. For Law, prayer begins with a "recollection of spirit" in which one closes one's eyes and in silence allows the soul to place itself in the presence of God.[58] All prayer commences with the singing of a Psalm which prepares the way for devotions. He stresses that Psalms should be sung, not simply read, since body and soul mutually influence one another through singing. According to Law's conception of the "union of soul and body," the outward or vocal practices of singing, reading, or praying, influence the inner dispositions of the heart, just as the inner movements of the heart influence our bodily actions. Law's conclusion is that "outward helps" and "inward meditations" serve to "fix habits of piety in our hearts." The singing of Psalms, involving soul and body, enable the messages to reach pray-ers at deeper levels.[59]

A.B. Simpson was one of a large company of witnesses who identified distractions as a major hindrance to the prayer of "stillness." These spiritual guides directed persons to the prayer of "recollection" which counteract this hindrance. In this prayer one employs Scripture, the devotional classics, meditation, vocal prayer, vocal reading, singing, as well as the imagination. In so doing, one places oneself in the presence of God where one can attend to the "still, small voice." The Christian "mystics" provide an historical context in which to assist our understanding of Simpson's experience of the prayer of "recollection."

PRACTICE OF THE PRESENCE

The devotee of contemplative prayer has the glorious possibility of using the heightened consciousness of God's presence, which is one fruit of this form of prayer, to bring Him into every thought and activity of life. It is true that He is present already whether we are aware of His presence or not. Nevertheless, the consciousness of His presence can make a profound difference to the actualization of the Christ life. The contemplative dimension of the Christian life can bring depth and direction to the active dimension of Christian living. The writers of spiritual theology affirm that the experience of contemplative prayer can so infuse one's life that all of life becomes the living out of one's prayers to God.

The writings of A.B. Simpson communicate a dynamic philosophy of "abiding in Christ." Faith for Simpson is active, not passive, since Christians have a vital role to perform in their spiritual enlargements. In his classic, *A Larger Christian Life*, he describes our participation as "a strenuous and unceasing energy on our part in meeting Him with the cooperation of our faith, vigilance and obedience."[60] We are to give "earnest attention" to the "provisions of God's grace." It is at the point of attentiveness to the provisions of grace that we work out "our own salvation," for the Christian life "is yet in embryo and infancy, an inward principle of life which must be worked out in every part of our life." It is to the work of growth that we must give earnest attention so as "...to make the most of our spiritual resources and opportunities."[61] In *Walking in the Spirit*, Simpson leaves no doubt about the importance of our cooperation in our spiritual growth:

> It would throw a flood of light on the perplexing doctrine of election if we would remember, when thinking of this subject, that we are elected by God, not unto salvation unconditionally and absolutely, but unto holiness. We are predestined to be conformed to the image of His Son. It is idle and unscriptural, therefore, to talk about being elected to salvation irrespective of our faith and obedience. We are elected to obedience and sprinkling of the blood of Christ, and are summoned, therefore, to make our calling and election sure, by pressing on into the fullness of the grace of Christ.[62]

For Simpson, the participation of the Christian in making "our calling and election sure" pertains to all of the dimensions of "abiding in Christ." A central element in Simpson's teaching on abiding is "practicing the presence of God." In *Echoes of the New Creation*, he declares,

> It is thus, beloved, in practicing the presence of God slowly and patiently, the habit of dependence is formed; it is there that we triumph or fail. Cultivate the habit of constant dependence. In everything let it be, 'Not I but Christ,' until at last it becomes so natural that you do it without thinking, that almost mechanically you will find yourself saying, 'Jesus for this,' 'What shall I do, Lord?' Thus we shall establish the habit of dependency upon Him for all the little details....Let us count everything sacred and divine and realize Christ is living His life in us.[63]

In *The Christ Life*, Simpson provides a definite structure for one's participation in the growth of the Christ life: one moves from "act" to "habit" to "breathing"[64] to "established character."[65] This movement begins with "definite effort," and with persistence becomes spontaneous."[66] Thus synergy—man cooperating with God—is central to Simpson's spiritual theology, but it is a synergy that flowed out of salvation and not toward salvation. It involves the working out of one's salvation in every area of life. Simpson describes the process in these words:

> This abiding must be established by a succession of definite acts of will, and of real, fixed, steadfast trust in Christ. It does not come as a spontaneous and irresistible impulse that carries you whether you will or not, but you have to begin by an act of trust, and you must repeat it until it becomes a habit. It is very important to realize this ...until at last it comes to be as natural as your breathing ...we must cultivate the habit of constant dependence on Him...if you would abide in Christ, you must cultivate the habit of always recognizing Him as near, in your heart of hearts.[67]

He expounds on his conception of synergy in an article entitled "Deeper":

> There is still a deeper depth where the act becomes a habit and the habit becomes the character. It is a law of the

182

inner life that when we repeat an act often enough, it becomes habitual, it comes to be a law of our nature and then back of it is the settled and established character of which it is the expression.... So of any ... spiritual exercise, the act induces the habit and the habit establishes the character. This is growing deeper. This is the rooting and grounding of the life and this is what the Holy Spirit is waiting to lead us into if we will dare to choose it and persistently follow Him in it.[68]

Simpson followed in the footsteps of many spiritual writers who taught that a central goal of prayer was the practice of the presence of God for the purpose of enriched worship and service. A panoramic view of the past may expand our insight into the "how" of the practice of the presence of God. One of the best known of these writers is Brother Lawrence who lived in the late seventeenth century. In his *Practice of the Presence of God*, Brother Lawrence testifies to having come to such an awareness of the presence of God that the "clatter" of the kitchen did not differ from the "time of prayer."[69] Through his own journey, he discovered that "in order to form a habit of conversation with God continually, and referring all we do to Him, we must at first apply to Him with some diligence; but that after a little care we should find His love inwardly excite(s) us to it without any difficulty."[70]

John Wesley (1703-1791), in *A Plain Account of Christian Perfection*, offers an eloquent description of "The Character of a Methodist" that includes the following characteristics:

For indeed he 'prays without ceasing.'...His heart is lifted up to God at all times, and in all places. In this he is never hindered, much less interrupted, by any person or thing. In retirement or company, in leisure, business, or conversation, his heart is ever with the Lord....He walks with God continually; having the loving eye of his soul fixed on him.[71]

For Wesley, "continual prayer" is a vital means of grace, not an activity that occurs only at periodic intervals, but rather a way of living.[72]

The anonymous author (nineteenth century) of *The Way of a Pilgrim* provides a way of practicing the presence of God through the Jesus Prayer. In this classic, a Russian peasant on a pilgrimage reaches a critical turning point in his journey when he encounters an elder who teaches him to pray without ceasing. The elder gives him this advice:

> The ceaseless Jesus Prayer is a continuous, uninterrupted call on the holy name of Jesus Christ with the lips, mind, and heart; and in the awareness of his abiding presence, it is a plea for His blessing in all undertakings, in all places, at all times, even in sleep. The words of the Prayer are: 'Lord Jesus Christ, have mercy on me!' Anyone who becomes accustomed to this Prayer will experience great comfort as well as the need to say it continuously. He will become accustomed to it to such a degree that he will not be able to do without it and eventually the Prayer will of itself flow in him.[73]

On his journey, the pilgrim encounters other persons who, like him, want to know how to pray without ceasing. He becomes a spiritual guide to them on the "prayer of the heart." On one occasion, the pilgrim counsels a seeker to harmonize the repetition of the Jesus Prayer with physical breathing:

> The next step, according to the writing of the Fathers, is to direct the flow of the Jesus Prayer in the heart in harmony with your breathing; that is, while inhaling, say 'Lord Jesus Christ,' and while exhaling, say 'have mercy on me.'...Thus, with the help of God, you will attain self-activating prayer of the heart.[74]

Thomas Kelly (1893-1941), in his *A Testament of Devotion*, suggests that there "is a way of ordering our mental life on more than one level at once." This mental ordering is imperative if we are to live integrated lives, if we are to live life from the "Center" in that "amazing inner sanctuary of the soul, a holy place, a Divine Center, a speaking Voice, to which we may continuously return."[75] Kelly offers the following advice for arriving at habitual inward prayer:

> There is no new technique for entrance upon this stage where the soul in its deepest levels is continuously at Home in Him. The processes of inward prayer do not grow more complex, but more simple. In the early weeks

184

we begin with simple, whispered words. Formulate them spontaneously, 'Thine only, Thine only.' Or seize upon a fragment of the Psalms: 'So panteth my soul after Thee, O God.' Repeat them inwardly, over and over again. For the conscious cooperation of the surface level is needed at first, before prayer sinks into the second level as habitual divine orientation. Change the phrases, as you feel led, from hour to hour or from forenoon to afternoon. If you wander, return and begin again. But the time will come when verbalization is not so imperative.... At first the practice of inward prayer is a process of alternation of attention between outward things and the Inner Light. Preoccupation with either brings the loss of the other. Yet what is sought is not alternation, but simultaneity, worship undergirding every moment, living prayer, the continuous current and background of all moments of life. Long practice indeed is needed before alternation yields to concurrent immersion in both levels at once.[76]

The reader may conclude that Simpson would not approve of practicing the presence of God in the form presented by the anonymous author of The Way of a Pilgrim and Thomas Kelly, and the reader may be correct. However, the reader should consider these two similarities. First, Simpson wrote a hymn entitled, "Breathing Out and Breathing In," which contains these words:

Jesus, breathe Thy Spirit on me,
Teach me how to breathe Thee in,
Help me pour into Thy bosom
All my life of self and sin.
I am breathing out my own life,
That I may be filled with Thine;
Letting go my strength and weakness,
Breathing in Thy life divine.

Breathing out my sinful nature,
Thou hast borne it all for me;
Breathing in Thy cleansing fullness,
Finding all my life in Thee.
I am breathing out my sorrow,
On Thy kind and gentle breast;

185

Breathing in Thy joy and comfort,
Breathing in Thy peace and rest.

I am breathing out my longings,
In Thy list'ning loving ear,
I am breathing in Thy answers,
Stilling every doubt and fear.
I am breathing every moment,
Drawing all my life from Thee;
Breath by breath I live upon Thee,
Blessed Spirit, breathe in me.[77]

Second, Simpson gave this advice for cultivating the habit of practicing the presence of God, as referred to earlier in this article, "In everything let it be, 'Not I but Christ,' until at last it becomes so natural that you do it without thinking, that almost mechanically you will find yourself saying, 'Jesus for this,' 'What shall I do, Lord?' Thus we shall establish the habit of dependency upon Him."[78]

For Simpson, as well as other writers on the spiritual life, the practice of the presence of God through inward prayer, and the bringing of His presence into every thought and activity of life and service was at the heart of the Christ life. Although the cultivation of inward prayer involves, for them, our cooperation with God, prayer without ceasing is an expression ultimately of the indwelling life of Christ. It is the gift of His presence. Simpson believed that the movement from "act" to "habit" to "breathing" to "transformed character," though it involves will and effort, is actualized by the enabling power of the Holy Spirit. He is the Actualizer of the practice of the presence of God.

DRAWING CORRECT CONCLUSIONS

It is inaccurate to conclude that this "old mediaeval message," which became one of the "turning points" of Simpson's life, led him to take a passive stance toward service. A reading of what remains of a surviving diary reveals otherwise. He was a man of action whose life represents an integration of the contemplative and active dimensions of the Christian life. Simpson was aware of the danger of imbalance in either direction:

There is a subtle danger, however, for intensely spiritual minds, to carry the internal side too far and to lose the perfect balance of character which includes the active and the practical, as well as the inward and the spiritual sides of our being. Mary and Martha together form the perfect combination; sitting at the feet of Jesus, and also serving with busy ministering hands; 'not slothful in business; fervent in spirit; serving the Lord.[79]

His discovery of the prayer of "stillness," and his commitment to the cultivation of the practice of the presence of God did not remove him from service, but rather, brought depth and direction to his service for Christ. As A.E. Thompson observes:

Dr. Simpson had solved the secret of service when he learned the mystery of prayer. In prayer he received a vision of God's will. Through further prayer he ascertained God's plans for the carrying out of His will. Through prayer, he was empowered to execute those plans. More prayer brought the supply of every need for the work. Continuing still in prayer, he was able to carry through what he had begun. Praying always, a spirit of praise and adoration welled up in his heart, and God received all the glory for everything that was accomplished.[80]

It is inaccurate to conclude that this "old mediaeval message" led Simpson to give Scripture a secondary role in his spiritual theology. Simpson believed in the pre-eminence of Scripture, although he did not believe it to be the exclusive means of discerning the voice of God. In other words, he believed that Scripture teaches that God speaks through "the still, small voice," as well as through people, circumstances, and even dreams.[81] In this way he upheld the pre-eminence of Scripture while affirming the other vehicles through which God speaks. Simpson was clear in his conviction that the enlargement of life and work relates consistently to an ever-deepening participation in the Scriptures:

We do not need a new Bible, but we need new eyes to read our Bible and brighter light to shine upon its deep and pregnant pages. We need to see not simply a system of exegesis or a system of Biblical exposition and criticism; a thorough knowledge of the letter and its wondrous framework of history, geography, antiquities and ancient languages; but a vivid, large and spiritual conception of what it means for us and what God's thought in it for each of us is. We want to take it as the message of heaven to the twentieth century and our generation, nay, the living voice of the Son of God to us this very hour, and to see in it the very idea which He Himself has for our life and work.[82]

From these words, one can conclude also that Simpson united the study of theology with the spiritual quest. He did not deny the essential element of sound "exegesis," but claimed that it was inadequate if placed outside the spiritual quest. For him, the purpose of spiritual theology is to integrate theology and spirituality. His writings represent a fine contribution to this integration.

From the above account, it is accurate to conclude that A.B. Simpson drank willingly from various streams of Christian spirituality, since these streams represented for him dimensions of biblical truth. His openness to other expressions of Christian spirituality suggests that he sought truth from wherever it could be found in the Christian tradition, even if he did not agree entirely with a doctrine of a particular writer. One may certainly conclude that the example of Albert B. Simpson provides a justification for the exploration of the rich treasury of devotional literature in the history of the Church, including the writings of Simpson himself. Is it possible that such a study might lead us to "turning points" in prayer also?

ENDNOTES

1. Richard F. Lovelace, *Dynamics of Spiritual Life* (Downers Grove: Inter-Varsity Press, 1977), p. 11.

2. The writer uses the terms spiritual theology and Christian spirituality interchangeably. What do these expressions mean? Richard Lovelace, in his *Dynamics of Spiritual Life*, describes spiritual theology as "a

discipline combining the history and the theology of Christian experience." He observes, "Catholic Christians have long recognized the existence and central importance of this study, and it is time that Protestants realized that they share with Catholics a deep interest and a rich heritage in Christian spirituality (p. 11)." Lovelace calls for a new interest in "the theology of the Christian life" among Protestants. He posits this interest as vital to the health of the church, "Since virtually all the problems in the church including bad theology issue from defective spirituality, the attention given to spiritual theology—that is, to the question of how to keep all the cells in the body of Christ in optimum health and running order—should culminate in a new vitality in the church" (p. 58). According to Louis Bouyer, in his introduction to the three-volume work, *A History of Christian Spirituality* (New York: Desclee Co., 1963), spiritual theology "instead of studying the objects of belief...in the abstract...studies the reactions which these objects arouse in the religious consciousness." Moreover, he suggests that spiritual theology "concentrates...above all on prayer and on everything connected with prayer...on religious exercises as well as religious experiences." It is not that the study of doctrine is unimportant to Bouyer. He admits that the study of doctrine is "the basis of spiritual theology" (Vol. 1, pp. vii-xi). Kenneth Leech, in his *Experiencing God: Theology as Spirituality* (San Francisco: Harper & Row, 1985), furnishes us with an excellent definition of spiritual theology, "the uniting of theological work with the spiritual quest...a transforming knowledge of God, a knowledge in which the seeker is deeply changed. All true theology is about transformation, about changing human beings and changing the world, in and through the encounter with the true God" (Preface). What are the sources of spiritual theology? The central and pre-eminent source is Scripture (2 Tim. 3:16-17). A secondary source of Christian spirituality, but important nonetheless, is the spiritual classics. Ernest Larkin, in his article, "A Method of Reading the Spiritual Classics," suggests their value lies not in their being an additional source beyond Scripture, but rather "derivatives of the Scriptures, reflections on that same light... refracted through the prism of particular times and persons and places. ...They do not occupy the same hallowed standing as the sacred books (Scripture)...(they are) commentary on the Christian reality...witnesses to the ever-recurring mystery of Christ present....They are a special hermeneutic, i.e., an interpretation of God's Word, offering enlightenment on the original revelation for different persons and circumstances" (*Review for Religious* 40 [May-June, 1981]: 388). For Neil Hamilton, in his *Maturing in the Christian Life* (Philadelphia: Geneva Press, 1984), the spiritual classics are commentaries on the "experience of Spirit," and invite us to participate in the multi-faceted experience of the Spirit in the history of the Church (pp. 105-107). Why should an evangelical Christian consult the great treasury of devotional literature formulated throughout the history of the Church? Part of the answer comes from "a representative group of evangelical leaders" who formulated a document entitled, "The Chicago Call: An Appeal to Evangelicals," which addressed the need for evangelical maturity. The statement begins with this confession: "We confess that we have often lost the fullness of our Christian heritage, too readily assuming that the Scriptures and the Spirit make us independent of the past. In so doing, we have become theologically shallow, spiritually weak, blind to the work of God in others and married to our cultures." In developing the call to spirituality, the participants declare: "We need to rediscover the devotional resources of the whole church, including the evangelical traditions of Pietism and Puritanism. We call for an exploration of devotional practice in all traditions within the church in order to deepen our relationship both with Christ and with other Christians," Robert Webber, *Common Roots: A Call to Evangelical Maturity* (Grand Rapids: Zondervan, 1978), pp. 251-256.

3. A.B. Simpson, *The Holy Spirit*, 2 Vols. (Harrisburg, PA: Christian Publications, Inc., n.d.), 1:160-162.

4. Ibid., 1:161.

5. Ibid., 1:162.

6. A.E. Thompson, *A.B. Simpson: His Life and Work* (Harrisburg, PA: Christian Publications, Inc., 1960), p. 181 (hereafter cited as *A.B. Simpson*).

7. Ibid., p. 171.

8. Ibid., pp. 171-183.

9. Henry Wilson, *The Internal Christ* (New York City: Alliance Press Co., 1908), pp. 8-9.

10. Thompson, *A.B. Simpson*, p. 185.

11. I Thess. 5:17 (NASV).

12. A.B. Simpson, *Days of Heaven on Earth* (Harrisburg, PA.: Christian Publications, Inc., 1945), p. 53.

13. Ibid., p. 197.

14. G.P. Pardington, *The Still, Small Voice* (New York: Christian Alliance Publishing Company, 1902), p. 175.

15. Thompson, *A.B. Simpson*, p. 181.

16. Arthur T. Pierson, *Forward Movements of the Last Half Century* (New York: Garland Publishing, Inc., 1984), pp. 11-12.

17. Ibid., p. 65.

18. Gordon S. Wakefield, ed., *The Westminster Dictionary of Christian Spirituality* (Philadelphia: The Westminster Press, 1983), p. 328.

19. Thomas S. Kepler, comp., *An Anthology of Devotional Literature* (Grand Rapids: Baker Book House, 1977), p. 460.

20. Harry Verploegh (comp. and ed.), *A.W. Tozer: An Anthology* (Camp Hill: Christian Publications, 1984), p. xi.

21. William Backhouse and James Janson (comp.), *A Guide to True Peace or The Excellency of Inward and Spiritual Prayer* (New York: Harper and Brothers, 1946), pp. vii, xi-xii.

22. Wakefield, *Westminister Dictionary*, p. 95.

23. Thomas Keating, M. Basil Pennington, and Thomas E. Clarke, *Finding Grace at the Center* (Still River: St. Bede Publications, 1978), pp. 35-36.

24. M. Basil Pennington, *Centering Prayer* (Garden City: Image Books, 1982), pp. 26-30.

25. Ibid., pp. 30-32.

26. Colm Luibheid and Norman Russell, trans., *John Climacus: The Ladder of Divine Ascent*, The Classics of Western Spirituality series (New York: Paulist Press, 1982), pp. 261-263, 268.

27. Ibid., pp. 269-270.

28. John Meyendorff, ed., *Gregory Palamas — The Triads*, The Classics of Western Spirituality series (New York: Paulist Press, 1983), pp. 1-4.

29. Douglas V. Steere, *Quaker Spirituality — Selected Writings*, The Classics of Western Spirituality series (New York: Paulist Press, 1984), p. 69.

30. Ibid., p. 83.

31. Ibid., p. 129.

32. A.B. Simpson, "The Secret of Prayer," *Living Truths* 4 (March 1904): 121.

33. A.B. Simpson, *Walking in the Spirit* (Harrisburg, PA: Christian Publications, Inc., n.d.), p. 39.

34. Ibid., pp. 40-42.

35. Ibid., p. 42.

36. Simpson, "The Secret of Prayer," pp. 125-126.

37. William Johnson, ed., *The Cloud of Unknowing* (Garden City: Image Books, 1973), pp. 48-49.

38. Ibid., pp. 48-49.

39. Ibid., p. 111.

40. Simpson, "The Secret of Prayer," p. 126.

41. Simpson, *The Holy Spirit*, 1:160-162.

42. Simpson, *Walking in the Spirit*, pp. 128-129.

43. Simpson, *The Holy Spirit*, 1:161.

44. A.B. Simpson, *The Christ Life* (Harrisburg, PA: Christian Publications, Inc., 1925), pp. 72, 74, 76.

45. Meyendorff, *The Triads*, pp. 42-44, 46, 49.

46. Johnson, *The Cloud of Unknowing*, p. 96.

47. Ibid., p. 114.

48. Ibid., p. 43.

49. Ibid., p. 99.

50. Ibid., p. 56.

51. Ford Lewis Battles, trans. and ed., *The Piety of John Calvin* (Grand Rapids: Baker Book House, 1978), p. 98.

52. Ibid., p. 99.

53. Ibid.

54. Peter Erb, trans., *Johann Arndt — True Christianity,* The Classics of Western Spirituality series (New York: Paulist Press, 1979), pp. xi, xv, 1-16.

55. Ibid., p. 120.

56. Ibid., pp. 268-269.

57. Ibid., pp. 268-270.

58. Paul G. Stanwood, ed., *William Law—A Serious Call to a Devout and Holy Life—The Spirit of Love*, The Classics of Western Spirituality series (New York: Paulist Press, 1978), pp. 198-200.

59. Ibid., pp. 209-216.

60. A.B. Simpson, *A Larger Christian Life* (Harrisburg, PA: Christian Publications, Inc., 1979), p. 142.

61. Ibid.

62. Simpson, *Walking in the Spirit*, p. 50.

63. A.B. Simpson, *Echoes of the New Creation* (Harrisburg, PA: Christian Publications, Inc., 1965), pp. 39-41.

64. Simpson, *The Christ Life*, p. 69.

65. A.B. Simpson, "Deeper," *Christian and Missionary Alliance Weekly* (October 6, 1897): 345.

66. Simpson, *The Christ Life*, p. 69.

67. Ibid., pp. 69, 72-73.

68. Simpson, "Deeper," p. 345.

69. Douglas V. Steere, ed., *The Practice of the Presence of God*, Living Selections From Devotional Classics series (Nashville, TN: The Upper Room, 1950), p. 24.

70. Ibid., p. 12.

71. Frank Whaling, *John and Charles Wesley—Selected Writings and Hymns*, The Classics of Western Spirituality series (New York: Paulist Press, 1981), pp. 303-306.

72. Ibid., p. 370.

73. Helen Bacovcin, trans., *The Way of a Pilgrim* (Garden City: Image Books, 1978), p. 18.

74. Ibid., p. 83.

75. Douglas V. Steere, ed., *A Testament of Devotion*, Living Selections From Devotional Classics series (Nashville, TN: The Upper Room, 1955), pp. 26-27.

76. Ibid., pp. 29-30.

77. *Hymns of the Christian Life* (Harrisburg, PA: Christian Publications, Inc., 1978), p. 251.

78. Simpson, *Echoes of the New Creation*, p. 40.

79. A.B. Simpson, "Editorial," *Living Truths* (July 1906), p. 385.

80. Thompson, *A.B. Simpson*, p. 185.

81. Ibid., pp. 119-121. Thompson documented a night dream that Simpson had, and considered its influence on his missionary vision. In a letter written by W.W. Simpson on Oct. 17, 1916, and addressed to A.B. Simpson, W.W. Simpson suggested to A.B. Simpson that God spoke through tongues in the new dispensation of the Spirit rather than through the "still small voice." W.W. Simpson declared, "The 'Still Small Voice' belongs to a past dispensation, the mighty sound of Pentecost suits this age better." A copy of the letter is located in the archives of Canadian Bible College/Canadian Theological Seminary.

82. Simpson, *A Larger Christian Life*, pp. 54-55.

DWAYNE RATZLAFF

Dwayne Ratzlaff received a B.A. from the University of Saskatchewan, an M.Div. from Canadian Theological College and, recently, a D.Min. from Asbury Theological Seminary. He has pastored Alliance churches in Dartmouth, Nova Scotia and Niagara Falls, Ontario. He is currently Assistant Professor of Pastoral Studies at Canadian Bible College, supervisor of the Preparation for Ministry program at Canadian Theological Seminary, and a Canadian Evangelist.

A.B. SIMPSON AND WORLD EVANGELIZATION

by

T.V. Thomas with Ken Draper

The life and work of Albert Benjamin Simpson cannot be considered without reference to his understanding of world evangelization. The following study will examine Simpson's life, theology and strategy of mission in the hope of enhancing our understanding of his contribution to the work of world evangelization and the vitality of the Christian & Missionary Alliance.

THE DEVELOPMENT OF A.B. SIMPSON'S PERSONAL CONCERN FOR WORLD EVANGELIZATION

Before he was born, A.B. Simpson's mother consecrated him to the Christian ministry and to missions.[1] He was baptized by the Canadian missionary, John Geddie, and many of his childhood heroes were among the greatest figures of missionary endeavour. Yet it was not until a decade into his ministry that he became interested in the evangelization of the world.

Simpson was a frail, sensitive boy who had been brought up in the full rigor of a strict Calvinism devoid of joy or humour. These early influences produced a young man who feared God

195

and wanted to appease Him. At fourteen, Simpson made his first conscious step towards God, but, as he admits, it came more out of duty than conviction.[2] His intense devotion to his high school studies led to a nervous breakdown at seventeen. Personal despair broke only after a chance encounter with a book entitled *Marshall's Gospel Mystery of Sanctification*. Here he read:

> The first good work you will ever perform is to believe on the Lord Jesus Christ...." The moment you do this, you will pass into eternal life, you will be justified from all your sins, and receive a new heart and all the gracious preparations of the Holy Spirit.[3]

He responded immediately to this invitation and experienced the conviction to reinforce the sense of commitment he had always had to the gospel ministry. In giving his life to Christ and claiming Christ's forgiveness and salvation, he did not find immediate release, but became nonetheless convinced that his salvation was sure. He regained his physical health soon after. In January, 1861, to confirm and solemnize his conversion, Simpson wrote a formal agreement covenanting his life to God.

Simpson's commitment to the ministry continued, and after teaching high school for a year, he entered Knox College in Toronto. Four years later, in 1865, he graduated, was ordained, married Margaret Henry, and took his first assignment as a Presbyterian pastor in the prestigious Knox Church, Hamilton, Ontario.

He soon gained a reputation as an able preacher and Knox Church grew steadily under his leadership, a sure confirmation to him of his call to the pastoral ministry. He was firmly committed to his church and his congregation, and to an understanding of the "regular work of the ministry"[4] which, in turn, motivated him to expend all his energies for the welfare of his own people. This localized view of the ministry led him to reject out of hand an opportunity to participate in an evangelistic campaign during his pastorate in Hamilton.

After eight years at Knox Church, Simpson had become an accomplished and respected pastor with a genuine love for the church, but as yet had none of the passion for evangelism that would soon overtake him. At this point, he answered a call to the Chestnut Street Church in Louisville, Kentucky. Chestnut

Street Church was even more prestigious than Knox and offered a generous salary. Besides, Kentucky's milder climate promised Simpson's always delicate health a reprieve from the harsh Canadian winters.

A series of crises precipitated the growth of Simpson's concern for the evangelization of the world.[5] The first of these occurred in 1874, in conjunction with an evangelistic campaign similar to the one Simpson had rejected while in Hamilton. He was one of the chief organizers of the campaign, and, impressed by its success, sought the spiritual power and infilling of the Holy Spirit to sustain him in his expanding ministry. Simpson called this experience a major turning point in his life.[6]

The renewed zeal for evangelism that resulted from this experience led Simpson to invite other Louisville churches to join together each winter for evangelism and revival. Although some declined his offer, he and his congregation took on the task of sponsoring public Sunday evening meetings. Simpson became so preoccupied with evangelization that it came to replace "the proper work of the ministry" in his mind. No longer content to be secure in a comfortable church of social equals, he sought to mobilize the whole church for evangelization. Thousands right in Louisville needed to hear the message of salvation and of life in Christ.

Perhaps the most dramatic move into which Simpson led his people was the building of a new and larger church building. He envisioned a plain, functional building to serve as a centre of evangelism, but his trustees had a more elaborate building in mind. The result was an impressive structure with a $50,000 debt. By this time, Simpson was so dedicated to evangelization that he refused to spend the money on buildings that should have been used to advance the gospel[7] and he would not dedicate the new Tabernacle until it was completely paid for. He left Louisville for New York in early 1880 in order to gain greater freedom to pursue his goal of evangelizing the masses. The Tabernacle remained debt-ridden and undedicated on his departure.

It was at this time that Simpson received his missionary vision. His first response was to go to China, but this proved impractical. More practical was his decision to advance the cause of missions by informing the Christian public of the need for and progress of world evangelization. He chose the illustrated periodical as his medium because of its growing popularity.

Simpson received his call to Thirteenth Street Church in New York City in 1879. Where else but New York, the North American centre of missionary activity would one go to launch a missionary magazine?[8] What better place to engage in the work of evangelization than the continent's greatest metropolis? Simpson agreed to take on the new pastorate on condition that the church officers would unite with him in a popular religious movement to reach the unchurched masses.[9] They agreed to it in principle, but found the practice rather less appealing, preferring their pastor to spend his time with the more socially advanced classes.[10]

After a little more than a year of very active ministry in New York, Simpson became ill and had to interrupt his pastoral duties. In 1881, he visited the famous convention grounds of Old Orchard, Maine, and heard Dr. Charles Cullis speak regarding divine healing. More impressive to Simpson than Cullis' sermons were the testimonies of the many who had been healed. Having heard the message, Simpson went directly to his Bible to confirm the teaching.[11] Convinced that the message of divine healing for the body "was part of Christ's glorious Gospel for a sinful and suffering world,"[12] he solemnly claimed this grace as he had previously claimed salvation and the power of the Holy Spirit.[13] He also dedicated himself to promoting this doctrine in his teaching. After this experience, Simpson remained free of the recurring health problems that had previously plagued his ministry.

From this time on, the message of the Lord for the body became one of the four pillars of Simpson's Gospel, yet he always kept it in perspective. For example, when the prominent teacher on healing, John Alexander Dowie, invited him to join in a cross-country campaign, he replied, "Dear Brother Dowie, I have four wheels on my chariot. I cannot agree to neglect the other three while I devote my time to one."[14]

Simpson's healing did not produce spiritual tunnel vision; if anything, it broadened his perspective, gave him the confidence to trust his Lord more completely, and provided him with the spiritual courage and physical confidence to set out on his own. In November of 1881, Simpson resigned his pastorate against the best advice of his church officers, his colleagues and his wife. His experience in Louisville and in New York had convinced him that established churches did not provide the kind of structure needed to launch an evangelistic work of the sort he had in mind.[15] Having given up his pastor's salary, house, and social position, Simpson set to work evangelizing the masses. He had previously published a missionary magazine, naming it *The Gospel In All Lands*. His ill health had forced him to relinquish control of this periodical, but he later founded a new one entitled *The Word, Work and World*, the purpose of which was to bring information about missions to a wide audience.

As Simpson's concern for world evangelization grew, his work expanded into a variety of ministries. Simpson's Tabernacle in New York City, soon after its inception, was organized as an independent church.[16] It served as a base for evangelistic meetings, including summer tent ministries.[17] It ran several rescue missions, an orphanage, a home for unwed mothers, and housed the Missionary Training School which provided trained workers for Simpson's evangelistic efforts.[18] Simpson was blessed in living to see much of his vision accomplished. He maintained an active role in the leadership of the Alliance until just a year before his death in October, 1919.

SIMPSON'S THEOLOGY OF WORLD EVANGELIZATION

Simpson was not a professional theologian nor did he claim to be one. He was a pastor, and the vast majority of his published material began as sermons presented in his own Gospel Tabernacle or at one of the many conventions he spoke at each year. His concern for world evangelization led him to develop an evangelistically-oriented theology. Having no need to be rigorously systematic, Simpson thought, wrote and spoke about the matters that concerned him most. In the process, he developed a unique theology of missions that provided direction for his effort and for a century of Alliance work around the world.

Simpson's theology of evangelization begins at the point of need: the world is cut off from God and thousands are in danger of eternal destruction. Man's sin has caused God's wrath to fall upon him and the lost must hear the message of salvation if they are to have hope. The preached word must therefore concentrate on hope, not wrath, and all the more so because Christ's saving love is the supreme principle of His life:[19] the love of God sent Christ into the world[20] and also sends Christ's followers out among their fellows[21] to proclaim what has been accomplished in Christ. Simpson made the principle of Christ's saving love the center of his theology.

Simpson's theology of mission stems from a trinitarian understanding of God. The Father sends the Son, Christ commissions His followers, and the Holy Spirit continues and completes Christ's work. Evangelization is a work of God in which the entire Trinity is actively involved. Yet God is pleased to accomplish that work through human agency. It is here, in partnership with God, that Simpson found his own field of endeavour.[22]

Simpson never intended that the Alliance he had formed in 1887 would become a separate denomination; thus, he did not provide a catechism or confession for his followers. Instead, he affirmed all of the accepted creeds and doctrines of the Protestant tradition.[23] Yet he had a keen sense of what was unique about the movement he led. He summarized the uniqueness of the Alliance as follows:

> First, it stands for an absolute faith in supernatural things and a supernatural God. It represents a Christianity which is out-and-out for God, and it gathers to it those and only those who believe something, and believe it with all their heart and soul and strength. In a word, it represents intense spiritual earnestness. And secondly, along with this as the outgo and overflow of this deeper life of faith and consecration, it represents intense aggressiveness in its work for God, and overflow and outgo that is ever-reaching on to the regions beyond, and seeking to pass on to others the blessings we have ourselves received.[24]

In 1887, the year the Christian Alliance and the Evangelical Missionary Alliance were formed, Simpson stressed that the Alliance was, above all, committed to evangelism.[25] He called for "self-denying efforts to reach the neglected classes at our doors by evangelistic and Christian work adjusted to reach and save them. And abroad ... to go into all the world and preach the

200

gospel to every creature."[26] The classical statement of Alliance distinctiveness is Simpson's Four-Fold Gospel. Christ as Saviour, Sanctifier, Healer and Coming King provided the focus that gave the movement identity from its inception.

Christ as Saviour

Simpson preached hundreds of evangelistic sermons.[27] He believed that in so doing, he was only fulfilling his obligation as one of the saved,[28] as one who had taken on the character of Christ. Indeed, for Simpson, every true Christian is a reincarnation of Christ,[29] and so has no choice but to show Christ's love and take His message to the world. The sheer joy of the gospel and its power to change lives provides the motivation to evangelize.[30]

In Simpson's view, the Church as a whole also has a responsibility to evangelize, because it is a people called out by God for service.[31] The Church provides the individual with the institutional as well as the spiritual support necessary for evangelization. It has received Christ's power through the Spirit and is equipped for this service.[32]

> The church is called to aggressive work for the world's salvation. This is the last great mission. It is to win souls, to rescue sinners, to evangelize the world, to gather in great multitudes from among the lost, and win them for Jesus and Heaven.[33]

Simpson believed that the North American Church of his day was squandering its resources because it was not actively involved in evangelization. In his view, the experience of salvation carries with it an obligation to work tirelessly to reach the lost so that they may receive the same benefits as the saved.

Christ as Sanctifier

Simpson stressed the connection between sanctification and evangelization even more than he did the connection between salvation and evangelization. He could not even conceive of evangelism apart from commitment to the consecrated life. In a

201

missionary sermon preached to the Nyack Convention of 1899, Simpson stated, "All missionary enterprise must have its source in deeper spiritual life."[34] With this in mind, he considered most North American churchgoers too worldly to be of any use as witnesses. He even went so far as to call their efforts counter-productive.[35] Without deeply committed Christians given entirely over to Christ, evangelization was certain to stall out on one of the many obstacles erected by the modern world.

Simpson also taught that true sanctification produces evangelistic zeal. "The result of [sanctification] is unselfish and aggressive work. No soul can receive this deep, divine over-flowing life and remain henceforth unto himself."[36] Sanctifi-cation is not a pleasure devised for the comfort of the Christian, but a call to, and empowering for, service.[37]

Acts 1:8, a favorite text of Simpson's, promises this empowering: "Ye shall receive the power of the Holy Ghost coming upon you, and ye shall be witnesses unto me both in Jerusalem, and in all Judea, and in Samaria, and unto the uttermost part of the earth."[38] Evangelism, therefore, is not "the exercise of our natural powers and talents, but the sense of the special gifts of the Great Paraclete."[39] It is not human ability that accomplishes the work, "...not power, but God Himself [working] in us and with us and beyond us and under-taking the great task with His own mighty hand."[40]

Simpson's realization of the need for the indwelling of God is evident in his continual call for believers to experience the filling of the Holy Spirit. However, his understanding of Acts 1:8 also convinced him that the giving of the Holy Spirit is conditional upon the proper use of His power:

> We do not get power as an abstract quality, but we receive the Holy Ghost, and He is the power. 'And ye shall be my witnesses unto the uttermost parts of the earth.' It is His last word, and it is connected with and dependent upon receiving the power. And connects the condition with the promise.[41]

Finally, the empowering of the Holy Spirit provides the motivation that makes service to God a joyful opportunity: "The baptism of the Holy Ghost is not worth anything if it does not fire your soul with a love like His, a love that forgets even your own spiritual need in pouring out your life like Him for others."[42]

202

Christ as Healer

Divine healing played a large role in Simpson's personal life and ministry. Although he did not explicitly link healing with evangelization, his emphasis on "the Lord for the body" brought his trust in God out of an exclusively spiritual realm and into the phsyical. Simpson believed that God cares about all aspects of life and wants the believer to appropriate His full provision. God can be trusted not only for bodily healing, but for a whole range of physical needs.[43] Simpson demonstrated his commitment to this teaching in his Berachah Homes. Here the sick could find rest, hear weekly teaching on biblical healing, and receive the laying on of hands for the restoration of health.

Despite the fact that he saw no explicit connection between healing and evangelism, Simpson believed in "power evangelism," namely, that healings and other powerful manifestations of the Spirit would accompany the preaching of the Gospel (Mark 6:17).[44] Acts, in particular, demonstrated to him the scriptural warrant for this contention. By 1894, he could report regarding Alliance overseas ministries "the healing of diseases and...manifestations of the supernatural power of God, as in Apostolic days, even in the midst of heathen darkness."[45] The combined testimony of Scripture and experience made him willing to claim signs and wonders as a part of preaching the Gospel in supernatural power. He challenged people to pray that such signs would accompany the Gospel wherever and whenever they would aid the work of world evangelization.[46]

Christ as Coming King

Simpson had an overwhelming sense that the Lord would return to earth during his own generation.[47] He believed that global events had reached a watershed and that the resulting opportunity for world evangelization would not be repeated.[48] As an ardent premillenialist, he did not share the postmillenial convictions of most Christian leaders of his day, for he could not find any evidence for this optimistic view, either in world events or in Scripture:

History laughs at our vain attempts and turns to

confusion our pretentions to save ourselves. Even Christianity is not going to gradually develop into a Millennium of Gospel light and universal righteousness. The prophetic picture of the New Testament tells us of a world growing worse as well as better, of the increase of wickedness on one hand and also of righteousness on the other, so that the true philosophy is Optimism and Pessimism. The bad is getting worse, the good is getting better. But they shall both move in together until that crisis hour when the Son of man shall come in startling suddenness and angel hands shall separate the good from among the bad.[49]

Simpson maintained that the role of the Church is not primarily to bring about social reform, but "to gather out of the nations of this world a 'people for His name.'" Similarly, he understood the purpose of the Gospel ministry to be: "To reach the people of every race and time who are to form the bride of the Lamb, and the one great millennial host who are to welcome Jesus at His coming and share with Him the dominion of the new age which His advent is to bring."[50] Through the work of evangelization, the Church will gather together the building blocks of the millennial kingdom and await the return of the Builder Himself.[51]

Simpson stressed that world evangelization would not only make ready a people for the King's return, but could in fact speed His coming. From Matthew 24:14 he argued passionately that Christ is ready and waiting to return as soon as the Church has fulfilled its obligation:

We know that our missionary work is not in vain, but in addition to the blessing it is to bring to the souls we lead to Christ; best of all, it is to bring Christ Himself back again. It puts in our hands the key to the bridal chamber and the lever that will hasten His return.[52]

The teaching of the Coming King lay as near to the heart of Simpson's theology of world evangelization as salvation and sanctification, and, like them, it also provided him with a great motivation to do missionary work: "I cannot understand how any man or woman can believe in the Lord's coming and not be a missionary, or at least committed to the work of missions with every power of his being."[53]

Simpson's eschatology gave shape and structure to his thinking about world evangelization and provided a basis for action to this end. He was committed to the evangelization of the whole word, and yet he was fully prepared for a limited response to the message. To bring about Christ's return the Church did not need to convert the whole world, but to call out a people whom God Himself had prepared.[54]

Simpson was also concerned to understand the unique light that each of the Gospels sheds on the Great Commission. Matthew demonstrates concern for nations rather than individuals (Matthew 24:14 and 28:19).[55] Simpson interpreted this concern as practical recognition of the problem of a limited response: the Church has a responsibility to ensure that all parts of the world have at least the chance to respond to Christ's saving love.[56]

> This great commission has never yet been fully realized. It contemplates a world-wide evangelization so glorious and complete that no nation, nor tribe, nor tongue shall be overlooked. It calls us, especially, to look at the nations rather than the individuals of the race, and to see that the unevangelized peoples are the first objects of our care....[57]

Simpson responded to Matthew's concern for the nations by looking for new and neglected areas of the globe to evangelize. However, he was never so caught up with this enterprise that he failed to be concerned for individuals. In Mark's Gospel, he found the commission to individuals: "Go ye into all the world and preach the gospel to every creature."[58]

From Luke's writings Simpson determined the order in which the work of world evangelization was to take place, "'to the Jew first' and the nations" (Luke 24:47; cf. Acts 1:8).[59] He discovered a complementary teaching in the parable of the King's supper (Luke 14:16-24). The invited guests are people already attending church. Those in the streets and the lanes are those unchurched in North America and Europe, and those in the hedges and highways are "the heathen and the lost" overseas.[60] Finally, from the emphasis on the believer's union with Christ in John's Gospel, Simpson concluded that Christians must recognize Christ Himself as the source of their power and authority in evangelism (John 20:21).[61]

Simpson's commitment to world evangelization stems from two overarching concerns: to bring salvation to the lost and to speed the arrival of the millennial kingdom. These constantly recur and intertwine in his writing and speaking. Underlying them is the central feature of Simpson's theology, the principle of God's saving love manifested in Christ Jesus. Yet Christ is not only Saviour but also Sanctifier, Healer and Coming King. Each of these components of the Four-Fold Gospel had its special significance for Simpson's program of world evangelization. Salvation and sanctification are necessary to and necessitate evangelization. Healing and other supernatural workings of the Spirit establish and confirm the work and the proclamation of this Gospel to every nation which will hasten the return of the Coming King.

SIMPSON'S STRATEGY FOR WORLD EVANGELIZATION

A.B. Simpson's strategy for world evangelization flowed out of his theological understanding of mission and consisted simply of two components: preparation and execution.

Preparation

Simpson believed that preparation for missions begins at home and that preparation for evangelization begins in the heart of each Christian. If the work was not being accomplished it was because Christian people had not been taking their salvation and sanctification seriously.[62] For world evangelization to begin in earnest, Christians in the homeland must experience revival and recommit themselves to holy living[63] and consecration.[64] Only then would the power of God be unleashed throughout the world.

For Simpson, home missions and foreign missions were part of the same work—calling a people to Christ. However, he believed that the greatest need for aggressive missionary action lay overseas and that the Bride of Christ was to be truly international. As a result, the Alliance has, from the beginning,

206

stressed overseas missions.

Simpson's ecclesiology defined the primary goal of the Church to be evangelization: "Every Christian owes it as a debt of common honesty that he shall give at least to one of the present generation of Christless men and women one chance for eternal life."[65] He believed that world evangelization begins with personal evangelism, each Christian active in his own sphere of influence.[66]

Simpson repeatedly stressed that the responsibility for spreading the Gospel did not belong exclusively to full-time Christian workers, but to every Christian: "[The Christian] is not obedient unless he is doing all in his power to send the gospel to the heathen world."[67] However, one can fulfill this obligation regardless of one's vocation[68] so long as one's resources and interests are focused on world evangelization.[69] Simpson urged that committed people called by God from every walk of life leave their business or trade and take the gospel to the lost. However, he realized that not everyone could go. He himself, despite his clear call and great missionary zeal, had stayed behind,[70] for he believed that those who "tarried by the stuff" were equal partners in the spreading of the gospel with those who went overseas.

Those who stayed in the homeland could exercise their role as partners primarily through prayer and financial giving. Only with the support of flourishing local churches, like the one at Antioch in New Testament times, could Alliance missions hope to succeed. For Simpson, this sort of cooperative arrangement was the only biblical model for the missionary enterprise.[71]

Simpson gave prayer a prominent role in the missionary enterprise of the Alliance, calling it "our greatest spiritual power."[72] He believed that evangelism was God's work and that only through constant prayer would the human activity of proclaiming the gospel indeed remain God's work.[73] Prayer ensures that the proper workers are raised up, that funds will be available to send them and that they will be empowered by the Spirit to do the work given them.[74]

As far as financial giving is concerned, Simpson believed that American businessmen had gained wealth and power with a divine purpose.[75] He contended that if the United States and the other wealthy nations of Christendom were to stop squandering their great wealth and use it for its true purpose, the evangelization of the world would be accomplished in one generation.[76]

Simpson also used educational means to mobilize local congregations for the task of world evangelization. Taking his inspiration from Acts 10 and 11, he concluded that as the Spirit had convinced Peter to evangelize the gentiles, so the leadership of the Alliance had to inform congregations of the plight of the lost overseas and lead them to action.[77] Simpson worked tirelessly to this end. He initiated the publication of the *Gospel In All Lands*, began *The Word, Work and World, Living Truths*, and the other Alliance periodicals, and even wrote a missionary travelogue. His many speaking engagements also constantly brought the need for missions before the Church. In addition, Simpson evidently invented that unique blend of Bible conference, camp meeting, evangelistic crusade and missionary promotion meeting that came to be known as the missionary convention.[78] Simpson held such conventions across North America, calling hundreds to Christ, to deeper spiritual life and to a commitment to world evangelization.

The final stage in Simpson's strategy of preparation for evangelization was to determine which areas of the world to evangelize.[79] Simpson used his many contacts with missionary associations[80] and relied on the advice of missions specialists as a basis for choosing the fields of greatest need and greatest opportunity. He refused to build on another's foundation, preferring to evangelize the, as yet, unevangelized. This was the essence of what he called "aggressive Christianity," which continued alongside the docile variety that prevailed during his day.[81] Moreover, because his eschatology promised the return of Christ when every nation had heard, he was constantly looking for those areas and peoples that had not yet heard the gospel.

Once the Alliance had selected a target area, it studied the condition, customs and needs of the people in the target area to determine a plan of evangelistic attack. Simpson kept detailed statistical records on unevangelized peoples from New York City to the ends of the earth. Thus, whenever he undertook an evangelistic campaign in New York City, he knew exactly where the greatest need lay and planned his activities to meet it.[82] Careful preparation, both at home and in the foreign field, were necessary if God's human agents in the work of world evangelization were to do their part.

Execution

In implementing his plan for world evangelization, Simpson revealed the practical man behind the visionary. Under his leadership, the Alliance movement spread across North America and became the base of operations for the work overseas. He organized both the home and overseas works according to the same principles.

Simpson's theology of world evangelization began with the saving love of God reaching out to lost man. His practice of world evangelization began at exactly the same place. Although he rejected the Social Gospel, Simpson could see the benefits of work to alleviate poverty. Therefore, he was actively involved among the poor in New York and sponsored agricultural services, orphanages, schools and medical facilities overseas. However, in so doing, he was not intending to change society but to change the lives of men and women:

> We are not called to a life of protest, to denounce evil and talk about righteousness. We are called to teach the children of God...the divine way of overcoming sin, the power of grace which God has revealed to us that will break the power of the law of sin and death.[83]

Simpson continued to rely on the "foolishness of preaching"; preaching alone could give men and women the chance for salvation and preaching alone would hasten Christ's return to earth. "Our work is to tell the simple story of His life, death and resurrection, and to preach the Gospel in its purity."[84]

Simpson considered love to be the first principle of Christ's life and believed that His ambassadors should have it as the driving force behind their own work. With this in mind, he rented theatres and abandoned buildings in unsavory neighborhoods in an effort to identify with and to reach the people in North America who had been ignored by established churches. He recommended this same principle to his workers overseas: "If [we] can better reach China by wearing Chinese dress and living in Chinese houses, [we] give up the customs and comforts of civilization that [we] may gain some."[85]

Simpson also managed to meet the need for both intensive and extensive effort in missions.[86] Alliance work was extensive in its attempt to proclaim the gospel to every nation and

209

intensive in providing for the long-term nurture of converts. Simpson sought to take a balanced approach to evangelization because, as we have seen, he considered the call to evangelize the nations and the call to evangelize individuals to be the essential components of the Great Commission. Moreover, these two emphases corresponded with his concern that believers take Christ as their Sanctifier as well as Saviour.

Simpson had a strong aversion to institutionalism and advocated simple and inexpensive methods of advancing the Gospel.[87] However, his commitment to planning and field research indicate that he did not believe in sacrificing orderliness for simplicity. At the same time, he had no fear that a well-administered organization would hinder his workers from relying on the spontaneous working of the Holy Spirit.[88] He simply sought an institutional framework that could lay the ground work for evangelization without making it top-heavy or unresponsive to the directives of the Spirit.

Simpson was able to devise such a framework because he understood evangelism to be the responsibility of the whole Church, not just one group or denomination. Thus he had the freedom to work in conjunction, rather than in competition with other outreach organizations.[89] In any event, he did not intend to create a denomination, but rather an interdenominational movement[90] of independent fellowships dedicated to living the deeper truths of Christ and to evangelization. To ensure the development of independent churches in North America and indigenous churches overseas, Simpson insisted on self-supporting local churches, training for new converts, and strong, capable local leadership.[91]

Simpson extended the principle of sacrificial giving[92] to Alliance branches overseas. He hoped, in so doing, to encourage new churches to mature in their responsibilities to God. Once they became self-supporting, such churches would be able to release funds for the further promotion of the Gospel. Simpson also introduced a new concept in funding missions. Although the Alliance was truly a "faith mission," Simpson believed that missionaries would be wasting both time and resources in trying to raise their own support. For this reason, he initiated a system of living allowances by which missionaries were to be paid according to need on the field rather than on the basis of skill, ability or experience.[93]

To train the "aggressive Christians" needed for the evangelization of the world, Simpson established the Missionary Training School in his Gospel Tabernacle in New York.[94] He also established Bible Schools overseas to train local Christians.[95] He placed a premium on local leadership, as we have already seen, and insisted that the North American pattern be duplicated overseas: "Native assistants, especially, should be afforded all possible help and encouragement; as they become able, they should be allowed to bear responsibility, and the element of foreign teaching, pastoral care, and supervision be gradually withdrawn."[96] This measure, more than any other, has ensured the development under the Alliance of indigenous independent churches overseas.

Simpson's descriptions of the peoples with whom Alliance missions worked contain the colonialist and paternalistic vocabulary that characterized the age of imperialism. Although modern Christians attuned to the present North/South debate and the contemporary language of international relations will find him offensive at this point, Simpson's brand of paternalism with its commitment to the building of indigenous churches was healthier than that of most of his contemporaries. While colonial governors and the majority of Protestant missions hesitated to give any real responsibility to nationals, Simpson insisted that Christians overseas take responsibility for an enterprise that lay close to his heart. Thus Simpson's theological understanding of the need for world evangelization and his commitment to evangelism as an activity of the entire Church ensured that his followers spread a Gospel devoid of many of the cultural accretions that Western missions tended to include in their presentations. Alliance missionaries were not to establish permanent mission stations, but to develop indigenous churches. As the church matured, the missionaries were to train local people to take their place. This released missionaries to penetrate as yet unreached communities.[97]

CONCLUSION

A.B. Simpson dedicated his life to God at seventeen years of age, and from that time was willing to follow God's direction.

That willingness led him to experience in his own life the sanctifying power of the Holy Spirit and the healing of his body, which were to form such a vital part of his message. Simpson was led by these experiences, first to vigorous efforts for evangelization in North America, and then to create an independent movement dedicated to this task around the world.

Simpson's thinking developed as he was actively engaged in pastoral and outreach work. A combination of significant experiences, careful study and an exceptional mind created a theology that was ideally suited to the work to which Simpson felt called. His theology demanded that the church fulfill Christ's mandate for world evangelization before His return. Simpson's goal was to help mobilize every member of the Church of Christ to be actively involved to this end.

Simpson's theological insights and organizational ability have bequeathed a healthy legacy to the Christian and Missionary Alliance. The Alliance is, in fact, a worldwide alliance of Christian individuals and congregations working to build Christ's Church. As Simpson required, the result of evangelization is not merely a head count of converts, but believers living holy lives and committed to service. The continuing Alliance commitment to building strong congregations and leaders engaged in the global task stands, more than anything else, as a tribute to Albert Benjamin Simpson.

ENDNOTES

1. A.W. Tozer, *Wingspread: Albert B. Simpson — A Study in Spiritual Altitude* (Harrisburg, PA: Christian Publications, 1943), p. 12.

2. Simpson's account of his conversion is recorded by A.E. Thompson in *The Life of A.B. Simpson* (Harrisburg, PA: Christian Publications, 1920), pp. 13-23.

3. Ibid., pp. 16-17.

4. Ibid., p. 44.

5. A.B. Simpson, "A Story of Providence," *Living Truths* 6 (March 1907): 150-151. (Hereafter cited as "Providence.")

6. Thompson, *Life of A.B. Simpson*, p. 65.

7. Simpson expresses this view rather strongly in an editorial in *Living Truths* 2 (June 1903): 299.

8. Tozer, *Wingspread*, p. 66.

9. "Providence," p. 150.

10. Tozer, *Wingspread*, p. 68.

11. Ibid., p. 79.

12. Ibid., p. 81.

13. Simpson wrote a solemn covenant with God on this occasion just as he had at his conversion. Thompson records this in his *Life of A.B. Simpson*, pp. 75-76.

14. Tozer, *Wingspread*, p. 135.

15. "The Gospel Tabernacle," *The Word, Work and World* 3 (March 1883): 45.

16. "Providence," pp. 152-153.

17. For an account of an organizational meeting planning strategy for tent ministries, see: "Tent Work in New York City," *Living Truths* 6 (June 1907): 345-352.

18. A summary of the current ministries at Alliance Branches was recorded in each issue of *The Word, Work and World*. See for example: *The Word, Work and World* 9 (special no., 1887): 84, for a view of the range of activities Simpson oversaw.

19. This theme is expanded by Simpson in "Christ, Our Model, Motive and Motive Power," *Living Truths* 2 (May 1903): 245-257. (Hereafter cited as "Our Model.") See esp. p. 249.

20. This is a favorite usage of Simpson's. For his most systematic treatment of it, see: A.B. Simpson, "Aggressive Christianity," *The Christian and Missionary Alliance Weekly* 23 (September 23, 1899): 260-262. (Hereafter cited as "Aggressive Christianity.")

21. A.B. Simpson, "Scriptural Principles of Missions," *The Alliance Weekly* 45 (March 4, 1916): 357. (Hereafter cited as "Scriptural Principles.")

22. See A.B. Simpson, "Partnership With God," in *The King's Business* (New York: The Word, Work and World Publishing Company, 1886), pp. 80-89.

23. A.B. Simpson, "Distinctive Teaching," *The Word, Work and World* 9 (July 1887): 1-5. (Hereafter cited as "Teachings.")

24. "Aggressive Christianity," p. 260.

25. "Teachings," pp. 2, 3.

26. Ibid., p. 3.

27. Two collections of such sermons have been published. *Evangelistic Addresses* (New York: Christian Alliance Publishing Co., 1926), and *Salvation Sermons* (New York: Christian Alliance Publishing Co., 1925).

28. A.B. Simpson, "Practical Consecration in Relation to the Evangelization of the World," *The Christian Alliance Foreign Missionary Weekly* 13 (July 13, 1894): 28. (Hereafter cited as "Practical Consecration.")

29. "Our Model," p. 255.

30. A.B. Simpson, "The Last Evangel," *The Alliance Weekly* 46 (August 26, 1916): 340. (Hereafter cited as "Last Evangel.")

31. A.B. Simpson, "Our Trust," in *The Challenge of Missions* (New York: Christian Alliance Publishing Co., 1926), p. 58. (Hereafter cited as "Our Trust.")

32. A.B. Simpson, "The Ministering Church," in *The King's Business* (New York: The Word, Work and World Publishing Co., 1886), pp. 142-143.

33. Ibid., p. 141.

34. "Aggressive Christianity," p. 260.

35. A.B. Simpson, "The Modern Evangelistic Problem and Its Solution," *Living Truths* 4 (September 1905): 539-544. (Hereafter cited as "Evangelistic Problems.")

36. "Aggressive Christianity," p. 260.

37. A.B. Simpson, "Motives to Service," in *The King's Business* (New York: The Word, Work and World Publishing Co., 1886), p. 187. (Hereafter cited as "Motives.")

38. A.B. Simpson, "The New Testament Pattern of Missions," *Missionary Messages* (New York: The Christian Alliance Publishing Co., 1925), p. 26. (Hereafter cited as "Pattern.")

39. A.B. Simpson, "Power for Service," in *The King's Business* (New York: The Word, Work and World Publishing Co., 1886), p. 336.

40. A.B. Simpson, "Pentecost and Missions," *The Christian Alliance Foreign Missionary Weekly* 11 (July 14, 1893): 23. (Hereafter cited as "Pentecost.")

41. "Scriptural Principles," p. 357.

42. "Last Evangel," p. 339.

43. "Pattern," pp. 30-31.

44. Ibid., p. 28.

45. "Practical Consecration," p. 29.

46. "Patterns," pp. 29-34.

47. This theme arises in many places throughout his writings. He was convinced that the resources of his generation could fulfill the mandate to preach to every nation and the return of Christ would follow immediately. See: "Our Trust," p. 61; "Pattern," p. 21; and "Teachings," pp. 2, 3.

48. This special nature of his time is treated in a two-part series entitled "The Kingdom and the Times," *The Christian and Missionary Alliance Weekly* 35 (October 22, 1910): 57-58, 62; and 35 (October 29, 1910): 73-74, 78. (Hereafter cited as "The Kingdom.")

49. A.B. Simpson, "Evolution or Revolution," *Living Truths* 4 (June 1904): 308-309.

50. "Our Trust," p. 62.

51. A.B. Simpson, "The Lord's Coming and Missions," *The Challenge of Missions* (New York: Christian Alliance Publishing Co., 1926), p. 48. (Hereafter cited as "Lord's Coming.")

52. Ibid., p. 55.

53. "Pattern," p. 37.

54. "Lord's Coming," p. 53.

55. "Scriptural Principles," p. 356.

56. "Lord's Coming," pp. 52ff.

57. "Pattern," p. 24.

58. "Scriptural Principles," p. 356.

59. Ibid.

60. "Pattern," pp. 25-26.

61. "Scriptural Principles," p. 357.

62. A.B. Simpson, "Tarrying by the Stuff," *The Christian Alliance and Foreign Missionary Weekly* 11 (October 27, 1893): 259. (Hereafter cited as "Tarrying.")

63. A.B. Simpson, "An Ancient Pattern for Modern Christian Workers," *The Christian and Missionary Alliance Weekly* 23 (June 10, 1899): 22.

64. A.B. Simpson, "The Coming Revival," *Living Truths* 4 (February 1905): 70. (Hereafter cited as "Coming Revival.")

65. "Our Trust," pp. 64-65.

66. Simpson's espousal of what today may be called "Friendship Evangelism" can be found in a number of places in his work. See esp. "Coming Revival," pp. 73-74, and *Heart Messages for Sabbaths at Home* (New York: Christian Alliance Publishing Co., n.d.), pp. 94-97.

67. A.B. Simpson, "Mission Work," *The Word, Work and World* 9 (special no., 1887): 104. (Hereafter cited as "Mission Work.")

68. A.B. Simpson, "The King's Business," in *The King's Business* (New York: The Word, Work and World Publishing Co., 1886), p. 283.

69. Ibid., p. 291.

70. Ibid., p. 107.

71. "Scriptural Principles," pp. 357-358.

72. "The Kingdom," p. 57.

73. "Pattern," p. 21.

74. See "Tarrying," p. 361 and A.B. Simpson, "The Ministry of Prayer," in *The King's Business* (New York: The Word, Work and World Publishing Co., 1886), pp. 53ff.

75. A.B. Simpson, "The Ministry of Giving," in *The King's Business* (New York: The Word, Work and World Publishing Co., 1886), p. 129. (Hereafter cited as "The Ministry of Giving.")

76. "Mission Work," p. 107.

77. "Scriptural Principles," p. 357.

78. Tozer, *Wingspread*, p. 96.

79. "Evangelistic Problem," p. 39.

80. Robert B. Ekvall, "A Missionary Statesman, Part II," *The Alliance Weekly* 72 (July 10, 1937): 436.

81. "Pattern," p. 39.

82. A.B. Simpson, "The Religious Wants of New York," *The Word, Work and World* 4 (January 1882): 26-28.

83. "The Kingdom," p. 58.

84. "Pattern," p. 30.

85. "Our Trust," pp. 67-68.

86. Robert B. Ekvall, "A Missionary Statesman, Part I," *The Alliance Weekly* 72 (May 22, 1937): 326.

87. "Mission Work," p. 108.

88. "Coming Revival," p. 74.

89. "Our Trust," pp. 58-59.

90. Editorial, *The Word, Work and World* 9 (special no., 1887): 110-111.

91. Robert B. Ekvall, "A Missionary Statesman, Part III," *The Alliance Weekly* 72 (August 28, 1937): 437. (Hereafter cited as "Missionary Statesman, Part III.")

92. This theme is common in Simpson's work. For a representative address on the subject, see: "The Ministry of Giving."

93. "Missionary Statesman, Part III," p. 436.

94. Simpson describes his motivations in beginning the Missionary Training School in the context of his other activities during the early 1880s in "Providence," esp. p. 157.

95. "Missionary Statesman, Part III," p. 437.

96. Ibid.,

97. Robert Ekvall's explanation of Simpson's policy in this respect is most helpful. [Simpson] summed up the underlying principle in a unique exposition of the essential impermanence of the mission as opposed to the essential permanence of the local church. The natural tendency of any form of activity is to make certain its own continuance, and its first concern is to perpetuate itself. And so with much of mission

activity, but the declared ambition of Alliance missions was to be merely a passing phase in the development and growth of the native church. The mission of each field was permanent only in a relative sense. The time limit of missionary occupation was not to be pre-determined by the life-span of the missionary, the resources of the society, or even the idea of continuance until the Lord's return, but would be definitely reached when the local church became a properly functioning independent church, having its own fellowship with other such churches in the same field. Thus when the church should become permanent, the impermanence of the mission was to be revealed. "Missionary Statesman, Part III," p. 437.

T.V. THOMAS

T.V. Thomas grew up in Malaysia, but completed his B.Sc. and B.A. Degrees at Nagpur University in India. He then obtained an M.Div. from Canadian Theological College. While in India, he served in various capacities with Campus Crusade for Christ. After moving to Canada, he served as a National Evangelist with the Christian and Missionary Alliance, and as Assistant Professor at Canadian Bible College, before assuming his current position as Director, Murray W. Downey Chair of Evangelism, at Canadian Bible College and Canadian Theological Seminary.

KENNETH L. DRAPER

Mr. Draper received a B.A. in history at Queen's University Kingston in 1982, a Teacher Certification at the University of British Columbia in 1983, and studied theology and Bible at Canadian Theological Seminary in 1983-84. He is currently supervisor of volunteers at the Plains Historical Museum and researcher for the Centre of Evangelism at Canadian Bible College and Canadian Theological Seminary.

RESTRICTED FREEDOM:
A.B. SIMPSON'S VIEW OF WOMEN

by

Leslie A. Andrews

Albert B. Simpson's attitude toward women must be viewed against the backdrop of his consuming passion to evangelize a lost world before the return of the King. He did not seek to placate those whose ecclesiastical agendas were, in his opinion, secondary to the task of world evangelization. If women furthered the primary mission of the Church to reach lost souls for Christ, then he enthusiastically endorsed their ministries to achieve that objective.

An incident in 1893 graphically illustrates his characteristic stance. Following a "great convention" in Atlanta, Georgia, a leading pastor of the city, supported by the ministerial association, sought to set "the community right on the subject of women speaking in public." Simpson chided the pastor as follows:

> The dear brother seems to have quite forgotten all the glorious results of that great convention, in the single fact that it had run across one of his ecclesiastical convictions and the opportunity of proving that the convention and the women were wrong in that one particular seems to have almost obliterated all the other effects of the convention and kept him and his brethren from reaping the glorious harvest of spiritual blessing that ought to have been gathered out of such a meeting....[1]

219

Simpson went on to describe the public ministry of women as "a little side issue of a purely speculative character, which God has already settled, not only in His Word, but in His providence, by the seal which He is placing in this very day, in every part of the world, upon the public work of consecrated Christian women." He concludes his rebuttal with the following exhortation: "Dear brother, let the Lord manage the women. He can do it better than you, and you turn your batteries against the common enemy."[2]

The views of the founder of The Christian and Missionary Alliance on the formal and public ministry of women will be explored throughout this article. Simpson's interpretation of the relevant portions of Scripture, the role played by women in Alliance congregations during Simpson's day, and of his relationship to Maggie, his wife, will form a triadic web for weaving together an overview of his position on the issue of women in formal ministry.

REFLECTIONS ON SCRIPTURE

In commenting on various biblical teachings, Simpson demonstrated, either directly or indirectly, a positive attitude toward women and their ministries.

Holy Spirit

In *When the Comforter Came*, Simpson included a chapter entitled "The Motherhood of God." In it, he presents a view of the Trinity that acknowledges the male-female duality of the Godhead:

The heart of Christ is not only the heart of man, but has in it also all the tenderness and gentleness of women.... He combined in Himself the nature both of man and woman even as the first man Adam had the woman within his own being before she was separately formed from his very body.[3]

In the Trinity, therefore, we have a Father, a Brother, and a Husband, and "One who meets all the heart's longing for motherhood."

"As our heavenly Mother, the Comforter assumes our nurture, training, teaching, and the whole direction of our life." He possesses in his teaching and guiding "considerate gentleness and patience," along with the motherly comfort, "discipline and faithful reproof which erring childhood so often needs."[4]

Thus, spiritual ministry, as modelled by the Trinity, requires the contributions of each of the sexes.

Marriage

In addressing the subject of communion with Christ, Simpson, on one occasion, used the marriage relationship as an illustration:

> When the wife is married, it is expected that she will act accordingly, and maintain the attitude of a wife by fellowship and dependence. When a partnership is formed between two human beings, they are expected to co-operate according to the agreement....[5]

Simpson here implies that the woman, as wife, is the dependent one in the "partnership." Yet, when asked:

> In how far must a sanctified wife 'obey in all things' her husband, and 'in all things be in subjection unto her husband,' as St. Paul commands, she having less light, spirituality, and being inferior in understanding and judgment? Must the wife take literally Paul's words and descend to a lower plane of intelligence? I can hardly understand divine wisdom in this.[6]

Simpson responded that a wife's relationship to God supersedes her responsibility to her husband, thereby qualifying his understanding of dependency:

> A wife's obedience applies only to matters pertaining to this life. In all matters of conscience as between her and God and affecting her supreme duty and love to God, she is free, and the higher law applies, 'We must obey God

rather than man.' In domestic affairs and her own personal relations to her husband, she is bound by the law of obedience, and if it requires her to stoop to a lower degree of intelligence, she should be very careful before contracting marriage to be sure that she is binding herself not to a lower, but to an equal, or higher intelligence.

In responding to a similar question regarding the same issue, Simpson stressed that "no wife is compelled to sin to obey her husband, and if she does, the sin is hers as well as his." He believed that it was "fallacious" to assume that the Lord may intervene, "or if He does not, it would still be all right as the sin would be on her husband,"[7] should a husband demand an obedience that would require his wife to commit sin. Thus, for Simpson, women maintain an independent status before God, despite their functioning as dependent partners in marriage.

Priscilla

Simpson used Priscilla as an example of the ministry of women. Priscilla, he insisted, "must not be forgotten." Her ministry was "all womanly" and "never apart from her husband." Although always mentioned together with Aquila, Priscilla was no mere cipher.

> Indeed, we can almost infer from the way the apostle speaks of this beautiful pair that she became at last the stronger nature of the two. In the first references to them, it is Aquila and Priscilla, but toward the last, it is Priscilla and Aquila, and the devoted and faithful woman moves to the front.[8]

Simpson then urged, "'Give her' and every noble woman 'of the fruit of her hands, and let her own works praise her in the gates.'" He warned, "Let no man hinder the ministry of woman within its true limitations. God has ever honored it and will yet more and more. 'Favor is deceitful and beauty is vain, but a woman that feareth the Lord, she shall be praised.'"[9]

Simpson was never able to resolve the ambiguity of his view of women. Woman is to be praised "in the gates" for her works. She is not to be hindered in her ministry. But it is a ministry with "true limitations." A woman's works are to speak for themselves, publicly, while at the same time they are to be restricted. The ambiguity revolves around woman's obvious giftedness—obvious because of her "works"—and the need to channel this giftedness.

Headship (1 Corinthians 11)

Simpson struggled diligently with the restricted freedom of women.

> Ever since Anna announced the incarnation, and Mary Magdalene heralded the resurrection, woman has been God's special instrument for publishing the glad tidings of salvation. We may regulate, but can never suppress her ministry. The best remedy for the abuse of anything is its wise and proper use.[10]

He sought to resolve the ambiguity of restricted freedom, in part, by appealing to the principle of headship. "The head of every woman is the man, the head of every man is Christ, the head of Christ is God. This is the Scriptural order of the sexes...."[11]

The appeal to headship, however, did not fully solve the problem for Simpson: "...this does not authorize the exclusion of woman from public work for the Lord." He concluded that the limitation applied to the "formal and official ministry of the Christian church in the strictly ecclesiastical sense." The "formal and official ministry" included the offices of pastor, elder, and bishop.[12]

Still Simpson wrestled: "...besides the official ministry and government of the Christian church, there is an infinite room for proclaiming a glad message of salvation." He concluded that the prophetic ministry had "undoubtedly" been given to woman and that this meant nothing less than speaking "unto men to edification and exhortation, and comfort." He concluded,

> Any word, therefore, of edification and exhortation is proper for a woman to speak in the Christian assembly, and anything the apostle may have said subsequently to this statement can never rescind or abrogate these admissions and permissions.[13]

223

Once more, though, Simpson modified his permission by suggesting that "the less formal her testimony is, the better. The more it takes the form of a simple story of love, the less like a sermon and the more like a conversation, the more effective it will be." Evidently, he wanted to maintain some distinction between the sexes in regard to public speaking and predicated this distinction on "the spirit of feminine modesty" which would add "more power" to what she said.[14] To this end, he differentiated between the Greek words *kerago*, "to proclaim officially with a trumpet," and *laleo*, "to talk." He claimed that *laleo* describes the ministry of woman, and *kerago*, the ministry of man. "Man," therefore, "is the official herald, woman is the echo of his voice, repeating it in a thou-gentler (sic) tones, until love bears it to every human heart." His questionable exegesis at this point probably reflects more his struggle to distinguish between the separate spheres of men and women in ministry than a concern for proper interpretation. His argument concludes with a reaffirmation of the significance of the ministry entrusted to women:

> While we place these gentle restrictions around the ministry of woman, as the Bible seems to teach, we do not say that they limit her work a single iota in any really practical and womanly way. We thank God for her precious ministry, and we pray God to raise up more and more of His daughters to proclaim abroad in their sweeter and gentler way the Father's love. The Lord Himself gave the Word, great was the company of women that published it. May the Lord speedily fulfill this, the true version of the grand old Psalm.[15]

Phebe and Persis

While preaching on the nature of service, Simpson referred to Phebe and Persis as examples of woman who, "too, has her ministry":

> Phebe is a servant or 'deaconess' of the church in Cenchrea, and 'the beloved Persis labored much in the Lord'; ever, of course, in a true womanly way and sphere, but with equal liberty in all except the pastoral office and the official ministry of the Christian church. God be

thanked for the enlargement and restoration of woman's blessed ministry, and let our beloved sisters awake and fulfill in these days the vision of three thousand years ago, 'The Lord Himself gave the Word, great was the company of women that published it. Kings of armies fled apace and she that tarried at home divided the spoil.'[16]

Once more, Simpson affirmed his commitment to an enlarged and restored "blessed ministry" for women. He extolled their labor so long as it was rendered "in a true womanly way and sphere, but with equal liberty in all except the pastoral office and the official ministry of the Christian church." He also urged women to "awake" in order to fulfill the mandate of the Psalmist to publish the good news.[17]

Much later, when writing about "New Testament Types of Missionary Characters," Simpson referred again to Persis: "The only person that gets a double mark of commendation in Paul's catalogue of his friends at Rome is 'the beloved Persis who labored much in the Lord.' The others labored, but she labored much. It is usually a woman who reaches the superlative degree." Persis, for Simpson, represented the epitome of devotion to the work of missions:

> Thank God, the race is not extinguished, but the missionary work of women is wider, deeper and more glorious today than ever before. No one can do more in promoting the idea of missions at home, no one can be such a recruiting agent for volunteers, especially in her own family, and no one can give and sacrifice as women do. God help you, 'beloved Persis,' still to 'labor much in the Lord.'[18]

Deborah

Deborah, according to Simpson, "is the first example of a woman called to public service by the Holy Ghost...called to exercise the public functions of a leader." She represents "a glorious multitude of noble women" who "have followed in her train! The great ministry of the church today is being done by holy women....They are the most potent spiritual and moral forces of our age....It is too late in the day to question the

public ministry of woman. The facts of God's providence, and
the fruits of God's Spirit, are stronger than all our theological
fancies."[19]

And yet, having acknowledged the extraordinary public role
that Deborah exercised in the life of Israel, Simpson proceeded
to moderate the effect of her example:

> The Holy Spirit has distinctly recognized woman's place in
> the church, not only to love, to suffer and to intercede, but
> to prophesy, to teach and to minister in every proper way
> to the bodies and the souls of men; and yet, when we have
> said this, all this, there yet remains a restriction which
> every true woman will be willing to recognize.[20]

In the light of Deborah's prophetic, public ministry of leadership in ruling an entire nation, Simpson's "restriction,"
reiterated in the following citation, seems particularly curious:

> After all that can be said on both sides of this question, it
> seems to remain as the practical conclusion of the whole
> matter that woman is called without restriction to teach,
> to witness, to work in every department of the Church of
> Christ, but she is not called to rule in the ecclesiastical
> government of the Church of Christ, or to exercise the
> official ministry which the Holy Ghost has committed to
> the elders or bishops of His Church: and whenever she
> steps out of her modest sphere into the place of public
> leadership and executive government, she weakens her
> true power and loses her peculiar charm.[21]

Simpson had a penchant for quaint phrases such as "modest
sphere" and "peculiar charm." He apparently used them in an
effort to uphold the distinction between the sexes, while simultaneously acknowledging the influential role women have been
given in ministry. He struggled to maintain a healthy tension
between the public and private domains of human sexuality.
Ultimately comparing Deborah to Moses, Simpson acknowledged the unique role Deborah exercised as leader of His
chosen people:

> Deborah herself, the first public woman of the ages, was
> wise enough to call Barak to stand in the front, while she
> stood behind him, modestly directing his work, *and proving*

in the end to be the true leader. It is no disparagement of woman's ministry to place her there. Who will say that the ministry of Moses as he stood that day on the mountain, with his hands uplifted to God, while Joshua led the hosts in the plain below, was a lower ministry than that of Joshua? He was the true leader and the real power behind the hosts of Israel, although he was unseen by the eyes of men. This was Deborah's high honor, and no one was more ready than Barak himself to acknowledge her pre-eminence (italics added).[22]

1 Corinthians 14, and 1 Timothy 2

Two of the more problematic passages regarding the public ministry of women are 1 Corinthians 14:34,35, and 1 Timothy 2:11-15. Twice Simpson responded to readers who inquired about these prohibitions.

Do the passages in 1 Corinthians xiv:34,35, and 1 Timothy ii:9,10 mean what they say? If so, what authority have the women of the C.A. [the Christian Alliance] for preaching or teaching in the churches?[23]

Six years later, a similar question arose:

How do you explain 1 Corinthians xiv:34, and 1 Timothy ii:11,12? Satan has kept me [sic] tongue tied by those two verses many times. Through Christ I have overcome; but I would really like to have you explain them.[24]

To the first query, Simpson replied:

The passages referred to mean what they say, but they do not say that the women of the C.A. must not preach or teach in the churches; and other passages, such as 1 Corinthians xi:11,5, distinctly recognize the right of woman to prophesy in public. *The great question is, whether the sister has anything worth saying.* If she has a message from God, God forbid that anybody should stop her delivering it, and there are plenty of Scriptural and womanly ways in which a true woman can represent her Master and speak for the edification of His people.[25]

To the second letter, Simpson simply responded, "We would refer our questioner to the previous passage in 1 Corinthians xi:5, where the right of woman to prophesy, provided she does it modestly, is clearly recognized."[26] Once more, the guiding criteria for Simpson seems to be the manifestation of the Spirit's presence in the ministry of the woman, whether it be preaching or teaching, and "womanly ways" of delivering the message.

Sixteen years later and near the end of his life, Simpson once more grappled with the public ministry of women. He appears to contradict his earlier statements when writing about "The Worship of the Church" and specifically "Women in Church Worship":

> ...any assumption of the place or prerogative of the man is improper, even though the woman be exercising the gift bestowed upon her.

As he did years earlier, Simpson based his reasoning on

> relationships or, to be more explicit, headship. The order is, God, Christ, Man, Woman (11:2-3). The woman is the glory of the man as the man is the glory of God (11:7). The man is not of the woman but the woman of the man. Neither was the man created for the woman but the woman for the man. Yet neither is without the other, for as the woman is of the man, so is the man also by the woman (9:8-12). Consequently [Paul] says, 'I suffer not the woman to usurp authority.'[27]

He concluded that woman's place in the worship of the Church is one of association with, rather than superiority to, the man. She may pray and even prophesy in the Church. When she speaks, however, she must do so "in modest and seemly manner" (11:5).[28]

Simpson understood the prophecy referred to in this epistle to refer to preaching, i.e., to speak "unto men to edification and exhortation and comfort" (14:3). Women may be endowed with the gift of prophecy (Acts 2:17). The evangelist Philip had four daughters who prophesied (Acts 21:9). According to Simpson's understanding, however, prophesying or preaching by women was not done in the context of the pastoral role:

It is, however, noteworthy that there is not an incident recorded in the New Testament of a woman exercising the ministry of the pastor, deacon, or teacher. Christ did not call any woman into the Apostolate though there were 'certain women who ministered unto him.'[29]

In his efforts to maintain a clear distinction between the sexes and to encourage while simultaneously "regulating" the public ministry of women, Simpson was not entirely accurate in claiming that "there is not an incident recorded in the New Testament of a woman exercising the ministry of the pastor, deacon, or teacher." For instance, Phebe was called "a servant (*diakonon*) of the church in Cenchrea," the same word used of "deacons" (*diakonous*) in 1 Timothy 3:8. And, of course, Priscilla had an important ministry of teaching along with her husband, Aquila.

Ministry by Exception

The Christian and Missionary Alliance, from its inception, has stressed healing as part of the Fourfold Gospel. Prayer for the sick accompanied by anointing with oil by elders of the church has been customary. On one occasion, a reader wrote to ask whether women have the right to anoint the sick for healing. Apparently, an evangelist had claimed that "no women have a right to anoint the sick for healing, but elders only." Simpson replied:

> We believe the teaching of the Scripture recognizes the elder as the proper one to anoint, but we do not consider that this should be carried to such an extreme that in the absence of a proper elder, a suffering child of God should be compelled to refuse the ministry of a believing woman simply on a technical ground. God's methods in matters of outward form are flexible enough to allow for exceptions and adjustments, and while every true woman will ever seek to take the more quiet place, yet we believe that where the regular officer is not available or even prepared for this ministry, that God will accept hers.[30]

The above commentary on James 5:13-16 is punctuated with

frequent "exceptions": "carried to such an extreme"; "in the absence of a proper elder"; "simply on a technical ground"; "God's methods in matters of outward form"; "flexible enough to allow of exceptions and adjustments"; "where the regular officer is not available or even prepared for this ministry." Simpson was concerned with expediency, in this instance that of divine healing for the sick, and he regarded the "form" of anointing with oil by the elders as servant to the function which the form served.

RESOURCES AND ROLES OF WOMEN IN THE ALLIANCE

Prompted by the suffrage movement in Great Britain, Simpson expressed his approval of women's franchise. He advocated it on the basis of what "fair and reasonable men" would do. Whatever "the increasing outrages of the suffragettes of Great Britain" were, he congratulated American women for disavowing "any sympathy with such extreme and unlawful methods." He evidently believed in conceding "the right of the franchise to every woman who really wants it" on the basis of expedience, since to do so "probably would bring about better political conditions."[31] Thus, pragmatic concerns regarding the role and responsibilities of women underlay even Simpson's political views. How much of the issue of women's suffrage influenced his thinking about the utilization of the resources of women in the church, is difficult to determine.

Simpson certainly placed a high priority, however, on women's ministry, declaring at one point: "Our women are perhaps our chief asset." As for the role of women in Alliance missions, Simpson had this to say:

Women's Missionary Societies are among the most helpful auxiliaries of the various churches. Perhaps the difference between these bodies and our work is that while in them the women help the work, with us the women are the work. But surely there...is room for still larger expansion in their great ministry of testimony, attractive influence and self-sacrifice and love.[32]

In spite of any hesitancy there may have been about "Woman's Ministry," women exercised widely divergent responsibilities during Simpson's days of leadership. "The Alliance is now fully organized in the General Board of Management, and the various States are beginning to form local auxiliaries."[33] With that introduction, the editor proceeded to publish under "The Work at Home," the revised Constitution and list of officers. In that list, forty were named as members of the "General Committee," and six of these were women: Miss E.S. Tobey of Boston; Miss Mary E. Moorhead of Pittsburgh; Mrs. Fanny H. Foster of Providence, Rhode Island; Miss Lottie Sisson of New London, Connecticut; and Mrs. Bryson of Montreal. Twenty-nine Vice Presidents were named, one of whom was Mrs. S.G. Beck of Pennsylvania. Miss Carrie F. Judd of Buffalo was cited as Recording Secretary.[34]

In the "First Annual Report to the members of The Evangelical Missionary Alliance," the Board of Managers listed six "Vice Presidents" of The Evangelical Missionary Alliance, three of whom were women: Mrs. Chas. Green of Baltimore; Mrs. S.G. Beck of Philadelphia; and Mrs. D.M. Bishop of New York. Miss Waterbury (Harriet, or H.A.) was listed as "Recording Secretary and Financial."[35]

Of the original officers under the "now fully organized" Christian Alliance and The Evangelical Missionary Alliance, several women continued in significant and prominent ministries in the years to come. Carrie F. Judd, the Recording Secretary for The Christian Alliance, wrote its "Annual Report" in 1889. During the annual Convention of 1889, she, along with Mrs. H.D. Walker of Providence, Rhode Island, and Miss Mattie Gordon of Nashville, Tennessee, was authorized by the Executive Board "to organize auxiliaries and branches of the Christian Alliance, in connection with their evangelistic labors in the various cities and towns where they may be called in the providence of God." In addition to her evangelistic ministries, Judd was also a recognized teacher and convention speaker.[36]

Mary E. Moorhead, member of the General Committee of The Christian Alliance, was used of God in extraordinary ways in the development of the work in Pittsburgh. "All through these years of loving work and obedience, the compassionate Christ came again and again to dear Miss Moorhead, telling her in tender accents that could not be doubted, that for His sake,

231

another step must be taken." And step after step she did take. Moorhead, an invalid for many years, had been healed in answer to prayer. In response to her healing, "a divine prompting filled her whole soul, to tell to others what God had revealed to her."[37]

First Moorhead donated the family mansion she had inherited from her father as a "Bethany home." "The suffering and burdened and storm-tossed" came and were taught and healed and paid only as they were able and were prompted by the Lord. Soon 250 were meeting in the expanded chapel of the mansion. Next, "Miss Moorhead felt an urgent call to open a place where books and tracts treating on these points [the Fourfold Gospel] could be found." The Bethany Tract Room, which was "eminently successful," was then opened, and a large correspondence ministry begun.[38]

The ministry of the Bethany home required trained Christian workers. To this end, a home and Bible school for these workers was annexed to Bethany. Moorhead's vision did not stop there, however. She pressed on to establish a mission ministry to "a very neglected locality" where "thousands of the burdened and bound" of Pittsburgh could be reached with the Gospel.[39]

A third woman of prominence among the early officers of the Alliance was Miss Harriet Waterbury, "Recording Secretary and Financial of The Evangelical Missionary Alliance." She taught Bible and Church History at the New York Missionary Training College.[40] In addition to serving as Secretary of the Christian Alliance, and of the Missionary Alliance, she was "assistant editor and business manager of the publishing office." She came into the Alliance from the Society of Friends, "where she had a position of considerable Christian influence, and was much respected and beloved." She had held a "high position in the public schools" where "she had the advantage of a professional education, and a large and valuable experience in literary work." She left that profitable and secure position to enter the work of the Christian Alliance "without any condition of remuneration." In an editorial following her death on April 20, 1891, Simpson eulogized her:

> She was a noble woman, and will ever remain one of the choice and inner circle of the Christian Alliance and Tabernacle workers. She has been in our work from a

232

little after the beginning....She was thoroughly methodical, painstaking, self-denying, and most efficient and capable in every way....Her work was a perfect joy to her. We need not say that her noble sacrifice was most fully repaid by her kind Master in every way, but this does not abate in the slightest the spirit of her own true self-sacrifice. She was wholly free from selfishness.[41]

Mrs. S.G. Beck, widow of a Philadelphian millionaire, was yet another prominent Alliance woman, serving as a Vice President of The Christian Alliance and as a Vice President of The Evangelical Missionary Alliance. She opened the evangelistic work and healing home in Philadelphia where there were three meetings a week in which "they had never failed to have the presence of God mightily."[42] Simpson described her as "Our dear friend, Mrs. Beck, who has been honored of the Master of His humble and shrinking instrument in all this work since the beginning...." She spoke at the New York Convention in the Gospel Tabernacle during March 10-17, 1890.[43]

Given Simpson's consuming passion to win a lost world to Jesus Christ, it is not surprising that women gifted evangelistically exercised prominent roles in the Alliance. In a sermon entitled "The Transformation," based on Psalm 68:7-12, and delivered at the Gospel Tabernacle, Simpson explains: "God multiply the army of the women that still are publishing His glorious Word."[44]

In addition to Carrie F. Judd, Mrs. H.D. Walker, and Miss Mattie Gordon, mentioned earlier as having been authorized by the Executive Board "to organize auxiliaries and branches of the Christian Alliance, in connection with their evangelistic labors in the various cities and towns where they may be called in the providence of God," other women served in officially recognized evangelistic ministries.[45]

Miss Mattie Perry served extensively throughout the southern states. Nine years after the first female evangelists had been officially recognized, and on two successive months, Simpson highlighted her ministry in his magazine:

She is an authorized evangelist of the Christian and Missionary Alliance in all the Southern states, and God has used her to build up the work throughout the whole field, and is now rewarding her by giving her a training institute in the mountains of North Carolina.

We desire to call special attention to the noble work of our dear sister....Her evangelistic field covers the entire vast region. She has been successful in commencing an important training institute.[46]

In Mrs. George Stahl's obituary, it was reported that she opened the work in Toledo. "She was the instrument used in leading thousands, no doubt, to see this truth and establish the work in Toledo...."[47]

In 1909, "Miss Mary G. Davies was added to our staff last year as a field evangelist and has rendered splendid service over a very wide field and under unusual conditions of labor and trying weather."[48]

Simpson did not praise all women so graciously. For example, when Miss Mattie Gordon preached at the Oberlin Convention held in the First Congregational Church, Simpson found her sermon disappointing:

...preached a long sermon, which did not give general satisfaction....Many were disappointed, who heard her a year ago and were then greatly delighted [sic].[49]

By 1890, the role of deaconess had assumed official status:

The work of deaconesses has assumed an important place. Homes for these workers have been opened at Cincinnati, New York and Boston.[50]

Miss Ellen A. Griffin, an "honored worker," was a deaconess of the Berachah Home in New York. In a twelve-page tribute to her in *The Word, Work and World* upon her death, Simpson extolled her life and ministry in glowing terms. She possessed a "quick, penetrating and logical mind"; she was "decisive," and had "rare executive ability." Having been converted under Sankey, she became "an earnest worker for souls" and "won them by the hundreds." She had a pastoral heart and acted "as a real Shepherd...nurturing many a feeble sheep and tender lamb in its early struggles and temptations." Having experienced divine healing herself, she was "fitted to be a peculiar help to persons seeking Divine Healing." She

at once rose superior to all weaknesses, weariness and fear, and for years, used to work unceasingly, night and day, in all kinds of weather, in season and out of season, without regard to clothing or inclemency, and with such a luxury and exhilarance of life service that she did not know what it was to be tired.[51]

Simpson regarded her as "one of the strongest and noblest characters we have ever known," especially in view of her "self reliance and energy" and the "quiet and unfaltering quality of her faith." After a "sharp and bewildering" struggle to enter into the "deeper and quieter lessons of His still and sanctifying presence...the great strong woman lay like a babe on her Saviour's breast. It was eternal peace. There never was another struggle or another cloud." Simpson summed up her life by identifying seven traits: (1) a strong character of "intense force and energy of will and intellect"; (2) a strong sense of justice; (3) a supreme loyalty to her convictions, the cause she espoused, and the Master she loved; (4) an absolute disinterestedness — she tolerated no selfish interest; (5) faith, which was the strongest spiritual quality of her life: "It was clear, simple and absolutely unwavering. It was, indeed, a mighty faith"; (6) love; and (7) hard work: "Let her work be her monument and her crown."[52]

Women were free to lead music in Simpson's conventions. Miss Louise Shepherd of New York "led the singing" at the Convention in Jacksonville, Florida (March 20, 1891), and participated again in the Convention in Fort Worth, Texas (June 3, 1892). According to A.B. Simpson, she, along with Mrs. Simpson, "as usual, have contributed, in testimony and song, the peculiar half which they have been so well able to render in all our Conventions."[53]

May Agnew Stephens was a song leader, pianist, and soloist. It was said that she could lead the congregational singing from the piano and could sway the audience with her singing. A few of her hymns are in Hymns of the Christian Life: "I Choose Thee, Blessed Will of God" (words); "Never Thirst Again" and "'Tis Better Far to Follow Jesus" (words and music); "O Love Divine" and "Living in the Glory" (music, with words by Simpson).

Simpson's relationships with women testify to the profound respect he had for them. Five-foot-one-inch Maggie, Simpson's wife, must march to the front of the line. She has been frequently misunderstood. A.E. Thompson, in his biography of Simpson, says that it was he who received the call to missions and to evangelism and not Mrs. Simpson. However, Maggie became, in time, one of her husband's most avid supporters and exercised considerable responsibility in his movement.

Simpson maintained a diary sporadically. The entries, which cover the closing of his ministry in Louisville, Kentucky, in 1879, and the beginning of his ministry in the 13th Street Presbyterian Church, in New York City in 1880, reveal something of the tension in their relationship.

Mrs. Simpson was concerned about the proposed move to New York because of having to raise her four children (and one expected) in that great metropolis. Her mood at the time is reflected in Simpson's references to her in the diary:

> M. took out the pages I had written for the past two weeks here — God so permitted her foolish and sinful hand. Poor child. I have prayed and prayed for her until of late I cannot pray without intense distress. I leave her with Him, trusting that He will lead her to repentance and salvation. She has suffered much of late. She is possessed of an intense bitterness, and I am full of pain and fear. I was much exercised as to whether I should ask my brethren of the Session to speak to her and beseech her to be reconciled, but after conferring with one of them, I found it would be vain, and I wait in silence upon God. I trust my own heart may be kept righteous, and merciful in everything.[54]

Just twelve days later, however, Simpson's description of life was dramatically different:

> Praise for much peculiar burden of prayer and spiritual blessing all day. Praise for my wife's kind and loving and altered spirit. God seems so to bless her as He leads me in the peculiar path He has of late so clearly shown.[55]

What remains of Simpson's diary is very fragmentary. Nevertheless, it does accent his own swings in mood, which in turn are reflected in his descriptions of Maggie. Dr. Simpson, along with his great spiritual heights, also had great spiritual depths which erupted in strong conflicts and feelings, even after he met the Lord in the deeper life. Mrs. Simpson, however, always stood by her husband.

Evidence of the strong working relationship which Dr. and

Mrs. Simpson came to enjoy, is evidenced in the fact that for ten years she filled the position of financial secretary of the Christian and Missionary Alliance, and for a number of years served as secretary of the Foreign Board.

CONCLUSION

Several things may be noted in conclusion about the public role that women held in The Christian and Missionary Alliance during its founder's lifetime. First, Simpson was thoroughly committed to the task of world evangelization and welcomed enthusiastically as co-workers, those women who shared his vision and supported the task. Women served as missionaries, evangelists, educators, teachers, preachers, and officers in the movement.

Second, Simpson had a profound respect for the spirituality, intelligence, and giftedness of women. He did not hesitate to praise them publicly, wholeheartedly, and widely for their ministries.

Third, Simpson struggled to maintain a delicate balance between the sexes in public ministry. His was an authentic struggle to reconcile differences of human sexuality. He sometimes resolved these differences in an apparently arbitrary manner owing to his highly pragmatic approach to ministry and his commitment to doing whatever promoted world evangelization. His view, maintaining that women must not be permitted to serve as pastors or elders, was not always supported by accurate and consistent exegesis. It did, however, reflect his genuine preoccupation with the tension between the manifested spiritual giftedness of women and the restrictions he perceived imposed by Scripture.

In his draft of the first constitution for "The Evangelical Missionary Alliance," Simpson cited five special features proposed in the movement.[56] One feature was "the ministry of woman." The movement's founder believed that Christ, "the great Head of the Church," desired "to emphasize and utilize it [ministry of woman] still more." The foreign mission, he stressed, needed 100,000 women right then and had "a place

237

for everyone."[57]

The question before the Christian and Missionary Alliance one hundred years later is, "Is there still a place for everyone?" If the answer is yes, the next question is, "What is that place for women?"

ENDNOTES

1. *The Christian Alliance* (December 29, 1893), p. 402 (hereafter, *CA*).

2. Ibid.

3. A.B. Simpson, *When the Comforter Came* (New York: Christian Publications, 1911), n.p.

4. Ibid.

5. *The Christian Alliance and Missionary Weekly* (December 4, 1891), p. 339 (hereafter, *CAMW*).

6. *The Christian and Missionary Alliance* (June 9, 1900), p. 385 (hereafter, *CMA*).

7. Ibid.

8. *The Alliance Weekly* (January 8, 1916), p. 230 (hereafter, *AW*).

9. Ibid.

10. *CAMW* (March 27, 1891), p. 195.

11. Ibid.

12. Ibid.

13. Ibid.

14. Ibid.

15. Ibid.

16. *CAMW* (February 3, 1893), p. 69.

17. Ibid.

18. *CMA* (September 8, 1906), p. 154.

19. *The Christian Alliance and Foreign Missionary Weekly* (December 7, 1894), p. 533 (hereafter, *CAFMW*).

20. Ibid.

21. Ibid.

22. Ibid.

23. *CAFMW* (April 20, 1894), p. 43.

24. *CMA* (March 24, 1900), p. 187.

25. *CAFMW* (April 20, 1894), p. 43.

26. *CMA* (March 24, 1900), p. 187.

27. *AW* (February 5, 1916), p. 294.

28. Ibid.

29. Ibid.

30. *CMA* (June 9, 1900), p. 385.

31. *AW* (March 1, 1913), p. 338.

32. *AW* (April 13, 1912), p. 20.

33. *CA* (August/September 1887), p. 112.

34. Ibid.

35. *CA* (January 1889), p. 10.

36. Ibid., p. 8.

37. *CAMW* (February 28, 1890), pp. 138-139.

38. Ibid.

39. Ibid., p. 140.

40. See *The Word, the Work and the World* (October 1886), p. 234 (hereafter, *WWW*); *CA* (September 1888), p. 136.

41. *CAMW* (April 24, 1891), p. 257.

42. See *CA* (August/September 1887), p. 112; ibid. (January 1889), p. 8; *WWW* (April 1887), p. 256; and ibid. (October 1886), p. 232.

43. See *CA* (February 1889), p. 24, and *CAMW* (February 28, 1890), p. 129.

44. *CMA* (July 11, 1903), pp. 71-72.

45. *CA* (January 1889), p. 8.

46. See *CMA* (October 19, 1898), p. 373, and ibid. (November 5, 1898), p. 421.

47. *CAMW* (January 3, 1890), p. 9.

48. *CMA* (June 5, 1909), p. 154.

49. *CA* (March 7, 1890), p. 172.

50. *CAMW* (January 10, 1890), p. 27.

51. *WWW* (February 1887), pp. 94-96.

52. Ibid., pp 94-98.

53. See *CAMW* (March 20, 1891), p. 177; ibid. (June 3, 1892), p. 354; and *CMA* (October 1, 1904), p. 273.

54. A.B. Simpson, personal diary (entry for Louisville, Kentucky, Monday night, 10 November 1879).

55. Ibid. (entry for Tuesday night, 16 December 1879).

56. *WWW* (June 1887), p. 367.

57. Ibid.

LESLIE A. ANDREWS

Leslie A. Andrews earned a B.A. from Nyack College, an M.Div. and D.Min. from Columbia Theological Seminary, and a Ph.D. in adult education at Michigan State University. Dr. Andrews has been director of Christian Education in Atlanta, Georgia, and Nyack, New York, having taught at Nyack College and Trinity Evangelical Divinity School. Currently, she is Assistant Professor of Christian Education at Canadian Theological Seminary.

A.B. Simpson and the Tensions in the Preparation of Missionaries

by

Jacob P. Klassen

It is a well-documented fact that Albert Benjamin Simpson brought together, in his life, excellent academic preparation, deep spirituality, a worldwide concern for the lost, and a sense of the urgency of sending forth workers. His philosophy of ministry had as its cornerstone the "multiplication factor," about which the apostle Paul wrote to his disciple: "And the things you have heard me say in the presence of many witnesses entrust to reliable men who will also be qualified to teach others" (2 Timothy 2:2, NIV). To this task of teaching and preparing candidates for ministry, the founder of the Christian and Missionary Alliance committed himself with his typical dedication and enthusiasm.

Walter M. Turnbull, author of the chapter, "A Christian Educator," in *The Life of A.B. Simpson*, the official Alliance biography, offers the following summary of Simpson's philosophy of missionary education:

> ...he himself considered that his highest and most fruitful service consisted in imparting divine truth and life through systematic training of the young and open-hearted. The schools he founded were not by-products of his ministry, but were conceived as an integral part of his

241

commission. Simultaneously with the dawning of his great vision of truth, and the beginning of his larger service beyond the borders of the accustomed, came the impulse to duplicate himself by giving special attention to the instruction of the plastic minds among his followers. Thus he strove to revivify not only the message but also the method of Scripture. His prophetic calling was never better exhibited than in the founding of his modern 'school of the prophets,' nor were his God-given wisdom and foresight anywhere more clearly shown than in the principles and aims which he adopted in connection with his training work.[1]

Dr. Simpson had followed with interest the development of the East London Training Institute for Home and Foreign Missionaries, established by Dr. and Mrs. H.G. Guinness in 1872. It set the pattern for the training center he founded some ten years later in New York City. Indeed, the two institutions were remarkably similar: both were begun in order to prepare missionaries; both were located in needy sectors of large cities; both stressed practical training in helping the poor, providing shelters for former prostitutes and homes for orphans; and both expected all students to participate actively in evangelism, and to be successful at soul-winning.[2]

Simpson's endeavor to send forth as many workers as possible as quickly as possible sometimes forced him to use what he called "irregular workers," an appellation he explained as follows:

> God has always done a great deal of His work out of season, as well as in season, irregularly as well as regularly....Early in the history of the church we find God sending forth laymen like Stephen, Philip and Barnabas to lead the great work of apostolic evangelization. We do not compete in this Institute with the regular theological seminary and the ordinary methods of taking the gospel ministry. We claim to be raising up a band of irregular soldiers for the vast unoccupied fields to supplement the armies of the Lord in the regions they cannot reach and work they cannot overtake.[3]

At other times, the writings of Dr. Simpson and his co-workers stress the need for a more thorough academic preparation:

> We find it...imperative to reach a higher standard of results in the training.... The Institute has reached blessed results in the past for present emergencies, but...with the increasing demands of the fields, many of our students fail to be equal to those demands. We are, therefore, grappling with the problems of a graded system of training....[4]

The reasons for these seemingly divergent emphases in Simpson's view of education will emerge in the course of the following historical study. This study will follow the three-fold division that Walter Turnbull proposes for the historiography of the early Alliance, namely 1882 to 1890, 1890 to 1897, and 1897 to 1920.[5]

1882 TO 1890

During this first eight-year period, the Missionary Training College for Home and Foreign Missionaries and Evangelists moved frequently. The course consisted of one year of study, including English, Christian Evidences, Bible Study and Interpretation, Church History and Christian Life and Work. The following is the first statement of character and purpose:

> This work originated in the felt need for a simple spiritual and scriptural method of training for Christian work for the large class of persons who desire to become prepared for thorough and efficient service for the Master, without a long, elaborate college course. It aims, through the divine blessing, to lead its students to simple and deeply spiritual experiences of Christ, and to recognize the indwelling presence and power of the Holy Ghost as the supreme and all-essential qualification and enduement for all Christian ministry; and to give to them a thorough instruction in the Word of God and a practical and experimental training in the various forms of evangelistic and Christian work; besides such other theological and literary studies as are included in a liberal course of education.[6]

243

Because Dr. Simpson published an illustrated Bible and missions magazine (it is now called *The Alliance Witness*), he soon was recognized as a missionary leader. These magazines kept the interest of missions in the forefront, reporting news of the Missionary Alliance and other missionary societies from around the world. He also used these publications as a tool to recruit students for the training institute. For example, a feature-length article in *The Word, the Work and the World* gave detailed coverage to the proposed course offerings of the New York Missionary Training College,[7] origin and objects of the course, entrance requirements, the hours for lectures and recitations and the type of practical training in mission work that the students could expect. Other issues contained full-length articles of commencement exercises, including the speeches of faculty, guest speakers and outstanding students. The public announcement of the opening of the third session of the Institute (New York Missionary Training College) in *The Word, Work and World* reiterated the statement of purpose which Dr. Turnbull recorded as the original statement for the Institute when it commenced in 1882.

The curriculum represented a balance between foundational studies and practical training in ministry. In 1885, the courses were listed under the following three divisions: (I) *Literary Department:* English Language and Literature, Rhetoric and Public Speaking, Logic, Mental and Moral Philosophy, Natural Science, Ancient and Modern History and Geography with special reference to Bible Lands and Mission Fields; (II) *Theological Department:* Christian Evidences, Bible Expositions, New Testament Greek, Systematic Theology, Church History, History and Biography of Christian Work and Pastoral Theology; (III) *Practical Department:* Christian Experience with special reference to the Enduement of Power, Exercises in Sermon Outlines and Bible Readings, Evangelistic Work and the conducting of Religious Services, Personal Work for Souls, Foreign Missions, Sunday School Work, Actual Mission Work under the direction of a teacher in City Missions two nights per week, and Vocal Music.[8]

In 1885, the original one-year course of studies was expanded to three years. A student could still attend for only one year, but it was "strongly recommended that all the students... endeavor to avail themselves of the thorough mental and spiritual training afforded by the three years' course."[9] Lectures were given from two o'clock until six o'clock during the week, and two evening classes per week were held for special studies and for those students who could not attend during the day because of work. However, the College expected students to spend mornings in missionary work or study. The emphasis was on practical training, as the following quotation from *The Word, Work and World* indicates:

> During the coming Winter, several new stations are to be opened, which will be connected with the college work; and the students will be engaged in these several evenings in each week, under the care of the Rev. Robert Roden, and with the view not only of useful work, but also of practical training in conducting meetings, in exhortation, and in leading souls to accept Christ. The work will include also systematic visitations in the destitute fields of the city. This may be made an invaluable part of the course.[9]

From such humble beginnings developed the present colleges and seminaries of the Christian and Missionary Alliance.

1890 TO 1897

Concerning the next years of education, from 1890-1897, Dr. Turnbull wrote the following summary:

> The second period, from 1890 to 1897, covers the years during which the Training College was located at 690 Eighth Avenue, where a substantial building was erected in connection with the Gospel Tabernacle. From this time the work developed rapidly. Many who are now labouring for Christ in the homeland and mission fields received their preparation in the old Training School at "690." In 1894, the name was changed to the New York Training Institute. The high price of land in New York, and the distractions to student life in the city, led to the choice of a rural site, when a larger building became necessary.[10]

Dr. Simpson sought to attract missionaries who were

committed to a simple lifestyle, spiritually dynamic and desired the support of a non-denominational mission through *The Christian Alliance*, an illustrated missionary magazine:

> Tenderly, but boldly, we are constrained to say that the ecclesiastical lines of our day have grown so rigid and the machinery of Christian work so elaborate and conservative that they have ceased to be fully adjustable to the world's great needs. Missionaries sent forth from such atmospheres carry with them to the foreign field the complexion of the home church, and reproduce abroad the features which, in the church at home, neutralize her highest usefulness. And therefore, God, in these last days, is gathering a great number of His consecrated children in all the churches into closer fellowship with Him, and from their midst is sending forth new missionary movements, undenominational, independent, simple and spiritual, which will carry to the heathen world the spirit of separation from the world, holiness of heart and life, entire consecration, self sacrifice and simplicity in Christian living, and a full belief in the supernatural power of God and in the speedy coming of the Lord Jesus Christ, all of which must bring about a new phase of missionary life and work and a corresponding seal of the Holy Ghost upon the work and workers.... The time has gone by for elaborate ecclesiastical missionary movements. We are in the day of spontaneous and simple Christian effort under the direct superintendence of the Holy Ghost and through men and women who are wholly baptized with His power. We believe most solemnly that the great movement today, which is calling together the consecrated children of God in every land in a closer fellowship of holiness and deeper spiritual life, is just the preparation of new missionary centres which are to cover the world before the close of the decade with an Army of simple self-denying messengers through whom the whole world will be evangelized and the coming of our Master hastened.[11]

During this second phase (1890-1897) in the life of the Institute, simplicity, spiritual experience in the fullness of the deeper life, and practical experience in soul-winning were stressed in the education and preparation of missionaries. It

246

was also stressed that the new thrust of missionary fellow-ships should not be encumbered by ecclesiastical structures and that missionaries should not impose North American ecclesiastical structures on churches planted overseas.

Undoubtedly, Dr. Simpson came by his qualms about denominational organizational restrictions honestly. He wanted to inspire the members of many denominations with his personal vision of evangelizing the world in his own lifespan, and thus have the largest scope possible to recruit workers in all denominations in an effort to "preach the Gospel in all nations, to bring back the King." Nevertheless, he thought he was not extracting members from existing denominations so as to form yet another competitive denomination of his own.

During this second period of the development of the Alliance, the need to reach the heathen and the urgent need for overseas workers received constant exposure in the magazine, *The Christian Alliance and Missionary Weekly*. This sense of urgency comes out in an editorial entitled "Why I Should Go Now."

> The King's business requires haste. The Lord's coming draweth nigh. The preaching of the Gospel to all nations must precede it. The time is short. There are many reasons why you should not wait. Under ordinary circumstances it might be very desirable to spend six or seven years getting an elaborate education; but if we really expect the Lord's speedy coming, what in the world are you going to do with all your elaborate preparation? After you have studied for six years at home and spent several years in learning the language abroad, and are just about ready for work, the century will have closed and 1900 will be here. Haste brother, haste, go out quickly into the highways and byways and constrain them to come in, that my house may be filled.[12]

The same editorial lists six compelling reasons for going immediately:

> (1) Go now, because souls are dying now; (2) Because the kind of workers most needed are not men and women with elaborate educations, but bold, simple, aggressive pioneers; (3) Because even with the utmost dispatch, it will take at least two years to get to work; (4) Because the only time we have is now; (5) Because the spirit of

247

promptness and service is one of the first qualities and is essential to the true soldier; and finally (6) Because now God is opening the doors in every way and is coming to the aid of His people. Our own Society already has much more money for missionary work than it has men. In heathen lands, there are hundreds of open doors not yet filled....God is hasting, time is hasting. Let us make speed and go into all the world and preach the Gospel to every creature."[13]

This sense of urgency and desire to bring back the King before the end of the century characterizes Simpson's writing during this period and account for his emphasis on speed over depth in the education of Alliance workers.

1897 TO 1920

The third period of education and preparation, according to Dr. Walter Turnbull, extends from 1897 to 1920. Notable achievements in this period, according to Turnbull, were the development of the Missionary Training Institute at Nyack, New York, and the short-lived Nyack Seminary. He gives the following indications of the extent of Dr. Simpson's influence in educating missionaries and pastors during this time:

> Dr. Simpson's educational ideals were expressed not only in the Nyack work, but also in regional schools which were modeled after the original pattern. Toccoa Falls Institute in Georgia and the Alliance Training Home in St. Paul are rapidly-growing institutions with the same aim and methods. The Pacific Bible School was also similar in character. Boydton Institute, Virginia, for coloured students, is now operating upon the same principles. In South China, Central China, West China, Indo-China, Gujarat in India, Berar in India, the Congo, and Palestine are offspring Bible Schools of far-reaching influence, manned by those who caught the vision of divine possibility in such enterprises from their great leader. These are some of the material monuments of Dr. Simpson's persevering labours.[14]

248

Clearly, Dr. Simpson believed that the evangelization of the world required the development of training institutions to prepare workers for North America and the mission fields of the world. Interestingly enough, articles in Alliance periodicals during this twenty-three year period reveal a tension between a perceived need to upgrade academic requirements and (even in the same issue of a periodical) a perceived need to promote far less demanding types of education and training. The Alliance continued to offer both types of education simultaneously. The following quotations serve to illustrate this either/or versus both/and training models in the Alliance:

> The enrollment has been larger and steadier than ever before, notwithstanding the fact that conditions of admission have been made more exacting and the requirements of the work of the school stiffer. This, however, is to be expected. The more we improve our standards, the more the institution will be appreciated....

> The spring term of the school will open on Monday, May 8, and close on Friday, June 23, a term of seven weeks. We wish to call special attention of possible students to it. Many of our present students have to leave after commencement for reasons of necessity, either financial, domestic or evangelistic. There will be a (sic) plenty of room for others to come in. It is a most delightful season of the year. The courses of lectures will be complete for the term and largely entirely new. There will be less rigor of study but no less value in the curriculum itself....

> We are glad to say that, simultaneously with our spring-term, a term will be carried on in New York, at 690 Eighth Avenue, the Alliance headquarters, under the superintendency of Pastor Kenning, consisting of forenoon lectures, afternoon house visitation and tract-distributing, and evening attendance upon the various missions of the city....

> Two things have been pressing upon the heads of the Institute very urgently: the need of further accommodations, and the need of advancing the standard of the training....Build larger we must. With this problem we are wrestling by prayer and consultation....We find it equally imperative to reach a higher standard of results in

249

the training. Both the foreign and the home fields call for it, demand it. The Institute has reached blessed results in the past for present emergencies, but there has been so much of immaturity left in the training of our students, that, with the increasing demands of the fields, many of our students fail to be equal to those demands. We are, therefore, grappling with the problems of a graded system of training, which, while not excluding applicants on stringent conditions of admission, will locate all students in their proper place in a graded system, and make graduation to be, not a matter of merely attending the school a certain length of time, and going over the curriculum, but without mature results, but a matter of reaching a worthy standard of mature preparation for home and foreign work.

In accomplishing this latter end, it is evident that it will be necessary to provide many of our students with an elementary course, preparatory to the full Biblical course, the former course to embrace elementary Biblical work and a large degree of elementary education of a general character, which many of our dear students lack, a lack that tells seriously against their success in mastering the higher Biblical work and in meeting the still sterner requirements of life's work at home or abroad. Thus, while not debarring students from the Institute by a high educational standard of admission, yet the Biblical course proper would not be entered upon until proper and needful requirements are met. Graduation, then, from the Institute will mean a fair standard of attainment, educational, Biblical and spiritual, whether it takes a longer or a shorter time to reach that standard.[16]

Dr. Simpson himself commented on the need to improve the course of studies as follows:

It is not divulging a close secret to say that plans are under careful and prayerful consideration for greatly changing and improving the present course of study in the Missionary Institute.

The session will probably be extended so as to include nine months, from September to June, embracing three terms.

There will be a full two years' course of Bible study, for which students must pass an entrance examination and matriculate as in other colleges. The standard will be raised much higher, as our home and foreign work demands continually a higher class of labourers in both mental and spiritual calibre. But in order to meet the needs of those who cannot pass this entrance examination, there will be a junior or preparatory course also covering two years. This may be shortened, however, by students who are more fully prepared and reduced to one year.

A full announcement of the plan of work and course of study will be made early in the season. The object of the Committee and the Board is to make our Missionary Institute as thoroughly efficient for the training and sending forth of home and foreign workers as the theological seminaries of the various churches are in connection with the work of the religious denominations. The time has come in our work when we need thorough and efficient labourers, and our Institute must supply them. Up to the present time, its work has been somewhat immature and tentative. It has reached its majority and it is fitting that it should now enter upon a stronger and more effective spiritual manhood.[16]

In spite of these strong calls to improve the academic standards, there are also indications that Dr. Simpson loved lay workers, and strove to provide them with training and spiritual nurture. Thus we read in the November 11, 1906, issue of *The Christian and Missionary Alliance:*

The classes of workers which have been added to the missionary staff have created a new constituency. There was a time when only the ordained preacher was acceptable as a missionary candidate. Today the lay missionary takes an equal place with his ministerial brother, and our women's missionary societies have established their place and the place of their sex in the very van of the world's evangelization. Above all these combined agencies is the developing of the native ministry, who have increased in the past quarter of a century until today they outnumber the workers from

251

Christian lands more than five to one. There is an opportunity today for any man or woman, who has the fire of God burning in his soul, to go forth as a herald of the cross to the heathen world.[17]

During the first thirty-eight years of its education, training and sending of missionaries, the Alliance experimented with a variety of models. The pendulum swung from the one extreme of very brief, elementary, practical preparation (in order to send the missionaries forth as quickly as possible), to the other extreme of much higher academic standards. Concurrently, throughout this period, we read of practical training in ministry in downtown New York. A number of issues of the *Christian and Missionary Alliance* magazine advertise correspondence courses offered by the Missionary Training Institute and the headquarters of the Mission in New York City. Toward the end of Dr. Simpson's life, the correspondence courses had to be suspended because of his failing energies. Throughout Dr. Simpson's ministry, we observe this scholarly missionary statesman wrestling with the tensions of preparing workers for the ministry. He appreciated the need to maintain high spiritual and academic standards for missionary candidates. Yet, at the same time, he strove to nurture and train lay people, his "irregulars," in order that the Gospel might be preached everywhere. He firmly believed that the higher institutions of learning could not possibly train enough witnesses to accomplish the task of world evangelization. This bipolarity produced some tensions as we shall see in the following section.

INITIAL DIFFICULTIES ENCOUNTERED IN PREPARING MISSIONARIES AND WORKERS

The Lack of Workers for North America

One of the recurring tensions that Dr. Simpson addressed repeatedly was the lack of workers for Alliance "branches" (congregations) in North America. Dr. Simpson summarized this need as follows:

Surely there never was a time when the Master's words were more timely, 'Pray ye therefore the Lord of the harvest that he would send forth labourers into His harvest.' Our cry has long been for workers for the home field and leaders for our Alliance branches, but not only for these, but for a yet higher type of labourer, men qualified to fill the breach and lead the hosts of the Lord in these strenuous days of opportunity and privilege....And yet the work of the Alliance, especially the oversight of the home field, requires qualifications of no ordinary kind. There must be experience, enabling the worker to thoroughly represent these precious truths. There must be culture and ability sufficient to impress and attract the religious world. There must be executive ability and the gift of leadership, and above all else, there must be such faith in God, such unselfish devotion and such self-sacrificing principle that the humble and unremunerative lot of an Alliance superintendent will outweigh the emoluments and honors which the world has to offer to the gifted men and women.[18]

In several other editorials and articles in the official magazine, Dr. Simpson appealed for those who would be willing to work in the branches teaching the fullness of Jesus, and supporting the evangelization of the world.

The Problem of Divine Healing

In the early days of the C&MA, several critical newspaper articles blamed the deaths of Alliance missionaries in the Congo and in the Sudan on Dr. Simpson himself.[19] In the latter instance, the missionaries had, according to *The Missionary Review of the World*,

decided to adopt 'simple manners of life, living as the natives in the hope that by so doing they [would] gain the confidence of the people....' Three members of the mission died....The doctors had the house quarantined and the remaining sick missionaries taken to the hospital. They were suffering from an infectious disease and with high fevers that had been neglected.[20]

Others echoed similar sentiments,

A more damning criticism came from Mrs. H. Grattan Guinness, whose husband had had such a profound influence on Simpson. She declared that the missionaries had died because...the notorious Dr. Simpson—who has already sent others to die in Africa and elsewhere from a similar cause—got hold of them and infused into them his fanatical views on the subject [of healing]....The responsibility for their deaths really rests on him who led them to believe error.[21]

In spite of these early discouragements, the Alliance had already become firmly established as a missionary society and had developed as an international influence for the missionary force.

The Problems of Money, Rapid Recruitment and Deployment

Dr. A.B. Simpson's spiritual life and missionary conferences had a continuing influence for the cause of international missionary activity. In fact, at one point, his young missionary organization appeared to raise so much financial support that there was added pressure to rush missionary candidates out to the fields. Daryl W. Cartmel discusses this problem as follows:

Another of the pains which twinged the society in the heyday of its growth was caused by the personnel it chose to send overseas. The sudden floods of dollars for missions was welcomed, but it was also embarrassing. After Round Lake and Old Orchard conventions of 1891, Simpson had money in hand for eighty missionaries and a gift of fifty thousand dollars to pay for their transportation, but where were the reapers to send into the harvest fields? By October, 1891, Simpson was sending out an urgent plea for men....The pressure to send the missionaries was so great that two or three years was too long to wait for the candidates' preparation. Qualifications of the candidates were examined, but the emphasis was upon willingness to move at short notice without waiting for years of academic training....The appeal for candidates was a constant theme of Simpson's editorials. He gave ten

254

reasons why a candidate would want to be a missionary of the Alliance and on the other side of the coin, what the Alliance expected of a candidate. None of the ten qualifications for missionary service had any reference to education.[22]

The C&MA learned some valuable lessons from the pressures of too rapid a deployment of poorly trained recruits. Dr. Simpson then adopted a strategy of more careful screening, more education and practical experience in the home land, and channeling finances through a central office. The C&MA today continues to function according to these principles.

The Impact of Dr. A.B. Simpson on Other Organizations

We have reviewed some of the tensions and pressures which Dr. Simpson and his young missionary society had to work through during the early years of the society's existence. However, despite these difficulties, Dr. Simpson was at the same time, able to play a key role in the development of Bible and missionary training institutes, and in the formation of other missionary organizations.

As noted above, Dr. Guinness of London, England, inspired Dr. Simpson to begin a missionary training institute in New York City. Simpson, in turn, inspired and encouraged the development of regional institutes whose leaders shared his doctrinal and missiological convictions. Soon other leaders, like D.L. Moody, also founded institutions which have trained thousands of missionaries throughout the past century. Dr. A.B. Simpson also played a direct role in the development of two mission organizations, as the following quotations indicate:

> ...through the undying persistence of one man, Rowland Bingham, SIM (Sudan Interior Mission) became one of the most dynamic mission ventures in Africa in the history of the Christian Church....Bingham returned to Canada, his faith renewed, determined to go forward with a mission to the Sudan. Realizing his own inadequacies for mission work, he took a basic medical course at a Cleveland hospital, and then in the Fall of 1895, he enrolled in A.B.

255

Simpson's Bible School in New York City....

(Peter Cameron) Scott enrolled at the New York Missionary Training College, founded by A.B. Simpson to prepare for missionary service in Africa. In November of 1890, at the age of twenty-three, he was ordained by Simpson, and the following day he sailed for the west coast of Africa to join the International Missionary Alliance in its work there.[23]

Scott later founded the Africa Inland Mission. Then, as now, the influence for missions of the C&MA was much greater than its numerical strength.

THE IMPLICATIONS FOR LEADERSHIP TRAINING TODAY

The multi-faceted approach Dr. Simpson used in the training of workers for the ministry has some implications for the Alliance today.

For North American Ministries

One may well pose the question: "If Dr. Simpson were training leaders for North American ministries today, whom would he train and what ministries would he train them for?" Certainly the Alliance needs seminary trained ministers, workers in cross-cultural ministry, and those who can address the needs of people in the inner city. He would probably devise a specialized core of workers who would be able to minister to the new waves of immigrants from the third world.

For Third World Churches

Dr. Simpson was a pioneer in the development of training institutes for national pastor and workers overseas. It is a safe assumption that the founder of the Alliance would today implement a variety of training programs, such as seminary training for some of the key leaders, as well as theological education by extension in its various forms to meet the demands of the preparation of leaders for the thousands of Alliance churches around the world.

For "Tentmaking" Missionaries

As we review the training program that A.B. Simpson devised for missionaries in his generation, we must ask ourselves how he would have found contemporary challenges to missions such as the fact that the Peoples' Republic of China does not permit regular missionaries to work in that country; that India currently is very restrictive in issuing visas for missionary activity; and that the Arab nations prohibit conversion from Islam. In the near future, 65 percent of our world, for all practical purposes, will be closed to the regular missionary. In view of Dr. Simpson's ability to adapt practically to a wide range of spiritual and physical needs in his own day, he certainly would be in the vanguard of preparing any type of missionary that the present world situation might demand. Hence he would doubtless have advocated the deployment of "tentmakers" to countries closed to professional missionaries. In this light, it is most encouraging to observe the development of the IPAP, the International Program of Alliance Professionals, the purpose of which is to provide theological preparation, prayer and moral support for Alliance members who are employed overseas in their vocational professions.[24]

In conclusion, it appears to this writer that in the areas of academic, theological and practical training for ministry candidates, the Alliance today is continuing within the early patterns developed by Dr. Simpson. We have benefited from experimentations in the rapid deployment of hastily-trained people followed by the shift to more comprehensive preparation. The latter is still Alliance policy today. Obviously there is always room for improvement. We must continue to stress and rekindle our traditional emphases on the fullness and power of the Holy Spirit, the utter commitment to the cause of reaching every people, tongue and nation for Christ, and the consecration of our financial resources.

Certainly the past century has bequeathed us a rich heritage in the preparation of missionary and pastoral candidates. May we strive to serve our generation and the next as well as Dr. A.B. Simpson served his and succeeding generations as we continue to train and commission ministry personnel for our world.

ENDNOTES

1. Walter M. Turnbull, "A Christian Educator," in A.E. Thompson, *The Life of A.B. Simpson* (New York: Christian Alliance Publishing Co., 1920), p. 214.

2. A.B. Simpson, "East London Training Institute for Home and Foreign Missions," in *The Word, the Work and the World* 1 (January-July, 1882): 93 (hereafter cited as *WWW*).

3. A.B. Simpson, "Editorial," in the *Christian and Missionary Alliance Weekly* 18 (April 30, 1897): 419 (hereafter cited as *CMAW*).

4. William C. Stevens, "Missionary Institute," *CMAW* 24 (April 1905): 205.

5. Turnbull, "A Christian Educator," p. 215.

6. Ibid., p. 216.

7. A.B. Simpson, "New York Missionary Training College," in *WWW* 5 (October 1885): 270.

8. Ibid.

9. Ibid.

10. Turnbull, "A Christian Educator," p. 218.

11. A.B. Simpson, "Editorial," in *The Christian Alliance and Missionary Weekly* 4 (May 23, 1890): 328 (hereafter cited as *CAMW*).

12. A.B. Simpson, "Why I Should Go," *CAMW* 8 (April 1892): 220.

13. Ibid.

14. Turnbull, "A Christian Educator," pp. 218-219.

15. Stevens, "Missionary Institute," p. 205.

16. A.B. Simpson, "Editorial," *CMAW* 24 (May 6, 1905): 273.

17. A.B. Simpson, "Opportunity, Achievement and Conflict," in *CMAW* 26 (November 11, 1906): 294.

18. A.B. Simpson, "Editorial," in *CMAW* 27 (February 22, 1908): 348.

19. A.B. Simpson, "Editorial," in *The Christian Alliance* 2 (April 1889): 50.

20. Daryl Westwood Cartmel, "Mission Policy and Program of A.B. Simpson" (M.A. Thesis, Hartford Seminary Foundation, 1962), pp. 64-65.

21. Mrs. H. Grattan Guinness, in *The Regions Beyond* 2 (August 1890): 309, quoted in Cartmel, "Mission Policy," p. 67.

22. Cartmel, "Mission Policy," pp. 88-89.

23. Ruth A. Tucker, *From Jerusalem to Irian Jaya* (Grand Rapids: Zondervan, 1983), pp. 291, 302.

24. Dr. L.L. King, in *The Open Line* 4 (September-October, 1985): 6.

JACOB P. KLASSEN

Jacob P. Klassen graduated from Canadian Bible College in 1960, and left two years later to serve as a missionary in Ecuador. He received an M.Miss. from Fuller School of World Mission in 1974, and in 1981, joined the faculty of Canadian Theological Seminary as Assistant Professor of World Mission and Evangelism. He completed a D.Miss. at Trinity Evangelical Divinity School in 1986.

EARLY ALLIANCE MISSIONS IN CHINA*

by

Paul L. King

In the late 1880s, when Christian and Missionary Alliance missionaries first arrived in China, the land already had a long history of contact with Europe and North America. For more than a millennium, China had held a fascination for people from the West, and from early times, China had been a special concern for Christian missions. By the seventh century, European traders and Christian missionaries were making their way to the Middle Kingdom. In the thirteenth century, the Church of Rome sent a new wave of missionaries to China. But, it was not until the seventeenth century that the Society of Jesus was finally able to establish a permanent Roman Catholic presence in the land.

By the early nineteenth century, when Protestant missions were begun in China, Western imperial powers were starting to carve out spheres of influence along the coast. As the century wore on, a declining Manchu dynasty was powerless to stem the tide of foreign privilege and presence that eventually spread to every corner of the land.

---

*This essay is an expansion of articles which have been published in *His Dominion* 11 (1985), 17-23, and *The Alliance Witness* (January 15, 1986), 7-10.

During the latter half of the nineteenth century, many church organizations, mostly North American and British, made China a special focus for missionary endeavor. The unequal treaties, with the provisions of extra-territoriality and most-favoured-nation status, made it possible for non-Chinese of all sorts to have free run of the land. But among the foreign missionaries, entrepreneurs, diplomats, and soldiers, the missionaries were the most salient, the most misunderstood, the most hated and feared. There were several reasons for this: they were the only foreigners that many Chinese saw; in some people's eyes they were vaguely identified with the opium trade; their religion was sometimes seen as a political threat; they looked like "foreign devils"; but mostly they were committed to a fundamental reordering of Chinese culture.

Alliance missionaries, at the turn of the century, were not always fully aware of what generated the intense opposition and violent persecution they encountered. They identified it as Satan defending his kingdom of darkness against the invasion of light, but they were sometimes ignorant of the historical antecedents and cross-cultural context that would not only have given perspective to the vicissitudes through which they went, but would also have profoundly influenced the formation of their policies and procedures.

For example, it is possible that a more critical evaluation of their status under extra-territoriality provisions of the unequal treaties would have resulted in mission policies and practices that distanced them from their imperialist compatriots. As it was, missionaries accepted the near-diplomatic immunity which was available to them, thus distancing themselves from the very people they wanted to win to Christ.

They, like us, were products of their age. It was the age of European colonial expansion, motivated in part by a desire to bring "Christian" civilization to the heathen world. Missionaries tended to see the unequal treaties as God's means of opening the door to China and while they took exception to some of the practices of Western powers and foreign traders, most of them uncritically took advantage of their special privileges and thus identified themselves with Western imperialism.

I am not sure that we would have done things any differently, and it will only be years from now that we or others will be able to look back and see the mistakes that we have enshrined in our pursuit of the heavenly vision. It is in the nature of things that we are blind to the future, myopic about the present, but often have 20/20 vision as we view the past. For instance, missionaries of the last century almost universally adopted a Great White Father attitude toward Chinese "natives," a stance which seemed appropriate and natural at the time. However, from the vantage point of historical perspective, we can look back to the nineteenth and early twentieth centuries and see that missionaries' failure to establish indigenous churches from the beginning placed a heavy burden on Chinese Christians, a burden which they are only now beginning to shake off.

It is with a clear vision of hindsight that one of those early twentieth-century missionaries is able to look back and concisely summarize the socio-political context of those years:

> The turmoil was that of a China awakening, a China reacting against many severe grievances, many involving foreigners: the power- and influence-grabbing of aggressive foreign governments; the greed of foreign businessmen; and even one foreign element in the name of religion.

> This was by no means all. China was suffering results of her own proud, ill-advised and bitterly anti-foreign actions; and her ages-old self-strangulating internal problems. Unrest existed all the more because of reforms that failed to become realities.[1]

ALLIANCE MOTIVATIONS FOR CHINA MISSIONS

China held a prominent place in the missionary vision of Dr. A.B. Simpson. That missionary vision had its roots in Simpson's early life in Canada. George L. MacKay, the Canadian Presbyterian pioneer missionary to Formosa (Taiwan), made an impact on him. While still a youngster, he had heard H. Grattan Guinness present a missionary challenge in Chatham, Ontario.[2] The examples and messages of these and other prominent missionaries of the day established a deep missionary concern that motivated Simpson throughout his life.

Years later, when Simpson established The Christian and Missionary Alliance, his vision was to send missionaries to places where the Gospel had never before been heard. The interior of China was one of the vast pioneer areas that beckoned to him, and China became one of the first fields of missionary endeavor for the C&MA.

Early Alliance missionaries were committed to one priority: evangelism. They went overseas with very spartan outfits, considering their inner spiritual preparation to be more important than any earthly goods or creature comforts that they could bring for their lives and ministries.[3]

Neither the pioneer spirit nor the modest outfits of missionaries were innovative. Many other Protestant missionary agencies of the time shared similar viewpoints and approaches in the task of world evangelization. Simpson's unique contribution to the missionary enterprise was the Faith Promise Pledge system. This has become a great motivator for Christians on the home front to give sacrificially to the cause of missions, and today C&MA churches continue to have among the highest per-capita giving rate in Christendom.[4]

Early Alliance missionaries were totally committed to fulfilling their call, even if it meant privation or death. They were individuals who had had a deep spiritual experience under Dr. Simpson's ministry, they shared his global missionary vision, and they were prepared to gladly pay the ultimate price in order to take the Gospel to the ends of the earth and thus hasten the return of Christ.

ALLIANCE BEGINNINGS IN CHINA

In 1887, Dr. William Cassidy, a Canadian, became the first Alliance missionary to sail for China. Back in Toronto, Cassidy had been first a school principal and then a medical student. Whether through education or medicine, he had a burning desire to help people and bring them to salvation in Christ. This became the basis for a strong missionary vision and eventually brought him into contact with Dr. Simpson. He received missionary training at the Missionary Training Institute in

New York City (now Nyack [NY] College) and he became the first missionary ordained by the Alliance.[5]

He travelled across the Pacific in steerage class out of a desire to meet Chinese, begin learning the language, and commence ministry to people from the country of his destination. However, he contracted smallpox and was put ashore in Japan, where he succumbed to the illness. He is buried in Japan.

Cassidy's untimely death came as a jolt to the mission-minded evangelical world, but it provided a powerful impetus for commitment of missionary candidates and their rapid deployment overseas. Less than a year after Cassidy's death, his widow, who had remained in the States pending his finding a location for language study and evangelistic work, sailed for China,[6] as did a number of other missionary women, and within a few years, a sizeable contingent of Alliance missionaries was beginning to establish itself in the interior.

265

In 1888, the first Alliance work was begun in Wuhu, Anhui Province, on the Yangtse River, and from that administrative base, spread further inland to Hunan and Hubei and to Sichuan and Guizhou provinces. Because communications and travel were so slow and difficult over such a vast territory, it seemed advisable, after some years, to move the field headquarters to a more central location, which was Wuchang, Hubei Province. Still later, because of expanding work in an area that stretched 1,200 miles from east to west, the field was divided into two administrative entities, Central China (Anhui, Hunan and Hubai), and West China (Guizhou-Sichuan Border).

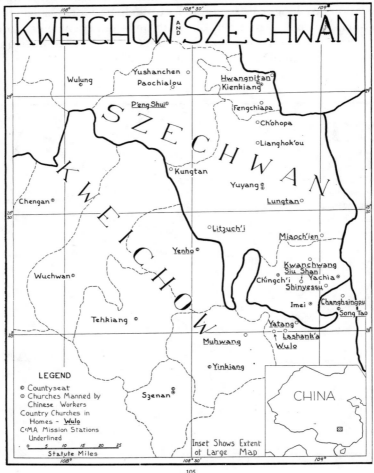

Changsha, the capital of Hunan Province, held a special challenge for Alliance missionaries. It was an extremely difficult city to enter as the population had an active hatred for foreigners. The missionaries viewed Changsha as a citadel of Satan, a spiritual bastion to be conquered. Around 1900, when Benjamin H. Alexander attempted to enter the city, he demanded legal protection for himself and his associates. When the local magistrate refused to provide such protection, he and his colleagues went ahead with colportage work, believing that God had sent them there to conquer the ramparts of Satan. They were savagely attacked and had to beat a hasty retreat to their boat. Alexander subsequently appealed to the U.S. Consul for protection, the Changsha magistrate was replaced, and Christian work was finally established in that city.[7]

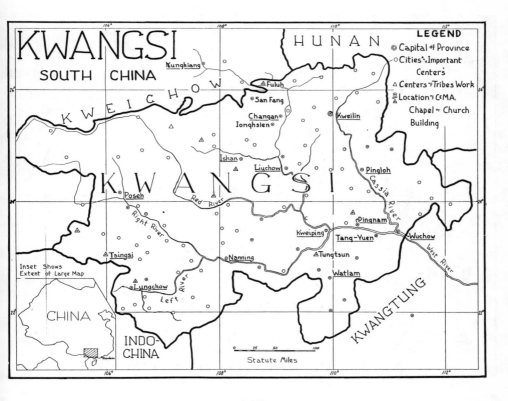

By 1895, a foothold had been gained in Guangxi Province, South China, an area which other missionary groups had abandoned because of violent local opposition.

Among the vast population of that province, the number of Alliance missionaries was only a drop in the bucket. Moreover, they laboured against great odds, battling tropical illnesses, risking bandit attacks, enduring both the curiosity and the indifference of the people. Nevertheless, they laid a foundation for a church which continues to this day.

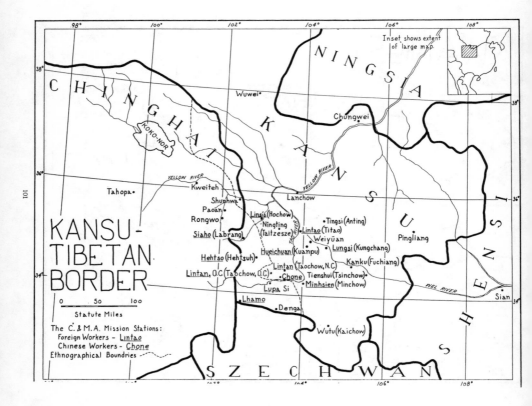

The Kansu-Tibetan Border area was the last Alliance field to be established in China. Around 1895, Reverend William Christie took a group on a trek of several months from Central China, to begin work in the Northwest provinces and Tibet. Mr. Christie was a stone mason from Scotland who later became Treasurer of the C&MA. He was assisted in China by W.W. Simpson (no relation to A.B. Simpson). Over vast distances and difficult terrain, among a population with a history of violence, and in an area where superstition had an especially strong hold on people, a Christian witness was established among Tibetans, Chinese and Moslem minority peoples.[8] Tibetans and Moslem minority peoples were hostile to Christianity, Chinese were hostile to foreigners, and the severe environment was hostile to human life.

For a time, the C&MA had a field of ministry in North China, an area encompassing Beijing, Shanxi Province, and Inner Mongolia. Unlike the other fields of ministry, which were all staffed by North American personnel, the North China Mission was comprised almost entirely of Swedes. They went to China in 1893 through an arrangement which Mr. William Fransen made with Dr. Simpson to support them. Mr. Fransen was a Swedish American whose missionary vision had been fired through association with Dr. Simpson. Because his missionaries had a more limited financial base in Sweden, they went to China with even more meager allowances and outfits than the North American missionaries had. They served with a spirit of joyful sacrifice and were beginning to see fruit for their labours.

Then, in 1900, a secret society known as the Boxers began to commit violent acts of aggression against foreigners in North China. The Boxers were a group within a larger secret society that had been in existence since the late eighteenth century. They were fiercely anti-foreign and believed themselves to be invincible.[9] With tacit support from the highest levels of government, they vowed to eliminate the imperialist presence from China, and Christians of every color were special targets of attack.

Christianity was viewed as the essence of imperialism, and Chinese Christians were considered "running dogs of the imperialists," traitors to their country. Unfortunately, the Swedish Alliance missionaries were working in the part of the country where foreigners and Chinese Christians were most savagely attacked by the Boxers. The entire mission was destroyed with as many as twenty-four adults and thirteen children brutally murdered, and the remaining personnel barely escaping, with great hardship, back to Sweden through Mongolia and Siberia. The North China Mission was never re-established, but out of the remnants of that group, The Evangelical Alliance Mission (TEAM) was founded.[10]

EARLY TWENTIETH-CENTURY ALLIANCE CHINA MISSIONS

After the horror of the Boxer Rebellion, a period of relative calm ensued, and missionaries all over China returned to stations from which they had fled at the time of the atrocities. With no way of knowing that the dynasty itself would fall in less than a decade, they saw that the Boxer Rebellion and subsequent Protocol had undermined the credibility of the Emperor, enhanced the prestige of foreigners, and increased people's interest in things foreign, including the foreign religion. Missionaries felt that they had entered on a new age of opportunity. For instance, Dr. Robert H. Glover, a distinguished Canadian missionary who would later become C&MA Foreign Secretary, wrote:

> If ever a dark storm-cloud had a silver lining, that of the Boxer uprising had. It has brought Missionary work into greater prominence and larger favour than ever before. By revealing the corruption of China's government and the hollowness of her superstitious systems, it has produced a wide-spread feeling of discontent with the old order of things, and an openness of mind toward Western thought and religion.[11]

Converts, baptisms, and churches showed a dramatic increase after the Boxer Rebellion.[12] In addition, the greater acceptance of foreigners and the increased curiosity about Christianity resulted in a great sense of optimism among missionaries all across China, a missionary challenge that they extended to youth in North America, resulting in an enthusiastic response from committed Christians at home. Dr. Glover called for ten new missionaries to be sent to each of the four China fields, and in October, 1904, a first group of eleven was commissioned for work in China. Two Canadians were in that group, Mr. Walter Oldfield and Mrs. M. Allward.[13] Mr. Oldfield served for 43 years on the South China Field.[14] Mrs. Allward was also sent to South China.[15]

A great drought occurred in South China just after 1900, and Alliance missionaries were very active in famine relief. It has been reported, for instance, that officials and gentry in Guiping, Guangxi, collected a large sum of money and handed it over to Alliance missionaries for distribution among needy farmers.[16] This makes an interesting commentary on the credibility and acceptance that missionaries had established for themselves, especially in view of the fact that thirty years before, Guiping had been a centre of violent anti-foreign opposition. In fact, all of Guangxi Province had been noted for banditry, a condition which had prevented other Protestant missions from establishing operations there. And it had only been with great difficulty that the Alliance had been able to begin any work in South China. Now, only a decade or so after beginning work, Alliance missionaries were being asked to coordinate relief efforts, a remarkable change indeed.

However, across the land, Chinese often identified missionaries with the hated foreign imperialists who were threatening China's sovereignty. Nor was such a connection entirely without basis. The French had forced the Chinese to give special concessions to the Roman Catholic Church in their Treaty of Tianjin (1860). The provisions of that and the other unequal treaties did provide special rights and immunities to Protestant missionaries and Chinese Christians, specifically in articles that had been formulated by missionary-diplomats such as W.A.P. Martin.[17] The current Chinese Communist view of Christian missionaries as being the religious arm of foreign imperialism and of Chinese Christians as "running dogs of the imperialists" is rather understandable.

EVOLUTION OF POLICIES AND PROCEDURES

In the difficult formative years of Alliance China missions,

271

policies and procedures were developed which set the pattern for the first half of the twentieth century. The primary policy was to win adults to Christ and to establish churches. The standard procedure was to buy property in a regional town or city centre where a mission station could be established as a base of operations. From that base, missionaries would do extensive itinerant evangelism in the area. Preaching points would be established where numbers of people responded to the Gospel, and chapels or churches organized where growing groups of Christians came into being. Auxiliary pursuits of colportage, literacy work, leadership training, and medical and relief activities were subservient means to the primary goals of evangelism and church planting.

At the same time, missionaries were very much aware that communication through the spiritual quality of their lives was more definitive in bringing people to Christ than any specific methodology. In 1900, Martin Ekvall, an Alliance missionary on the Gansu-Tibetan Border, wrote, "The results of missions in China were brought about more effectually by the Christian life exhibited by the missionary living among the natives rather than by merely travelling and preaching in the towns once or twice, and passing on." [18]

Thus, one of the first procedures to emerge was for Alliance missionaries to live among the people to whom they ministered and to identify with them as much as possible. Some adapted more than others to Chinese ways (e.g., Alexander wore a queue in the Manchu style of the day). But their modest allowances and meager outfits did force them to live closer to a Chinese economic level than was true for many other foreigners in China.

A second policy grew out of the principle of equality. One advantage of the Faith Promise Pledge system was that all personnel received the same allowance. The principle of equality of stipend level was strictly adhered to, thus reducing individual jealousies, hardships, and economic advantages. [19]

A third policy and procedure is related to leadership training. Theological education for Chinese leaders was an early priority for Alliance missionaries. Just after the turn of the century, Drs. R.H. Glover and R.A. Jaffray, both Canadians, were instrumental in establishing the Alliance Bible Seminary in Wuzhou, Guangxi Province. Dr. Glover proclaimed that the school's purpose was to produce "men more thoroughly trained in head and heart,"[20] a goal which continues unchanged today at the school's location in Hong Kong, where it is one of the premier seminaries of the colony.

From the beginning, the Alliance Bible Seminary had a formidable and useful curriculum. In 1902, just two years after the school was founded, Dr. Glover reported curriculum content and other activities designed to equip students for ministry:

> Old Testament—the Pentateuch and Joshua; New Testament—the Life of Christ, Acts, Romans, I and II Corinthians, Pilgrim's Progress with scripture proofs taken as a basis for Bible Theology, Dr. Martin's 'Evidences of Christianity,' Dr. Grave's 'Homiletics,' and Church History up to the Reformation. Written sermons or analyses of given texts have been required fortnightly. Instruction has been given by my Chinese colleague, Mr. Young, in Chinese classics, history, and composition. Elementary geography and arithmetic have also been taught. Each student has preached once every week in the street chapel, and all have taken part in the nightly meeting for personal work.[21]

Theological education in well-established institutions was never viewed as the main purpose or activity for Simpson's missionary enterprise. Rather, it was a means to help achieve the primary purpose for Alliance missions, namely, the evangelization of the country and the establishing of churches. Thus, while a few missionaries were teaching in resident Bible school programs, most of their colleagues were directly involved in activities that would bring their vision to reality. The established policy and procedure are described by Dr. Robert A. Jaffray, the distinguished missionary from Canada:

> The method of our work has been, after the necessary itinerating, to secure permanent stations, to take possession of the great centres of population as far as possible, and from these strategic points to extend the Gospel light into the darkness all around.[22]

One policy that has changed over the years had to do with the acquisition of real estate. From the beginning, and for many years thereafter, Alliance missionaries did not like to rent property, preferring instead to buy or build their own residences and places of ministry.[23] Today, in Hong Kong and Taiwan at least, the Mission prefers to rent property, partly because the cost of real estate is so high, but primarily in order to underscore and make easier to implement the conviction that the mission is temporary while the local church is permanent.

In the early years of Alliance China missions, missionaries had to deal with the problem of "rice Christians," Chinese who wanted "to join the Missions because of the temporary advantages supposed to come to them through the favorable influence of the missionaries in their social and civil disputes."[24] At least in part because of the "rice Christian" problem, a procedure of rigorous screening of baptismal candidates came to be practiced. New believers were considered "inquirers" until they were baptized, and between the time of conversion and the time of baptism, they went through a lengthy probationary period during which they were to successfully complete a catechism course and demonstrate that their new faith had made a difference in their lives.

The same policy has long since become standard procedure in China Protestant churches everywhere, not only where missionaries are still working, but also in the Peoples Republic of China. Though baptismal regeneration is not part of the church's faith, a believer is not considered to be a Christian until he has been baptized and thereby joined the church.

LATER DEVELOPMENT

In 1911, Sun Yat-sen's revolution overthrew the Qing Manchu dynasty and ushered in the Republican era, which continued until 1949. Those 38 years were among the most turbulent in Chinese history, filled with political revolution, iconoclastic ideologies, literary breakthroughs, and foreign invasion.

During those years, the missionary enterprise in China flourished, reaching its peak in 1927. Early in that year, some 6,000 Protestant missionaries were in the land. But within a few months, the Nationalist-Communist coalition government collapsed, civil war erupted, and about 4,000 missionaries fled to their homelands. During the next two decades, as China disintegrated under Nationalist-Communist-Japanese war, missionaries filtered back to the country, but there were never again as many missionaries in China as there had been in early 1927.

The C&MA maintained its work through all those difficult years, carrying on itinerant evangelism, helping in relief programs, establishing churches, and training Chinese church leadership. While many missionaries had a colonialist-imperialist world view, the C&MA, as early as the 1920s, adopted a policy of establishing indigenous churches. Though truly indigenous churches were not a reality before 1950, significant steps in that direction were made, particularly during the war years. From our vantage point today, that was truly a forward-looking policy, attested by the many former Alliance ministers who are still in ministry there today.

In 1949, the Communist armies defeated the Nationalists and established Marxist rule in China. The foreign presence was expelled and the bamboo curtain brought an end to the age of Protestant China missions.

CONCLUSION

Early Alliance history in China is a record of heroism and martyrdom in a cataclysmic clash between cultures. Missionaries were emissaries of Christ, but also products of a colonial age as they confronted a declining dynasty in a century of revolution.

Today, we can look back and recognize their heroism, and admire their vision and dedication, while deploring their imperialistic connection and the paternalism which many of them had toward the Chinese. They, like we, had victories and defeats, did some things right and other things wrong, went in the name of Christ and were products of their age. Today there are no missionaries resident in China, but a church is there because missionaries went there, and Christ is continuing to build His church on the foundation laid through their efforts.

ENDNOTES

1. Matthew Brown Birrel (1869-1957), "An Autobiography" (unpublished paper, n.d.), p. 23.

2. Paul H. Bartel, "An Overview and Evaluation of China Alliance Missions" (unpublished document, n.d.), p. 152.

3. Bartel, op. cit., p. 153.

4. Ibid., p. 160.

5. Lindsay Reynolds, *Footprints* (Beaverlodge: Buena Book Services, 1982), p. 99.

6. Reynolds, op. cit., p. 101.

7. *Christian and Missionary Alliance Weekly*, August 12, 1905, pp. 504-506. (Hereafter cited as *CMAW*).

8. Birrel, op. cit., p. 16.

9. Li Chien-nung, *The Political History of China, 1840-1928* (Stanford: Stanford University Press, 1978), p. 173.

10. *CMAW*, October 20, 1900, pp. 215, 216.

11. Ibid., September 3, 1903, p. 191.

12. Kenneth S. Latourette, *A History of Christian Missions in China* (NY: Paragon Book Gallery, Ltd., 1929), pp. 567ff.

13. *CMAW*, October 1, 1904, p. 273.

14. Reynolds, op. cit., p. 333.

15. Ibid., p. 332.

16. *CMAW*, October 3, 1903, p. 246.

17. Ralph Covell, *W.A.P. Martin: Pioneer of Progress in China* (Washington: Christian University Press, 1978).

18. *CMAW*, October 13, 1900, p. 202.

19. Ibid., June 28, 1902, p. 44.

20. Ibid., July 5, 1902, p. 44.

21. Ibid.

22. Ibid., February 1, 1902, p. 61.

23. Ibid., October 17, 1903, pp. 274, 275.

24. Ibid., May 13, 1905, p. 297.

(NOTE: Maps are hand-drawn and appeared in the Missionary Atlas [Harrisburg, PA: Christian Publications Inc., 1950].)

PAUL L. KING

Paul L. King serves as Director of the Centre for Chinese Studies and Assistant Professor of Sociology and Chinese Studies at Canadian Theological Seminary. He is also Adjunct Professor of Computer Science at the University of Regina. Dr. King received an M.A. and Ph.D. from Cornell University, an M.P.S. from Alliance Theological Seminary, and a B.S. from Nyack College. He was a Christian & Missionary Alliance missionary to Taiwan for eleven years, and as a research scholar and consultant, has made four extended visits to the Peoples Republic of China in the last four years. He is the primary inventor of a Chinese electronic word processor and the author of several published papers pertaining to linguistic considerations in Chinese data entry.

PUBLICATIONS OF A.B. SIMPSON

by

John Sawin

Simpson's publications may be divided into ten categories. The word "publications" is used in preference to "writings" because sixty-seven of his books were not written as books, but are sermons preached at the Gospel Tabernacle and various conventions. They were recorded stenographically and then printed in his periodicals. It is doubtful that Simpson did much editing, although some sermons were severely edited, but probably by another hand. By contrast, A.J. Gordon's well-known books, *The Ministry of the Spirit* and *The Ministry of Healing*, were written documents. As an author or writer, Simpson is at his best in the editorials and articles in his periodicals. Readers, therefore, should remember that when reading such books as *Wholly Sanctified* or *A Larger Christian Life*, they are in reality listening to Sunday morning discourses preached at the Gospel Tabernacle.

Too many people assume that Simpson's books were written commentaries, such as the *Christ in the Bible* series, and evaluate them as such, but most of them were sermons. Simpson was a prince of preachers in his generation, and sought to impart to his audiences spiritual truth that would elevate their Christian experience and motivate them to such commitment to Christ that the Gospel would be preached to neglected people everywhere and thus hasten the day of Christ's return.

The following is a list of ten categories of Simpson's publications. The total number (101) will be less than the total

279

number of Simpson's publications listed later, due to the fact that some of his sermons in one book were later re-published in a book or books with different titles. For example, *Danger Lines of the Deeper Life* (1897) reappeared in 1902 as the first ten chapters of *Christ in the Bible*, Vol. IV *(Judges-Samuel)*.

(NOTE: There is a detailed study of this on file in the A.B. Simpson Historical Library, Nyack NY.)

CATEGORIES	NUMBER OF PUBLICATIONS
1. Biographies: *Michael Nardi* *Josephus Pulis* *Henry Wilson* *A Cloud of Witnesses*	4
2. Commentaries	5
3. Correspondence Course	1
4. Devotional (includes *Is Life Worth Living?*)	8
5. Doctrinal (healing: 2; prophecy: 1)	3
6. Hymn Books The three hymn books were also published in various combinations including Hymns of the Christian Life, 1, 2 & 3, 1908.	3
7. Poems	3
8. Promotional	6
9. Sermons	67
10. Travelogue (trip around the world, 1893)	1
TOTAL	**101**

Herewith is a list of all the titles published by Mr. Simpson. He may not have been the primary compiler of some of the books, but, at very least, oversaw their compilation, as was the case with *The Story of the C.&M.A.*, 1900, and *A Cloud of Witnesses*, 1887. The publisher in each case was Simpson's publishing house, which bore three different names throughout its existence:

1. *The Word, the Work and the World*
2. *The Christian Alliance Publishing Company*
3. *The Alliance Press*

Titles of the books, the number of pages, the date (not necessarily the copyright date, but either the time they were preached or originally composed), as well as any helpful comments that may increase understanding, are listed below. below.

TITLE	PAGES	DATE
1. *All in All* or *Christ in Colossians* (Later it became part of the *Christ in the Bible* series.)	65	1901 March
2. *Apostolic Church, The,* or *I Corinthians* (Later it became part of the *Christ in the Bible* series.)	238	1897 November 1898 March
3. *Back to Patmos* or *Prophetic Outlook on Present Conditions* (Probably is a written document.)	103	1914
4. *Berachah Year Book, The, for 1886* (Readings for each month and promotional articles re: the work of the Gospel Tabernacle.)	40	1885 December
5. *Berachah Year Book, The, for 1887* (It is advertised in the periodicals but a copy has not been found.)	?	1886 December
6. *But God*	112	1889 June/July
7. *Challenge of Missions, The* (Five missionary sermons selected after Simpson's death.)	68	1926
8. *Christian Alliance Year Book, The, for 1888* (A promotional book similar to numbers 4 & 5 above, but now on behalf of the Christian Alliance and the Missionary Alliance.)	72	1887 December
9. *Christian Alliance, The,* and the *International Missionary Alliance Year Book for 1893* (Similar to number 8.)	70	1892 December

(continued on next page)

Continued

	CHRIST IN THE BIBLE Series, Nos. 10-35, in the order of the books of the Bible.		
10.	Genesis and Exodus, Vol. I. (The original edition includes a section of homiletical hints and illustrative materials to aid fledgling preachers. Some of the material Simpson used in the Missionary Training College. An octavo volume, 9 x 6 in.)	394	1888 November
11.	Leviticus - Deuteronomy, Vol. II (Classroom material, an octavo volume.)	412	1889 December
12.	Joshua, Vol. III. (Time ran out in Simpson's schedule. Sermons; an octavo volume.)	272	1893 September to 1894 February
13.	Judges to Samuel, Vol. IV. Of the 15 chapters, ten sermons were taken from Danger Lines in the Deeper Life, 1897, and five sermons from Making Jesus King, 1897.	243	1902
14.	Samuel, Kings and Chronicles, Vol. V. Of the 19 chapters, thirteen are from Making Jesus King, 1897. (July and August)	279	1902
15.	Kings and Prophets, Vol. VI	291	1902 November to 1903 March
16.	The Psalms. A CPI publication, a reprint of Jesus in the Psalms (January-April, 1892).	158	1920s
17.	Isaiah, Vol. VII	401	1904 November to 1905 May
18.	Life of Christ, Vol. VIII. Similar to numbers 10 & 11, class lecture material. An octavo volume; not reprinted.	400	1888 December

(continued on next page)

Continued

19. *Matthew to Luke*, Vol. IX. An octavo volume similar to No. 18. It wasn't reprinted. Homiletic hints were printed in the back.	343	1889 November
20. *Matthew*, Vol. XIII. A book of sermons.	339	1903 October to 1904 April
21. *Mark*, Vol. XIV. At this time, Simpson preached 22 sermons based on Mark's Gospel. Only 9 were published in this book.	183	1909 November to 1910 March
22. *Luke*, Vol. XIV B. Sermons, not a reprint of part of Vol. IX.	216	1905 October to 1906 February
23. *John-Acts*, Vol. X. Another octavo volume, classroom material.	367	1891 December
24. *The Gospel of John*, Vol. XV A reprint of the first section of Vol. X, edited slightly. The periodicals published approximately 60 sermons based on this Gospel which are not printed in any book.	301	1904
25. *Acts*, Vol. XVI. Sermons, not a reprint of second section in Vol. X.	203	1902 January to April
26. *Romans*, Vol. XI. The last octavo volume; sermons, not classroom materials.	274	1894 February to July
27. *I & II Corinthians*, Vol. XVIII A combination of *The Apostolic Church*, 1898, and recent sermons on II Corinthians; except that chapter 10, *The Grace of Giving*, was preached at Old Orchard in 1899.	395	1904 April to June
28. *Galatians and Ephesians*, Vol. XIX A reprint of *Free Grace* (March-April, 1901), and *The Highest Christian Life* (March-May, 1898).	254	1904

(continued on next page)

Continued

29.	*Philippians, Colossians and Thessa-lonians*, Vol. XX. These are sermons printed first in *The Sweetest Christian Life* (October-December 1899), *All in All* (March 1901), and *The Epistles of the Advent* (February 1901). The last chapter was preached in August, 1894.	290	1903
30.	*Philippians and Colossians.* A CPI reprint of two sections of Vol. XX.	124	1920s
31.	*Thessalonians, Timothy and Titus* A CPI publication. Thessalonians is a reprint of Section 3, Vol. XX. The other sermons were found in the periodicals, 1894, 1901, 1908 and 1912.	127	1920s
32.	*Hebrews*, Vol. XXII. A CPI reprint of *Within the Vail* (January-March 1890).	157	1920s
33.	*James*, Vol. XXII A. A CPI reprint of *Practical Christianity* (April-June 1901).	117	1920s
34.	*Peter, John and Jude.* A CPI reprint of *Words of Comfort For Tired Workers* (October-December 1901), and *Messages of Love* (April-June 1900).	197	1920s
35.	*Revelation*, Vol. XXIV. A republi-cation of *Heaven Opened* (November 1898-February 1899).	299	1905

Revelation concludes the *Christ in the Bible* series. Simpson didn't complete the schedule of books he envisioned in 1888-89. His busy schedule caused him to substitute sermons for written commentaries on Christ in all the Bible.

(continued on next page)

Continued

36.	*Christ in the Tabernacle*	117	1888 July/August
37.	*Christ Life, The.* The original edition had 5 chapters. Simpson added a new first chapter in 1912. It was an Easter sermon of 1900. In 1925, Walter Turnbull added chapters 7 and 8 taken from chapters 1 and 2 of *The Self Life* and *The Christ Life*, September 1896, and February 1897.	99	1888 May/June
38.	*Christ of the Forty Days*, the eight sermons; small format.	311	1890 April/May
39.	*Cloud of Witnesses, A.* Thirty-seven testimonies of Divine healing.	253	1887 July
40.	*Colportage Library, The* From his own publications, and some other books that his publishing company had printed, Simpson began in January, 1899, to reprint two paperbacks every month. They were intended to send out the message as quickly and cheaply as possible. A year's subscription cost $2.50 and brought to one's home 24 volumes annually. This program continued until postal regulations changed in mid-1901. Simpson published 62 paperbacks. Thirty-five of these were from Simpson's own books. The reprints were not always a full copy of the original book, and sometimes the title was changed. There is not any new Simpson material in the Colportage Library.		
41.	*Coming One, The.* Chapters 1-3, 8-10 & 13 are sermons published in the *Alliance Weekly.* The source of the other eight chapters are unknown. Some of them bear a resemblance to material in *The Gospel of the Kingdom.*	228	1912 January to March
42.	*Correspondence Courses.* These studies were intended to be a three-year study course. There were four subjects: (1) Bible Commentary; (2) Christian Doctrine; (3) Deeper Truth and Life; and (4) Homiletics.		1916-1918

285

(continued on next page)

Continued

43.	*Cross of Christ, The.* Sermons preached over a period of seven years, 1903-1909.	157	1910
44.	*Count Your Blessings.* A Bible prayer and promise for each day.	154	1900
45.	*Danger Lines in the Deeper Life.* Republished in *Christ in the Bible,* Vol. IV.	156	1896 November to 1897 January
46.	*Days of Heaven on Earth* Three hundred and sixty-four one-page sermonettes for each day of the year. Old Testament, 116 sermonettes; New Testament, 248 sermonettes.	371	1897 December
47.	*Discovery of Divine Healing, The* Ten of the 13 chapters were reprinted from *Friday Meeting Talks,* No. 3. The entire book was republished in 1925 under the title, *The Lord For The Body.*	146	1903
48.	*Divine Emblems in the Book of Genesis*	194	1888 February to March
49.	*Divine Emblems in Exodus*	207	1888 April/May
50.	*Earnests of the Coming Age* Twenty chapters of sermons (17) and articles (3) collected and edited by Walter Turnbull. Chapter 15 was taken from II Corinthians, ch. 8. All the chapters can be found in the periodicals 1902-1910, and 1916 and 1917.	222	1921
51.	*Echoes of the New Creation* or *Messages of the Cross, the Resurrection and the Coming Glory.* Chapters two and three were published in other books.	166	1903
52.	*Elim, Its Wells and Palms.* Readings for twelve months and seventy years.	147	1905 December

(continued on next page)

Continued

53.	*Epistles of the Advent* or *Christ in Thessalonians.* Chapter 4 was added in later editions, a sermon preached in August 1894. The four chapters became part of the *Christ in the Bible* series.	66	1901 February
54.	*Evangelistic Addresses.* An attempt to preserve some of Simpson's evangelistic messages. Unfortunately, he printed very few of his evangelistic sermons in the periodicals. Chapter one is a reprint of chapter seven in *A Larger Christian Life.*	96	1926
55.	*Fourfold Gospel, The.* The original edition had only four chapters. They were sermons delivered shortly after the formation of the two Alliance organizations. Two chapters were added in 1925.	106	1887 November/ December
56.	*Free Grace* or *Christ in Galatians* Published later as part of *Christ in the Bible* series.	65	1901 March/April
57.	*Friday Meeting Talks, No. 1* Messages given at the Friday afternoon healing and consecration meetings.	187	1894 November
58.	*Friday Meeting Talks, No. 2* or *Divine Prescriptions for the Sick and Suffering*	135	1899 March
59.	*Friday Meeting Talks, No. 3.* Except chapter three, these messages were published in *The Discovery of Divine Healing,* 1903, and *The Lord for the Body,* 1925. In the September-December issues of the periodical, there are four more Friday Talks not in this book. See 207, 249, 277 and 361.	111	1900 January to May

(continued on next page)

Continued

60.	*From The Uttermost To The Uttermost* The life story of the converted drunkard, Joseph Pulis. He was one of the original "seven" and served on the Board of Managers until 1912.	80	1914
61.	*The Fullness of Jesus* or *Christ Life in the New Testament.* Sermons preached when Simpson's congregation moved into the Church of the Disciples.	226	1886 May to November
62.	*The Gospel of Healing* (first edition) The first five chapters were first published in booklet form and also in the periodicals, ch. 1-3 in 1883, and 4-5 in 1885. They are not sermons. Later there were several editions and some editorial changes including deletions. The fourth edition appeared in 1890 and was revised in 1915. Probably more copies of this book were sold than any other Simpson publication.	167	1886
63.	*The Gospel of the Kingdom.* Simpson's first published sermons on prophecy. He presents considerable detailed information.	288	1886 October to 1887 April
64.	*Great Missionary Movement, A* The book is in two sections of 88 & 62 pages. The first section is a reprint of a series of tracts regarding Alliance missionary work. The second section contains the 1891 Annual Report of the Missionary Alliance and the Constitution and Bylaws of the same.	150	1892 March

(continued on next page)

Continued

65. *Heart Messages For Sabbaths At Home* Four sermonettes for each month of the year, plus a 13th month on the Fourfold Gospel.	233	1899 December
66. *Heavenly Vision, The*	125	1896 July to November
67. *Heaven Opened* or *Expositions of the Book of Revelation.* Later reprinted in *Christ in the Bible* series.	299	1898 November to 1899 February
68. *He Is Risen*	75	1887 March/April
69. *Henry Wilson, One of God's Best* Chapters 5-9 were written by A.B. Simpson; the others by Wilson's daughter, Madele.	195	1908 December
70. *Highest Christian Life, The* or *Expositions of the Book to the Ephesians.* Republished in the *Christ in the Bible* series.	100	1898 March to May
71. *Holy Ghost Ministries.* A reprint of seven chapters in *The King's Business*, 1886.		1901 May
72. *The Holy Spirit* or *Power From On High*, Vol. I, *Old Testament.* At Old Orchard, 1894, Stephen Merritt urged Simpson to write a "book of the Holy Ghost." He began the series at the Gospel Tabernacle in September.	394	1894 September to 1895 April
73. *The Holy Spirit* or *Power From On High*, Vol. II, *New Testament.*	392	1895 May to 1896 April
74. *Hymns of the Fourfold Gospel and the Fullness of Jesus.* Lyrics only.	130	1890
75. *In Heavenly Places* Sermons preached between March 1891, and April 1892.	247	1892

(continued on next page)

Continued

76. *Inquiries and Answers.* There are two parts: (1) thirty-seven questions and answers (30 pages) and (2) replies to Rev. A.F. Schauffler, Dr. A. Hodge, and Dr. J.M. Buckley (107 pages).	137	1886 July to December
77. *In the School of Christ* or *Lessons From New Testament Characters* (12).	250	1889 August to October
78. *In the School of Faith.* Lessons from Old Testament characters (18) (1907 edition). Chapters 1-7 were published in 1886. The title: *Seven Stars in the Firmament of Faith.*	336	Winter of 1885, 1886 and 1889 1890 January
79. *Is Life Worth Living?* Studies in Ecclesiastes. Brief articles, not sermons.	54	1899 January/ February
80. *Jesus in the Psalms.* Later reprinted in *Christ in the Bible* series.	340	1892 January to April
81. *King's Business, The.* Final sermons at the 23rd Street Tabernacle.	384	1886 January to April
82. *Land of Promise, The* or *Our Full Inheritance in Christ* (second edition). The congregation had just moved into Standard Hall.	273	1888 September to November
83. *Larger Christian Life, A.* The first sermon was preached at Old Orchard, the remainder at the Gospel Tabernacle.	432	1890 July to October
84. *Larger Outlooks on Missionary Lands* Simpson's diary of a round-the-world visit to mission fields. They were first printed in the periodicals.	595	1893
85. *Life More Abundantly* Devotional readings for 31 days.	134	1912 November
86. *Life of Prayer, The* (small format)	268	1890 May to July

(continued on next page)

Continued

87.	*Lord For The Body, The* Twelve chapters (1-11, 13) from *The Discovery of Divine Healing.* One chapter from *Inquiries and Answers,* Part I. Also Henry Wilson's healing experience.	142	1925
88.	*Love-Life of the Lord, The.* Sermons from the Song of Solomon.	213	1890 November/ December
89.	*Making Jesus King.* Reprinted in *Christ in the Bible* series, Vol. IV and V.	288	1897 February to June
90.	*Memorial Names.* The book is advertised, *Christian Alliance and Missionary Weekly* (March 1890), p. 145, but has not been found. The four sermons were printed in the periodical.		1890 January/ February
91.	*Messages of Love* or *Expositions of John's First Epistle.* Later reprinted in the *Christ in the Bible* series.	160	1900 April to June
92.	*Michele Nardi, The Italian Evangelist* His life and work.	175	1916
93.	*Millennial Chimes.* A collection of 62 poems covering five subjects: The Christ life, invitation, healing, hope, missions and travel. Some were later set to music and were included in *Hymns of the Christian Life.*	155	1894 December
94.	*Missionary Messages.* Probably selected by W. Turnbull from more than one hundred missionary sermons.	131	1925
95.	*Names of Jesus, The.* Not included in the book were three sermons on the same subject that were preached during the same period and were printed in the February, May 1891 periodicals. See pages 83, 131 and 275.	285	1891 January to June

(continued on next page)

Continued

96. *Natural Emblems of Spiritual Life* (small format)	356	1887 June to December
97. *The Old Faith and The New Gospels* Addresses about Christianity and modern thought delivered at Old Orchard.	161	1911 August
98. *Paul — The Ideal Man and Model Missionary* (small format)	73	1896 May/June
99. *Practical Christianity* or *Expositions of James' Epistle*. Later was re-printed in *Christ in the Bible* series.	162	1901 April to June
100. *Present Truth*. A series of sermons delivered at the New York October Convention. The emphasis is on the supernatural: God, book, life, church, body, hope and work.	151	1897 October
101. *Providence and Missions* The essence of sermons preached during the time in Chicago and elsewhere.	44	1898 March to June
102. *Salvation Sermons*. A collection chosen by Walter Turnbull.	123	1925
103. *Self-Life and Christ Life, The* All of these sermons appeared in other books.	89	1896 September 1897 February/ March
104. *Service For The King*. Seven sermons from *The King's Business*.	181	1900 July
105. *Seven Stars in the Firmament of Faith* This book has not been found. Its contents comprise the first seven chapters of *In the School of Faith*.		1885 December to 1886 February
106. *Songs of the Spirit*. One hundred and sixteen poems by A.B. Simpson published after his death. Some had been previously published ' and some had been set to music.	160	1920

(continued on next page)

Continued

107.	*Standing On Faith* or *Talks On The Self-Life*. Published and edited by Marshall, Morgan & Scott. They are a selection of sermons from six previously published books.	121	1932
108.	*Story of the Christian and Missionary Alliance, The.* A promotional publication relating some Alliance history, information of seven Alliance missionary areas, a list of Alliance officers and missionaries, and the Alliance financial statement of March 31, 1900.	98	1900 April
109.	*Sweetest Christian Life, The* or *Expositions of Philippians*. Later reprinted in *Christ in the Bible* series.	159	1899 October to December
110.	*Walking In Love*	270	1892 September to December
111.	*Walking In The Spirit*	297	1889 January to March
112.	*We Would See Jesus* Devotional readings about Jesus for thirty-one days.	62	1910 December
113.	*When The Comforter Came* Devotional readings about the Holy Spirit for thirty-one days.	126	1911 February
114.	*Wholly Sanctified*. A sixth sermon was added in recent editions.	189	1890 January to March
115.	*Within The Veil*. Expositions of Hebrews. Later reprinted in *Christ in the Bible* series.	256	1900 January to March
116.	*Words of Comfort For Tried Workers* Expositions of I Peter. Later reprinted in *Christ in the Bible* series.	130	1901 October to December

APPENDIX I

INTRODUCTION TO CHRIST IN THE BIBLE Series

When Dr. Simpson inaugurated this series, he stated that the proposed volumes were not "an attempt to compete with valuable works" published in the last few years. Rather, his intent was "to unfold the spiritual teachings of the Scriptures, especially with reference to the Person and work of Christ." (Preface, *Genesis, Exodus,* 1888 edition, p. vii.) Accordingly, he planned three parts for each volume:

1. An analysis of the spiritual teaching of the biblical book

2. Original and selected homiletic helps and illustrative materials

3. Historical and geographical papers illustrative of the various books and subjects (ibid., p. viii)

He also stated that "two causes have chiefly led to the publication of these volumes":

1. The desire of friends "to obtain, in a permanent form, the substance of the Bible teaching given at the Missionary Training College where most of these lectures were originally delivered."

2. "The call that comes to help the increasing number of consecrated Christians who are hungering for a deeper spiritual life and for a more profound acquaintance with the Word of God as it unfolds the fullness of Christ as Saviour, Sanctifier, Healer, and Coming Lord." (ibid., p. viii)

It is instructive to note the time of the above statements, 1888. The Christian Alliance and the Missionary Alliance had just been organized at Old Orchard in August of 1887. Simpson desired to help in increasing constituency. But "the times" also explain why the original impulse was never completed. The burgeoning Alliance demanded more and more of Simpson's time and his literary efforts suffered. Notice in column one of the chart which follows, that only seven volumes were published and two of those were not according to the proposed pattern. They were sermons. Five volumes appeared in 1888, 1889, and 1891, but two other sermons waited until 1894. Then the series went on the "back-burner" until 1902, no doubt because an abundance of other responsibilities was consuming his time and energies.

In 1902, Simpson set out to re-issue this series in five sets of six volumes per set, i.e., 30 volumes. They were to be uniform in binding and sell for $1.00 per volume, or $5.00 for a set of six. The first set was to go from Genesis to David/Solomon [see *Christian Alliance* (June, 1902, p. 318)]. In the *Christian Alliance* (September, 1908, p. 398), Simpson announced that the New Testament series was to be issued. It would cover all of the New Testament and be published in twelve volumes. Needless to say, his purposes were never realized.

The second column indicates Simpson's attempt to complete the series at least with sermons. He did re-publish previous volumes I-III, X (John only) and XI, but with the ommission of the homiletical helps. Between 1894 and 1902, most of Simpson's sermons were gathered and published as books. Some of these books were re-titled and included in the Christ in the Bible series. Others, like the sermons on the Synoptic Gospels, were published immediately as part of the Series. (This is true also of Isaiah, Acts and II Corinthians.) The bibliography will supply more details.

In the third column are the volumes of the series published after Simpson's death. The publishing company moved to Harrisburg, PA, and soon thereafter changed its name to Christian Publications, Inc. (This name continues to the present.) Note that the majority of the volumes are identical to column number 2. However, a number of new volumes were added; these consisted of books previously published under another title. One volume was dropped (i.e., Revelation). Timothy and Titus were published for the first time in book form with Thessalonians. (Note: the Pentateuch and the Gospel of John remained virtually the same in the three periods (no sermons). However, Simpson did preach a number of sermons on these biblical books.

Following is a list of the probable three distinct publication periods of the Christ in the Bible series. Note that there are some changes in the volume numbers.

CHRIST IN THE BIBLE

Series

1888-1894	1902-1910	circa. 1929-present
I. Genesis, Exodus (1888) —394 pages —large & small format	I. Genesis, Exodus (1902) —316 pages	I. Genesis —136 pages IA. Exodus —134 pages

(continued on next page)

Continued

II. Leviticus- Deuteronomy (1889) —412 pages —large format	II. Leviticus- Deuteronomy (1902)	II. Leviticus —125 pages IIA. Numbers- Deuteronomy —416 pages
III. Joshua (sermons) (1894) —272 pages —large & small format	III. Joshua (1902)	III. Joshua
	IV. Judges to Samuel (1902) —243 pages	IV. Judges to Samuel —243 pages
	V. Times of David & Solomon (1903) —279 pages	V. Samuel, Kings & Chronicles
	VI. Kings & Prophets of Judah & Israel (1903) —291 pages	VI. Kings & Prophets of Judah & Israel —291 pages
		Psalms —158 pages
	VII. Isaiah (1907) —401 pages	VII. Isaiah —401 pages
VIII. Life of Christ (1888) —400 pages —large format		
IX. Matthew-Luke (1889) —343 pages —large format	XIII. Matthew (new) (1904) —339 pages	XIII. Matthew (1929) —339 pages

(continued on next page)

Continued

	XIV. Mark (new) (1910) —183 pages	XIV. Mark (1928) —183 pages
	XIV.B Luke (new) (1906) —216 pages	XIV.B Luke —216 pages
X. John, Acts (1891) —367 pages —large format	XV. John (1904) —301 pages	XV. John —301 pages
	XVI. Acts (new) (1902) —203 pages	XVI. Acts —203 pages
XI. Romans (sermons) (1894) —274 pages —large & small format	XVII. Romans (1904) —298 pages	XVII. Romans —298 pages
	XVIII. I & II Corinthians (1904) —395 pages	XVIII. I Corinthians —164 pages
		XIX. II Corinthians —127 pages
	XIX. Galatians, Ephesians (1904) —254 pages	XX. Galatians, Ephesians —171 pages
	XX. Philippians, Colossians, Thessalonians — 290 pages	Philippians, Colossians —124 pages
		Thessalonians, Timothy, Titus —127 pages

(continued on next page)

Continued

	XXII. Hebrews —157 pages
	XXII.A James —117 pages
	XXIII. Peter, John, Jude —197 pages
XXIV. Revelation	

APPENDIX II

COLPORTAGE LIBRARY

(1899-1901)

At the close of the 19th century, paperbacks were becoming increasingly popular. The postal service offered the same cheap rates to mail them as they did for periodicals. The secular press capitalized on this and flooded America with a variety of paperbacks. Mr. Moody was the first religious person to take advantage of the situation.

Dr. Simpson joined Moody and initially published four paperbacks:

1. *The Gospel of Healing*
2. *The Christ Life*
3. *The Four-fold Gospel*
4. *Wholly Sanctified*

He wrote in June, 1899, that tens of thousands of copies of these four paperbacks had been sold in the last two years. (*CMAW* June, 1899, p. 8). Then he proposed to issue two copies of paperbacks every month, twenty-four in a year, at an annual subscription price of $2.50 (ibid., p. 41). One wonders the extent of his profit. From 1899 through 1901, Simpson published The Colportage Library. These publications ended in October, 1901, when the Post Office changed its regulations. Several authors contributed to The Library, but below only those books of Simpson are listed. (See the main bibliograpic list for particulars concerning the books of which the paperbacks are copies.)

A.B. SIMPSON'S CONTRIBUTIONS TO
THE COLPORTAGE LIBRARY
(listed alphabetically)

TITLE	PART	SCRIPTURE
Apostolic Church, The	I	I Corinthians
Apostolic Church, The	II	
But God!		
Emblems of the Holy Spirit (from *The Holy Spirit* or *Power From On High*, Vol. I, ch. 1-8)		
Friday Meeting Talks, No. 1		
Friday Meeting Talks, No. 2		
Friday Meeting Talks, No. 3		
From Faith to Faith	I	Romans 1-6
From Faith to Faith	II	Romans 7-16
Fullness of Jesus, The	I	
Fullness of Jesus, The	II	
Gospel of Healing, The		
Gospel of the Kingdom, The	I	
Gospel of the Kingdom, The	II	
Heaven Opened	I	Revelation
Heaven Opened	II	
Heavenly Vision, The		
Highest Christian Life, The	I	Ephesians
Highest Christian Life, The	II	
Holy Ghost Ministries (from *The King's Business*, ch. 4, 6-11)		
In Heavenly Places		
In the School of Christ	I	
In the School of Christ	II	
In the School of Faith	I	

(continued on next page)

Continued

In the School of Faith	II	
King's Business, The (ch. 1-3, 13, 16, 17)		
Land of Promise, The	I	
Land of Promise, The	II	
Love-Life of the Lord, The		Song of Solomon
Messages of Love		John's Epistles
Self-Life and the Christ Life, The		
Service for the King (from *The King's Business*, chs. 5, 12, 14, 15, 18-20)		
Sweetest Christian Life, The		Philippians
Walking in the Spirit	I	
Walking in the Spirit	II	

NOTE: Twenty-three of Simpson's books were thus reprinted in The Colportage Library, plus eight chapters of a 24th book, i.e. *Emblems of the Holy Spirit*.

COMPLETE COLPORTAGE LIBRARY

Volume I (1899)

NO.	TITLE	PART	AUTHOR
1	The Gospel of the Kingdom	I	A.B. Simpson
2	The Gospel of the Kingdom	II	A.B. Simpson
3	The Highest Christian Life	I	A.B. Simpson
4	The Highest Christian Life	II	A.B. Simpson
5	Walking in the Spirit	I	A.B. Simpson
6	Walking in the Spirit	II	A.B. Simpson
7	Eleventh Hour Laborers		F.L. Chapell
8	Heavenly Vision, The		A.B. Simpson
9	The Fullness of Jesus	I	A.B. Simpson
10	The Fullness of Jesus	II	A.B. Simpson
11	The Gospel of Healing		A.B. Simpson
12	Heaven Opened	I	A.B. Simpson
13	Heaven Opened	II	A.B. Simpson
14	But God!		A.B. Simpson
15	Friday Meeting Talks	I	A.B. Simpson
16	The Love Life of the Lord		A.B. Simpson
17	Stories of Salvation		A.B. Simpson (compiler)
18	Friday Meeting Talks	II	A.B. Simpson
19	Christ's Healing Wings		G.M. Peak
20	Heavenly Vision, The		A.B. Simpson
21	Modern Fads and Fanaticisms		W.B. Riley
22	Apostolic Church	I	A.B. Simpson
23	Apostolic Church	II	A.B. Simpson
24	Jesus is Coming		W.E. Blackstone

(continued on next page)

301

COMPLETE COLPORTAGE LIBRARY
Volume II (1900)

NO.	TITLE	PART	AUTHOR
1	The Sweetest Christian Life		A.B. Simpson
2	The Sun Bathed Life		M.A. Hawkins
3	Divine Healing	I	A. Murray
4	Alliance Arrows		F.W. Farr
5	Christ Our Power		H.S. Bainbridge
6	A Cloud of Witnesses		S.A. Lindenberger
7	Divine Life for the Body		K. MacKenzie
8	Divine Healing in the Light of Scripture		J.H. Oerter
9	Friday Meeting Talks	III	A.B. Simpson
10	Divine Healing	II	A. Murray
11	In the School of Christ	I	A.B. Simpson
12	In the School of Christ	II	A.B. Simpson
13	The Seven Churches of Asia		W.B. Riley
14	Messages of Love		A.B. Simpson
15	Addresses on Divine Healing		E. Baxter (Mrs.)
16	Lips Touched With Fire, or Pentecost for Me		O.E. Mallory
17	The King's Business, chs. 1-3, 13, 16, 17 (of No. 17)		A.B. Simpson
18	The Life of Praise		C.J. Montgomery
19	Holy Ghost Ministries, chs. 4, 6-11 (of No. 17)		A.B. Simpson
20	Limiting God		D. LeLacheur
21	Service for the King, chs. 5, 12, 14, 15, 18-20 (of No. 17)		A.B. Simpson
22	A Waiting Bride		F.C. Easton
23	In the School of Faith	I	A.B. Simpson
24	In the School of Faith	II	A.B. Simpson

COMPLETE COLPORTAGE LIBRARY

Volume III (1901)

NO.	TITLE	PART	AUTHOR
1	Transformed, or The Life of Jerry McAuley		A.C. Morrow (Mrs.)
2	The Land of Promise	I	A.B. Simpson
3	The Land of Promise	II	A.B. Simpson
4	Christ's Atonement		F.E. Marsh
5	The Self-Life and the Christ Life		A.B. Simpson
6	In Heavenly Places	I	A.B. Simpson
7	In Heavenly Places	II	A.B. Simpson
8	Texts Illuminated, or God's Care		J. Fuller (Mrs.)
9	Emblems of the Holy Spirit (chs. 1-8 of Vol. I, *The Holy Spirit* or *Power From On High*)		A.B. Simpson
10	From Faith to Faith, Romans 1-6		A.B. Simpson
11	From Faith to Faith, Romans 7-16		A.B. Simpson
12	Anti-Christian Supernaturalism		K. MacKenzie
13	Streams From the Valley of Berachah		S.A. Lindenberger
14	Not I, But Christ		I. David

APPENDIX III

Simpson began the *Christ in the Bible* series with homiletical hints and illustrative materials, with a desire to help his students become adequate preachers. The studies were prematurely ended at the beginning of the third year, due to Mr. Simpson's ill health.

PERIODICALS BY A.B. SIMPSON

(1880-1919)

DATES	TITLE	FREQUENCY
1880 February- 1881 October	*The Gospel in All Lands* (50-80 pp. per issue)	monthly
1882 January- 1887 December	*The Word, The Work & The World* (48 pp. per issue, sometimes more)	monthly
1882 February- December	*·The Work And The World* (32-64 pp. per issue) Materials printed on cheaper paper and sold for $1.50 less per year.	monthly
1888 January- 1889 June	*The Christian Alliance* (16 pp. per issue) The title of this·periodical and succeeding titles attempted to coordinate with the names of the new and enlarging Society.	weekly
1889 August- 1893 December	*The Christian Alliance &* *Missionary Weekly* (16 pp. per issue)	weekly
1894 January- 1896 December	*The Christian Alliance and* *Foreign Missionary Weekly* (24-28 pp. per issue)	weekly
1897 January- 1898 November	*The Christian & Missionary* *Alliance Weekly* (24 pp. per issue)	weekly
1898 December- 1899 May	*The Christian & Missionary* *Alliance Weekly* (32 pp. per issue)	monthly
1899 June- 1911 September	*The Christian & Missionary* *Alliance Weekly* (16 pp. per issue)	weekly

Continued

1902 July– 1907 September	*Living Truths* (64 pp. per issue) Simpson published this periodical incognito. He hoped in this way to enter homes that resisted the higher/deeper Christian life truth. He encouraged *Alliance Weekly* readers to subscribe to *Living Truths* for such friends.	monthly
1911 October– 1919 December	*Alliance Weekly* (16 pp. per issue) This periodical continued after the demise of Simpson and is with us today under the title of *The Alliance Witness*. It is now issued bi-monthly and consists of 30 pages per issue.	weekly

A